Ql 92   25-
                          ID

DEMOCRACY AND GHANA

DEMOCRACY AND GHANA

SELECT SPEECHES OF
PRESIDENT HILLA LIMANN

REX COLLINGS · LONDON · 1983

First published in Ghana by
Westcoast Publishing House Ltd, Box 6606 Accra
and in the United Kingdom by
Rex Collings Ltd, 6 Paddington Street, London W1

ISBN 086036 190 X

Typeset by Malvern Printers Ltd
and printed in Great Britain by
A. Wheaton & Co. Ltd., Exeter

Contents

Introduction

KENNETH MACKENZIE

This selection of the speeches of President Hilla Limann of Ghana was to have been called *Ghana Rebuilds*. It was intended to celebrate the first two years of civilian rule after Flight-Lieutenant Jerry John Rawlings had handed back power to an elected government on 24 September 1979. However, on 31 December 1981, while this book was with the printer, Flight-Lieutenant Rawlings seized power again. Instead of being a hopeful record of a beginning—the first half of what might have been the first of two presidential terms for Dr Limann—the book became something much more melancholy: a story with an unhappy ending, a source for historians investigating why Ghana's third attempt at democracy foundered. For the supporters and admirers of Dr Limann, who at the time of my writing this was under a sort of house arrest at Akosombo, the book will stand as a part answer of the allegations now being made against the Limann government and as an indictment of the military for their unconstitutional and morally unjustified act in taking power from the elected representatives of the Ghanaian people. If the government was failing to solve the problems of Ghana (and a reading of the speeches indicates that Dr Limann was sharply aware of how much distance still had to be travelled), then the people would soon have had an opportunity at an election to have rejected the Limann government and chosen an alternative. If there were provable instances of corruption and malfeasance, then there were processes of impeachment and trial available. Dr Limann repeatedly committed himself to accepting the rule of law and the verdict of democracy. The military seizure of power is a rejection of both these concepts. Flight-Lieutenant Rawlings claims to speak for the people but his only qualifications are that he has the power of the gun behind him.

Near the beginning of his term in office, President Limann saw the possibilities that were before Ghana. In a speech on 3 November 1979 (see page 211), he said: 'Our country stands at the crossroads of history today. After passing through many abuses and hardships, we now have the opportunity to chart a new way of life that shall lead to peace, progress and prosperity. Failure to do so will shatter our confidence in ourselves as a people capable of solving our problems. Indeed, it will open the floodgates to unmitigated disaster. . . .'

Dr Limann was relatively unknown in Ghana when he became a

presidential candidate in 1979: 'Dr Who' his opponents called him. He was a compromise candidate chosen after several leading men of the People's National Party had been banned from standing for election because they had been mentioned by previous commissions and committees of inquiry. The party was looking for someone untainted by any hint of corruption. Dr Limann is a man from the north of Ghana, which was likely to be a crucial area in the election, and the fact that he came from the same village as the late Imoru Egala, father of the party, was significant.

The village was Gwellu, in the Upper Region, and Dr Limann was born there in 1934. He trained and practised as a teacher after leaving school and then in 1955 he came to Britain to seek further education. He was notably successful in this, obtaining a B.Sc. (Econ) from the London School of Economics in 1960, a B.A. (Hons) in history as an external student of the University of London in 1964, and a Ph.D. in political science and constitutional law from the University of Paris. From 1965 he pursued a successful career in the Ghana foreign service, holding a senior post in Geneva when he was called to stand as President.

He is thus a learned man, as at home in French as he is in English. In these speeches he has quotations from Coleridge, Alexander Pope, John Stuart Mill and Matthew Arnold, phrases of Latin as well as French. During an official visit to Britain in May 1981, he surprised his hosts with his detailed knowledge of British constitutional history. There are few rulers in the world with a comparable theoretical grounding in economics. Critics claimed that he lacked charisma, or the ability to hold and electrify an audience. There is some truth in this. What he had to say was often witty, original and wise, but he usually read his speeches in a rather dull voice. This had the serious consequence that he was rarely able to inspire Ghanaians or convince them that the sacrifices he was demanding and the hardships they were undergoing were part of a noble struggle towards the rebirth of a better Ghana. A related criticism made by some was that his limited political experience—he had been a member of the Tumu District Council for a few years in the 1950s—made it difficult for him to dominate the tough and case-hardened politicians in his party; these were mostly rich businessmen, associated with the scandals and failures of the past. In the last months of civilian rule there were bitter controversies about alleged monetary malfeasance within both the ruling and the main opposition parties. Dr Limann is himself a man of total integrity, but he was not altogether successful in his efforts to rid Ghanaian politics of the taint of corruption, to convince the men of his party that it was necessary to be seen to be placing national interest above business interest.

The economic difficulties that Dr Limann inherited when he assumed power were huge, mostly due to the economic mismanagement of successive military regimes and made worse by the brief period of Rawlings rule and so-called 'house-cleaning' that preceded the handover. The idea that all economic problems could be solved by ending corruption was dangerously naive. Dr Limann was acutely aware of the complexity of Ghana's difficulties and of the fact that there was no simple magic formula for ending them. In January 1981, he spoke of Ghana's rich resources and of her 'prostrate economy, struggling for survival', and went on to give this explanation:

> . . . previous Ghana governments to varying degrees of neglect or guilt, failed to provide the right climate and conditions for putting these enormous natural resources and comparative advantages to good use in the interest of all and for social justice. Lack of sensitivity and proper direction, mismanagement and bureaucratic callousness have also added their contribution to this sad situation. Thus, those in permanent positions of trust and responsibility have not developed any real concern for, or responsiveness to, the needs of their fellow-citizens. Ghanaians therefore progressively became over the years rather disillusioned, bewildered at their sorry plight in the midst of abundant natural resources and cynical. They are ingenious only in cheating their fellows or the public in order to survive at all. Ghana's economy has also been plagued by factors outside her immediate control. These have included galloping, imported as well as locally-induced, inflation and, especially, the rapidly-increasing cost of fossil fuel as well as the inflated cost of imported equipment and other manufactured goods. . . . (Page 34)

President Limann's government, abjuring instant or gimmicky solutions to these grave problems, thought long and hard and took much expert economic advice before devising a long-term strategy. The first priority was agriculture. In announcing a two-year crash programme for agriculture on 14 May 1980, President Limann said agriculture was 'the cornerstone on which are short-term, medium-term and long-term development policy will rest, since this is the key to our economic recovery, long-term national prosperity and dignity' (see page 20). Other essential requirements were the expansion of other sources of foreign exchange, apart from cocoa which itself needed to be revived, and the attraction of investment capital. Ghana's rich gold reserves seemed the answer to the first problem, and the President organized a most successful international seminar in September 1981, on how to exploit Ghana's gold endowment. The government also introduced an Investment Code which provided generous terms to overseas investors and set up an Investment Centre to ensure that Ghana gained maximum benefit from them. This was a constant theme of Dr Limann's travels: as President he visited in Europe Britain, Yugoslavia, Rumania and West Germany, and in Africa Nigeria, Mali, Senegal, The Gambia, Benin, Upper Volta, Guinea, Togo and Kenya, speaking at OAU and ECOWAS summits and doing much to restore Ghana to her proper place in world affairs.

His critics claimed that the government was slow to act on economic problems. In a speech at Cape Coast towards the end of 1981 the President made this explanation and counter-attack:

. . . at the national level the People's National Party administration is leaving no stone unturned in its efforts to introduce major and permanent changes in the unenviable economic situation we have inherited. The changes are designed to promote continued stability, social transformation, greater progress and prosperity for all Ghanaians, who have suffered for far too long from the effects of self-centred, ill-conceived and short-sighted decisions, fits and starts and makeshift policies which have proved only too detrimental to all aspects of our national life. In our determination to arrest further humiliations and indignities, we have had to analyse carefully all aspects of our national problems in taking decisions affecting the vast majority of our people. This determination, this policy, is also meant to check those who had long plundered the nation but now make cheap political stunts, saying that we are slow, while carefully hiding the fact that when they had the opportunity they were very quick only in destroying the economy through sell-outs and the reckless abandonment of viable and socially beneficial projects throughout the country. . . .' (Page 219)

These speeches show Dr Limann continually aware of the need to combat corruption. In his first address to the nation in September 1979 (page 117), he said:

Those who engage in trade malpractices, popularly known as *kalabule*, must refrain from these nefarious and anti-social activities. I must warn all those who may think that the departure of the Armed Forces Revolutionary Council opens the sluicegates and provides an invitation to them to return to such anti-social activities. There is no place for such people in the new Ghana. I am determined to stamp out bribery and corruption, smuggling and indiscipline, and to revive public spiritedness. . . . We must all resist the temptation to cheat, plunder and rob our country and our fellows.

In his second anniversary address to the nation in September 1981 (page 240), he said:

XII

Election Day: The President speaks after declaration of the result.

President (centre) with Vice-President and President Sekou Touré of Guinea at Kotoka Airport 23 September 1979.

The Asantahene greets the President.

*The President seated between His Holiness Pope John-Paul II and
Dr Runcie, Archbishop of Canterbury in Accra, 9 May 1980.*

*The President and President Siaka Stevens of Sierra Leone,
February 1981.*

President Arap Moi of Kenya and Dr Limann, March 1981.

President Saye Zerbo of Upper Volta and Dr Limann, September 1981.

We still have a long way to go in making a lasting success of civilian democratic rule in Ghana. My purpose is not to paint a picture of despair or doom. Indeed, civilian rule is very much alive now, but lawlessness and too much complacency, if allowed any further scope, can turn it into a sour and sterile system. We should not forget so soon the harrowing experiences and humiliations we have endured before regaining our present liberties. My administration has been particularly worried about too much complacency, indiscipline and graft which have taken deep roots in our public life. . . .

Three months after that speech the soldiers brought civilian democratic rule to an end in Ghana. The peace and stability which were essential if international confidence were to be restored and the Limann recipe for economic recovery were to work have vanished. Flight-Lieutenant Rawlings and his associates have different ideas. Whether they will succeed in alleviating the economic hardships of the Ghanaians (or in effectively containing corruption), or whether their coming will prove the 'unmitigated disaster' predicted by Dr Limann only the future will reveal.

DG—B

1

Legonman Housing Project

On the occasion of the opening of the Legonman Housing Project, the President stressed in his address the Government's hopes for implementing housing schemes designed to cater for needs where they are greatest, namely for the homeless and helpless.

The Redco, a subsidiary of the Bank for Housing and Construction, is a new concept in real estate designing and construction. It is planned to provide for a self-contained community, complete with facilities for recreation, shopping and school education. It is situated ten miles outside Accra on the Aburi Road, opposite Madina.

I feel highly honoured to have been invited to inaugurate this pilot scheme of the Legonman Housing Project which is likely to make a unique, profound and far-reaching contribution towards efforts aimed at solving or at least minimizing our perennial housing problems in the cities as well as in the rural areas. Your invitation as well as my acceptance to attend this function testifies to and underscores the great importance we both attach to such a carefully worked out pioneering scheme and the gravity of the situation it has been designed to tackle.

Only yesterday, almost at about this time, I was privileged to be shown round the Matadi Housing Project near Monrovia in Liberia. I hope that when completed your project will greatly improve upon what I have already seen in terms of conception, design, construction, integration, finish cost and the variety of customers and their needs for whom you will cater. Indeed, I hope that your project will attract much more worthy dignitaries and visitors than me. I wish you in advance all the success you so eminently deserve in your initiative, boldness of conception, foresight and innovation.

My Government is acutely aware of the need to provide decent shelter for our people at reasonable rents or outlay cost. In fact, we have underlined this point in the Manifesto of the People's National Party which was endorsed by the electorate for implementation. In that document we have studiously avoided the use of the term 'Low Cost Houses' because mention of it stimulates such a sour taste in the mouth.

Our housing policy is heavily weighted in favour of rental units and the increasing use of such local material as burnt bricks and tiles. Your project therefore falls squarely in line with our plans and priorities.

As sketched in my Sessional Address in Parliament last November, subventions and grants to state Housing Agencies shall not be allowed to be used for subsidizing house ownership schemes of the semi- and fully-detached type any more because, apart from the exorbitant cost which puts them far above the reach of ordinary, honest mortals, they waste land, material, energies, patience and our fund of social equity and justice. Above all, they only enrich those who are already relatively affluent or worsen the plight of those who do not possess initial capital or assets to serve as collateral for bank overdrafts or loans.

I have dwelt at length on the merits and benefits of the Legonman Housing Project. I will, therefore, not bore you further by repeating them. I am, however, worried that the scheme seems to contain too large a number of the bungalow-type units and is also silent as to whether or not it will serve some of the pressing needs of the University of Ghana, Legon. I hope that it will still be possible for you to take account of these points even at this late though initial stage of the Project, if indeed, this has not been done. I also wish to draw very serious attention to the need to keep the cost of burnt bricks and tiles very low otherwise our shift of emphasis in this direction will become meaningless or silly.

I have already visited the Tema Brick Factory to which you have made reference in your statement. I hope that you will not be disconcerted when I confess that I was not impressed with the unit cost *ex loco* of the hollow bricks; which also suggested a very high incidence of breakages in loading, transportation and unloading. Perhaps, if such factories do not aim at amortizing the over-capitalized infrastructure of buildings and complex machinery in a rather short time.

Kindly allow me to sound an even more specific word of warning or caution to your management about the sort of house allocation systems of the past which has repeatedly and systematically negated the policies of successive governments of this country namely, those of providing reasonably cheap and decent shelters for people in the low income brackets. Houses built under such schemes with public funds have always found their way into the hands of the wealthy and affluent few who have always only turned round and rented them to workers at exorbitant rents. The sad history of the 'low-cost housing scheme' need not be retold here. Suffice it to say that such houses were so highly priced that it was absolutely impossible for the average Ghanaian to acquire his own shelter. Low-cost housing therefore lost its meaning long before graft, bribery and corruption and other injustices gave the *coup de grâce* to that otherwise laudable concept. My word of warning therefore is that Government will not allow this sort of thing to happen again.

Legonman Housing and similar Projects should endeavour to meet the needs of the ordinary Ghanaian in reality and not just in theory as other

2

schemes have done in the past. I hope that they will not become mere promising projects which will yield nothing equitable in the end.

Government wants to ensure that many Ghanaians realize their cherished ambitions of getting decent accommodation wherever they live and work within the country. Consequently, I do hereby declare our support for such projects as would greatly and quickly contribute to the solution of the acute housing problems facing many of our people.

Recognizing that one major problem which has hindered housing development is the inadequate supply and frequent shortages of building materials, ample steps are being taken towards the long-term development of local building material resources as an effective way of solving this problem. Emphasis will be placed on the production and use of such local building materials as timber and burnt bricks throughout all the Regions within the framework of rural development and industrialization programmes. The Ministers concerned are working out the details of these plans. Housing and its related facilities play a very important role in economic and social welfare development. Government shall therefore find out and remove other obstacles and/or implement other plans aimed at reducing the constraints which have hitherto hindered this important aspect of our national development.

In conclusion, let me now congratulate the Bank for Housing and Construction for the initiative in launching the Legonman Housing Project which, I hope, will be emulated by other banks, agencies and organizations for the benefit of their employees and the public at large. I shall watch the progress of this pilot project with keen interest. As a pioneering project, I wish it the unqualified success that it deserves. To this end, we shall do all within our power to help, encourage and promote your objectives.

2

Two-Year Crash Programme for Agriculture

On 14 May 1980, the President launched the Two-Year Crash Programme for Agriculture Development at Oyarifa on the Aburi Road. In the speech the President spelt out his government's policy options on the matter of food production and agricultural development. He explained his vision for agricultural activities to the thousands of citizens who attended the launching ceremony.

I have the pleasure to launch today the first phase of the New Deal for agricultural production in our attempts to arrest and eventually reverse the past phenomenon of food shortages repeatedly experienced in Ghana, a country so richly endowed with fertile soils, water resources and varied geographical zones.

From the authorities and the records I have consulted, this phenomenon has been with us, on and off, since the early 1920s. Attempts to unravel or solve it have admittedly also been repeatedly made. We must therefore now be more resolute, consistent, and persevering than ever before if we want to succeed in our renewed efforts to execute plans and production programmes in this all-important area of our economic activities. Publicity and propaganda there must be, but, this time, let our actions speak louder than words!

POLICY OPTION

As I have made the position crystal clear since last November, the agricultural policy option is the cornerstone on which our short-term, medium-term and long-term development policy will rest since this is the key to our economic recovery, long-term national prosperity and dignity.

In line with some of the stated objectives outlined in the Manifesto of the PNP which my Administration has been given the mandate to implement, the aim of this policy is to:

(a) eliminate our present large food deficit by increasing production so as to raise the nutritional levels of all Ghanaians;

(b) embark on a comprehensive and well-planned agricultural programme of rural development in order to raise rural incomes and also provide the grass-roots basis for our industrial growth;

4

(c) step up production of agricultural raw materials to provide our domestic needs and have a surplus for export.

ACTION PROGRAMME

A comprehensive agricultural programme, with production targets, which concentrates on food production, has been prepared, thanks to the efforts and assistance of a team of concerned citizen experts who have been working on it since last November. The details and strategies for its implementation will be outlined throughout the Regions by the Minister of Agriculture and other Ministers of State.

But, perhaps, I ought to re-emphasize from the outset that one practical manifestation of this policy has clearly been shown in my Sessional Address and the 1979/80 Budget presented to Parliament. In line with the Address, the Budget allocated ₵148 million to the Ministry of Agriculture alone from our own meagre resources. This represents an increase of 74 per cent over that of the previous financial year and does not also include funds allocated to the cocoa industry from our own resources, nor those from foreign sources for joint agricultural projects with international agencies.

I hope that over-hasty critics or carping theorists may now re-examine the records more closely and impartially for a fairer picture of these plans and efforts made within very severe financial constraints and numerous other competing and unavoidable demands on the budget. It may also be helpful for all of us to realize that what we have repeatedly lacked in the recent past are not ideas, theories and criticisms. which have always flowered in profusion, but political direction, will-power, realism, decisiveness, hard work, consistency, practical and sustained implementation of good ideas and sound programmes.

Let us, for once, now learn from hindsight and be guided by the dictum than 'Deeds are better than Words' in our attempts to salvage our shattered economy and regain our lost national respect and dignity. The lack of fair comment, honest dissent and constructive criticism in the past has not been beneficial to our socio-economic and political health and should therefore now be allowed and tolerated, but this can also produce negative and harmful results if it degenerates into irresponsible licentiousness.

LESSONS

We can draw useful lessons and inspiration from our own history which is replete with noble achievements even in adversity. Thus, in the early 1920s some of our forebears had to take a firm stand and even burn their cocoa to demonstrate their determination to defend their long-term interests and save the national economy rather than submit to local and foreign manipulators and cheats.

Earlier still was the Bond of 1844 and the remonstrances of the Aborigines' Rights Protection Society on the land issue made to Queen Victoria, the most powerful monarch of the then known world who reigned over 'the empire on which the sun never set'. This is part of the proud record of our ancestors and forefathers. We must therefore now return to the sources and the Founding Fathers, as I have said on an earlier occasion, if we want to understand and defend our present existence as a politically independent and sovereign nation and to maintain our present struggle to recover and eventually to win our economic emancipation.

We can also draw inspiration, moral strength and renewed determination from the past, particularly, from the fact that the Founding Fathers did not always sit back unconcerned, criticize or talk endlessly in the face of advertisy or national crises. Rather, they took such practical steps that repeatedly saved the country from either economic depression or political oppression. In the fullness of time, they even succeeded, led by the late Osagyefo Dr Kwame Nkrumah of blessed memory, in pulling the country through to be the first in Africa to wrest independence from colonial rule and domination.

Given this brief, proud historical background to our present nationhood; drawing the correct lessons and the necessary moral courage and strength from the bitter experiences of our recent past; with resolute determination, sustained efforts and hard work, we can win again against the odds now facing us at home and abroad. Needless to say that we must succeed. Indeed, we can succeed, we shall succeed! As I have often said since last September and even earlier, 'we dare not fail' again in our renewed resolve to win the mastery and control over our political and economic destinies as an independent, free, sovereign and united national community.

RESOURCE USE

My Administration is determined to make Ghana produce not merely adequate staple foodstuffs to satisfy our domestic needs but eventually surpluses for export. Our rich variety of arable lands, soils, seasons and geographical zones and our enormous water resources are the envy of others even within our own West African sub-region. Yet those others seem to produce more crops and livestock and are able to sell some of them to us. If vegetables and even flowers can now be grown in arid, even desert wastes, why can we not grow the same crops in our more fertile, wetter and lush country.

With imaginative and purposeful planning, consistency and hard work we can take the lead again in the crusade against poverty, hunger and disease and the economic emancipation of our country. We should all therefore now minimize diversionary tactics and antics and rather start to contribute our widow's mite towards our economic recovery and national revival. As a people we can no longer stand idly by or preside over a situation where only 11 per cent of available arable land is under cultivation, out of which no more than five per cent is under food production.

All concerned and patriotic citizens should therefore now start to take advantage of our rich natural resources to help in the collective effort. As I have said on an earlier occasion, it is futile for us to sit back with folded hands and only cry interminably of being 'hungry' or that we want 'food to eat'. We must ban such humiliating and undignified utterances from everyday use since they make others disrespect us. We should remember also that the mere cries for 'bread, bread' could not save ancient Rome from collapse and final destruction. We must all bestir ourselves and help produce more food for our own use since no one else will do so for us even if we cry our lungs out.

The past achievements of our country amply demonstrate that we can rise again to the new challenges facing us since we have never meekly succumbed to adversity—rather, hard times have always brought out the best in us. Consequently, we must now resolutely adopt sincere attitudes and new habits of work in our homes, offices and farms if we want to feed ourselves as responsible citizens with a sense of our self-respect and dignity. Neither manna from on high nor alms here below is possible without hard work. Even God helps only those who help themselves.

COLLECTIVE SELF-RELIANCE

Judging from the atmosphere of the recent Lagos Economic Summit, all OAU member countries are determined and stand poised, as we are, to concentrate on agriculture in order to put an end to their over-dependence on food imports or foreign food aid. Given our enormous natural resources we can hold our own or even take the lead again in this new struggle for the economic emancipation of our continent.

Strangely enough, the Lagos consensus was reached without any prior consultations between the Heads of State and Government of OAU member countries. Indeed, due to bitter past experiences all African countries have now realized that no one else will rescue us from our economic troubles and that we have to help ourselves, at least, in the areas where results can easily be achieved at little cost. Moreover, the results of our own efforts and hard work will also directly benefit us.

As a self-respecting people, we cannot forever expect others to work hard, economize, sacrifice and then lend their funds to us, with crippling strings attached, only for us to burn such funds away overnight on food imports, without any hope of repayment, on items we can ourselves produce more cheaply for our own use, sustenance and even for export.

Moreover, the rest of the world owes us neither our living nor any legal or moral duty to spend time and money on our importunities. Indeed, no genuine investor will lend us money only for food imports. In any case, we should start to move away from the tricky and bad habit of un-wittingly importing unemployment into our society by accepting food aid or assistance when we have not been struck by natural calamities such as earthquakes, locust visitations or droughts. Such habits are harmful to the productive sectors of our economy, unhealthy for our moral fibre and destructive of our political independence.

IMPACT

In order to make the desired impact within our projected agricultural development years, and also lay the foundations for comprehensive long-term economic recovery and development, government has decided to concentrate greater efforts and available scarce resources on selected areas which enjoy natural comparative advantages of crop cultivation, without, of course, neglecting other, less fertile or disadvantaged areas—far from it, such areas shall also greatly benefit directly from this policy option or shift of emphasis, and indirectly from its spill-over or multiplier effects.

Countrymen, the success of these policy options, consequential plans and scarce financial resources management requires the active support, material involvement and physical participation of all the able-bodied among us. Such a commitment and activity will be warmly welcomed, encouraged and supported by Government.

Our banks and other financial institutions, our chiefs, sturdy farmers and fishermen, public and para-statal agricultural organizations, schools, colleges, service institutions; in short, all Ghanaians have a civic duty to help and take advantage of these plans and of the budgetary allocations to be made available for inputs to ensure their successful implementation. We invite all to become alive to this duty. We also appeal to private owners of all available implements, from tractors to the simplest traditional farming tools, kindly to use them effectively them-selves or hire them out at reasonable charges to others for optimal use in this programme.

Those who do not want to work, as with tramps even in developed countries perhaps, prefer to go hungry by making this choice. If so, then they should equally have the courage of their convictions, accept the logical consequences of their free choice of idleness and therefore stop complaining.

We should always remember that in the larger sense, Government is the creature of all nationals, not their creator, or an occupying foreign power we must heckle, or a rich grandmother to do for us things we can do for ourselves. We cannot be responsible citizens if we expect Government to take the initiative in all things or do everything for us from the cradle to the grave. Yet even some of our traditional rulers who should know better and help mobilize their people for productive work, are now becoming one source of serious problems for the Government, the dissipation of scarce funds and the sapping of our energies and time.

I repeat my appeal to Ghanaians of all walks of life and status including our traditional rulers to realize that we must take our destiny into our own hands and not allow it to be taken away from us any more. This is part of the fuller meaning of freedom, self-government, independence and national sovereignty. Their price is hard work and the eternal vigilance of all citizens.

For those who want to live honest, decent, rewarding and fulfilling lives, agriculture has certainly been the field of the greatest opportunities since last November. Yet quite a number of people have failed to realize and take advantage of this. I wish once again to renew my appeal to such citizens to start to do so now in their best, enlightened self-interest. May I also re-emphasize that the past system of chits, authority notes and preferential treatment which enabled a few unproductive agents and even malingerers to make unearned incomes or windfall fortunes should now be forgotten, since my Administration will not encourage it. Indeed, any official indulging in it will, no matter his status, be drastically dealt with if this comes to my notice.

In contrast, agriculture can be the open sesame to the success of individuals, collectivities and the country at large because of the substantial resources to be allocated to it and the high demand for its products, both at home and abroad. Again, I invite and/or appeal to all and sundry to take advantage of this New Deal. Given our vast hinterland, and the relative lack of water resources and fertile soils of the latter, we can even earn a lot of foreign currency from food exports in future to supplement earnings from cocoa which is now declining in production whose price is also often fluctuating unpredictably and uncontrollably with harmful effects on our planning and economic development.

CROPS AND LIVESTOCK

Under the new agricultural policy option, the following food crops and livestock shall receive maximum attention and increasing financial support, within the scarce resources available to Government:

  i. Cereals—Maize, rice, guinea corn and millet.
 ii. Roots and Starchy Crops—Cassava, yam, plantain, cocoyam.
iii. Legumes and Beans—Ground-nuts, cowpeas, soya and other beans.
 iv. Vegetables—Tomatoes, onions/shallots.
  v. Livestock—Poultry and pigs.
 vi. In addition to the production of such traditional crops as cocoa

9

and coffee, sunflower and soya bean production shall also be greatly encouraged and intensified for their domestic and export potential.

Production targets of all these crops have been detailed in the Action Programme. Information about soil types and the areas where each crop can be cultivated to greatest advantage, and also seeds, can be readily supplied by the Ministry of Agriculture and other related Research Institutions.

Government is aware of, and greatly concerned about, large yearly post-harvest losses throughout the country. To minimize such losses, the Ministry of Agriculture has been instructed to erect storage structures equipped with preservation facilities in food-producing areas. In the case of easily perishable commodities such as tomatoes, the canning factories at Kpawlugu and Wenchi shall be vigorously encouraged to embark on large scale processing. I have personally observed annually since 1975 that State Fishing and Meat Marketing Corporation deep freezer vans are being used in carting charcoal. This strange practice should now cease forthwith and the vans rehabilitated and reverted to their proper function of carting perishable food items such as meat, fish and tomatoes. The general public should help enforce this directive.

INPUTS

Every effort shall be made to provide the inputs needed to boost the production of the above listed crops at reasonable prices. Such inputs should not be resold as has been done in some cases since January. They should be devoted to or applied strictly to their proper uses.

Already, as a modest beginning and following my rapid tour of the Regions and complaints received, the following inputs have, since January, been sold and distributed to farmers and fishermen at control prices:

 (a) Nearly three hundred thousand pieces of cutlasses,

 (b) Thirty thousand hoes,

 (c) Over one thousand outboard motors,

 (d) Nearly five thousand maxi bags of seed maize,

 (e) Nearly eight thousand maxi bags of seed rice,

 (f) About five thousand maxi bags of seed ground-nuts,

 (g) Twenty thousand bags of fertilizers,

 (h) Twenty thousand more tons or about half a million bags of fertilizers have also now arrived for additional distribution.

I wish to emphasize that all these efforts have been quietly made already in the nature of emergency measures which had to be taken in response to complaints received during my tour of the Regions and that every step has faced unbelievable bottlenecks, apathy, lack of data and numerous institutional inefficiencies confronting us. We have so far not made any noise about these efforts and difficulties in order to avoid raising false hopes of more food crops too soon or sounding unduly unfair, especially to those who have been working hard, some of them really very hard indeed, under the most difficult and trying conditions.

Due to overseas supplier and shipping space difficulties over which we have no control, the arrival of additional consignments of inputs ordered since last October and their distribution into the system in more adequate quantity, is only just slowly beginning to get under way. These expected inputs form part of the total of ₡52 million worth of licences made available for their importation. I hope that the combined effects of all these initial efforts will soon begin to be visibly seen.

OFFICIALS AND THE PUBLIC

We are all justifiably impatient about our economic recovery for which some of us have been quietly working day and night. However, as I have often said, destruction, which is easier than construction, has taken fourteen years to reach its present stage and cannot be reversed overnight, especially when public finances have also greatly dwindled. I hope that all related institutions and responsible personnel will however now grasp this sense of urgency and high expectation, bestir themselves and greatly improve upon their past performance which has left very much to be desired.

Indeed, as officials we must all henceforth closely rescrutinize the performance of our duties in this light so that those who cannot keep pace with the tempo at which we are expected to move may give way to those who can and are prepared to do so. Over-leisurely and complacent attitudes to duty and work or the lack of imagination and initiative on the part of officials in our present critical situation should change for the better before it is too late. A word to the wise should be enough.

We have patiently absorbed all unfair, often uninformed or even malicious criticisms of slowness only because we want to give everyone the time and the chance to adjust to the new civilian experiment rather than rush into taking panic measures which could only have worsened an already bad situation. Government's mandate and aim is to find jobs for people, not to dismiss them unnecessarily. However, we are also accountable to Parliament for every peswa spent and therefore have a duty to check those in official positions who do not co-operate or frustrate our efforts.

We can therefore no longer tolerate delays, negligence, leisurely work attitudes, indifference, insensitivity and unresponsiveness to public opinion, and above all, obstruction and incompetence. We appeal to the public henceforth to help check all such unhealthy and unhelpful attitudes by standing up against known wrongdoing by officials or being prepared to substantiate allegations of such wrongdoings since we cannot

11

effectively discipline anyone on mere unsubstantiated allegations or fabrications made out of spite, envy or malice.

Countrymen, it is in the interest of each and every one of us fully to be engaged in the agricultural programme on which we are determined to make optimum use of our present very scarce financial resources. We should all try, individually and as organizations, to contribute our bit to the objective of collective survival, economic recovery and national advancement. It is within our power and not beyond our ability, to succeed. No contribution from any citizen in this respect will be too small; no sacrifice from us in Government will be too great.

IRRIGATION

We cannot depend on rainfall alone for the success of the plans for increased and, especially, sustained agricultural production since rains have often been unseasonable and failed us in the past. Irrigation shall therefore necessarily play a vital role in our efforts in this field; maximum use shall start to be made of all available irrigation facilities for the cultivation of rice, vegetables and tomatoes, especially, during dry seasons, in order to curtail seasonal shortages of these items. All officials concerned should start to plan ahead now so as to avoid the recurrence of what has happened to tomatoes produced in adequate quantities this season. Private individuals and small-scale farming organizations living near water shall be helped in the importation and use of simple and less costly irrigation equipment to enable them to engage on all-season farming and realize the objectives of the Programme and also their personal aspirations.

Furthermore, we want to lay a sound infrastructural base not only for more widespread and even large-scale irrigation in order to ensure continuous production of basic food items, irrespective of rainfall.

We have already started to re-activate irrigation projects which had, like the Peki, Dawhenya and other model farms, been neglected to advancing bush or totally abandoned. The Ejura Farms, at present the single largest maize producers, shall receive every support to enable them greatly to increase their acreage and output. They will also benefit from the Lome II Convention. Official obstructions, if any, to their efforts shall therefore be drastically checked. It is hoped that the Botanga irrigation project near Tamale will also start shortly.

I must repeat that we ought to take advantage of our enormous water resources, and also that the habit of killing viable projects by starving them of inputs and/or taking them over only to be managed, not on the site, but by officials or uncommitted and uninterested citizens from the cities, shall be discouraged. All projects taken over in the past and destroyed shall be revived and managed more efficiently. We hope also greatly to speed up project formulation and implementation compared with what we have found on assuming office. All officials concerned in these fields should therefore take note and act accordingly.

Fellow Ghanaians, my Administration is directing keen attention to the livestock and fishing industries since we cannot enjoy our kenkey, banku, ampesi, akple, fufu or tuonsafe without fish or meat. We have, in the past, not fully exploited even our existing potential of livestock production, due, partly to inadequate supplies of feed, drugs and water, especially in the dry savanna regions where cattle are left unattended and unused until they are frequently stolen and driven away across our borders in large numbers. The loss of such national assets has not been making news headlines, but it is substantial. Similarly, the poultry industry which caught on very well, has, since 1975, been gradually starved to death unnoticed. The press should take up such issues in future and highlight them for national debate and governmental action.

In the immediate future, attention shall be concentrated on the production of poultry, pigs, sheep and goats, right down to the village level and also, where possible to backyards in the cities and towns. Wherever possible local materials and other inputs should be used to produce shelter for animals and birds and also for their feed.

FISHING

Inland fish farming shall be greatly encouraged, but since 60 per cent of the present annual fish catch is made by our canoe river and sea fishermen, we shall intensify our efforts to provide such necessary inputs as outboard motors, nets and mending twines to enable them to increase their output. As mentioned earlier, over 1,000 outboard motors have already been made available to canoe fishermen in the hope of their bringing home their catches. We shall naturally advise ourselves if they fail us by selling off such catches abroad.

In fact, I have already begun to wonder why with so many outboard motors already put into the small scale fishing industry since January, no visible improvements have as yet started to be seen even in the markets of the coastal regions. I hope that the public will now take up and seriously pursue this matter rather than complain or blame Government while others take undue advantage of such complaints to cheat the consumer and taxpayer whose hard-earned foreign currency pays for importing such equipment.

ACTION PROGRAMME AND COMMITTEES

Compatriots, under the Action Programme which spells out the detailed strategies and production targets for achieving our objectives, Regional and District Agricultural Committees shall ensure its successful implementation. In each Region, the Programme shall be operated by the Committee, under the overall supervision of the Regional Minister, accountable to me through the Minister of Agriculture. Each Committee shall be expected to determine and implement one annual national Agricultural Production Day Show with incentive-oriented price awards for high performance. The Committee shall need your co-operation and active support, not interminably negative criticisms.

GRATITUDE

Finally, I wish to place on record my personal gratitude to the banks and other organizations which have lent their equipment such as cutlasses for use pending the arrival of consignments ordered. In particular, I wish to express my deep appreciation to local manufacturers such as those of crocodile matchets, Bibiani Metals and Mechanical Lloyd for the manner in which they heeded and responded positively to our appeals by working hard to meet some of our pressing needs. I commend such understanding, goodwill and patriotic efforts.

At least, while others who also had no instant solutions or even constructive plans to solve our problems merely distorted facts and talked viciously, these organizations did their best to help. Hoping that they will not relent but even improve upon their recent past performance, I invite all other enterprises to emulate their example.

In order to augment and speed up these efforts, I have instructed that all equipment and other inputs imported with licences allocated to the Ministries of Agriculture, Trade and Industries should, as an interim measure, be distributed under Government control, accountable to me personally, through the respective Ministers.

SUMMARY

Fellow Countrymen, our Nation is endowed with the requisite human and natural resources for adequate and sustained agricultural production, growth and eventual take-off. Government plans to utilize these resources effectively to produce food in such quantities as would adequately feed our fast-growing population, with even net surpluses for export in the future.

All Africa is now engaged in a new crusade for economic emancipation, the eventual creation of an African Common Market and an Economic Community. We can therefore become pace-setters again in this field.

Indeed, even our present plight, plans, appeals, public expectations and a few negative individual reactions to them also strangely recall the circumstances and the atmosphere of the Osagyefo's epoch-making Dawn Broadcast. In this connection we in Ghana seem to have learnt nothing since 1961 while all other African countries are now the wiser

14

from the needless bitter experiences of the last twenty years. But can we really afford the posture of such forgetfulness or inability to learn from our past bitter experiences? Certainly not. We must go along with the rest of Mother Africa.

To achieve our objectives the Ministry of Agriculture shall reorganize its manpower distribution so as to strengthen decision-making and pro-gramme implementation at the Regional, District and sub-District levels.

The organizations and agencies concerned with food production and distribution shall also be drastically reorganized and redirected to enable them perform their proper functions efficiently.

The unemployed and the youth should also all be mobilized for massive agricultural production. These plans and objectives therefore require the support and co-operation of all of us. Please help the Ministry of Agriculture to help you and the country at large.

Traditional rulers can, particularly, help to mobilize their people for productive work by refraining from disputes and faction-fights which only dissipate scarce resources and sap our energies.

Social and industrial peace and stability are also needed for economically productive activities which will moreover reassure others, particularly abroad, that we are prepared and can save ourselves. Foreign investment is not and can never be string-free largesse. It is certainly not available or forthcoming anymore for perishable com-modities or the sort of fast disappearing goods usually found in the shops and large department stores in industrialized countries, where even such commodities now cost much more than we are often prepared to pay for them in Ghana. Moreover, we should always remember that the im-ported goods for which we all yearn, even without hard currency to pay for them, are produced by others who are willing to work. Such imports therefore only keep our own people unemployed, our resources unused or exploited cheaply by others and taken away from us in a Valco, or a Firestone type of naked and conscienceless exploitation of poor, un-developed countries by rich, developed countries.

Certain productive activities require no more than the willingness to work a bit for the things we need. Thus, rather than buy pepper, vegetables, tomatoes and many other similar items, we can all grow them in our backyards during our spare time at no great financial cost, which may even make substantial savings in our pay packets for other, more important, purposes such as school meals and means of transport.

Investment in costly machinery and other unmanageable inputs without the knowledge of their use and maintenance or the willingness to work and/or put them to full use, can only waste our scarce foreign currency resources to no other purpose than the interest of the manufacturers who dump such equipment on us.

Farmers and Fishermen, distinguished guests, fellow citizens, at this crossroad of our existence as a nation, I have the honour and the pleasure to declare the Action Programme for Agricultural Development and our economic recovery formally launched on the slogan of:

'GROW MORE FOOD FOR THE PEOPLE'

Weeks after the official launching of the Two-year Crash Programme for agricultural development, the President carried the challenging news to the North, Bontanga, Tamale to be exact.

It is a great pleasure for me to launch the first phase of my Government's Agricultural Development Programme in this Region today and at the site of the Region's first medium-sized irrigation project, for at this function we are also launching the commencement of work by Messrs Taylor Woodrow Ltd on the Bontanga Irrigation Scheme.

The site has been chosen for this launching ceremony in order to emphasize once more my Government's determination to develop our natural resources, such as water, for the benefit of our rural communities and the nation as a whole. It also indicates the importance of irrigation in the overall strategy for our eventual agricultural development and take-off.

As I have made it abundantly clear, my Government's first priority is agriculture. I am convinced that until we stop spending almost all our foreign earnings on food and fuel and begin to produce enough food locally we shall continue to see even our remaining essential services such as education and health services depreciate more and more until they totally disappear. This was, perhaps, how ancient Ghana ceased to be. I believe that the nation's life-blood is its agricultural wealth and potential.

Gallant farmers and fishermen, you are the major component of that wealth. You produce over 70 per cent of our life-sustaining foods. It is what your toil and sweat yield which keeps the cities alive. You have dutifully and painfully served the nation for years unaided. That is why we are convinced that you should now be helped. Please help us to help you.

The programme is aimed at increasing food production during 1980–1 and in subsequent years so as to avert our perennial food shortages. If we are to succeed, we have to be resourceful and industrious. We must mobilize and effectively commit all available resources to the production effort.

In order to make any meaningful impact on the food situation within the shortest possible time and thereby lay the foundation for more comprehensive long-term programmes, we have decided to concentrate efforts on the cultivation of selected food crops which include most of the major crops of this Region, namely, rice, yam, maize, sorghum, ground-nuts, millet and beans.

Poultry and fast breeding livestock such as pigs, rabbits, goats and sheep will also receive special attention. Veterinary services will be provided for them and also for cattle.

Fish production in this Region can be of greater significance than has generally been recognized so far. Ten per cent of the area of the Volta Lake is in the Northern Region. In terms of fish production, this represents an estimated annual catch of 4,000 tonnes. Again, the Region is drained by the Oti River, the Black and White Voltas and their tributaries which can yield another estimated 3,000 tonnes of fish annually.

As of now only ten outboard motors have been sold to the fishermen of the lake system this season, although spare parts have been ordered for the rehabilitation of the old motors. Fishing nets and twine are also expected to arrive soon. In contrast, over one thousand outboard motors have been put into the coastal fishing system, though this has not yet yielded any appreciable results.

Agriculture in this region, as in many parts of the country, depends largely on rain, the onset and distribution of which are, however, unpredictable. The hazards of the weather have been particularly severe in the past five years. To circumvent this problem, development of irrigation will be given greater attention than before. The first phase of the programme will ensure that all completed small irrigation projects in the region are fully utilized. The present total irrigable area includes Nasia, Golinga, Bunglungu, Libga and Yendi.

As I have already emphasized in my Sessional Address to Parliament and at the launching of the National Agricultural Crash Programme at Oyarifa, Government will ensure that maximum use is made of all available irrigation facilities in the country for stable and increased agricultural production.

In this connection, I am particularly happy that exactly a month after launching the national programme, I am here to cut the sod for the Bontanga Irrigation Project—one of the four medium-sized irrigation schemes identified in this region since 1963.

This project involves the construction of a 13-metre high earth dam across the Bontanga River with a length of 2,000 metres and capable of impounding 20 million cubic metres of water for the irrigation of 800 hectares of land directly below the dam. The main crops to be cultivated under the scheme when completed will be maize, rice, legumes, vegetables, cotton and tobacco. The dam will also produce facilities for about 20 hectares of fish ponds and it will support livestock development within the project area.

It is in order to complete this project quickly that Government has

17

approved the award of the contract to a reputable firm, Messrs Taylor Woodrow International Limited. I urge the contractors to complete their contract ahead of schedule, say within twenty-four instead of thirty months. Government will give them all the assistance needed to keep to this deadline.

The Northern Region is very important agriculturally both in what it actually produces already and in its potentialities. The Region is the leading producer of yams and rice and it is second in the production of sorghum, millet, ground-nuts, goats, sheep, cattle and fowls. The production of these major crops, livestock and poultry should be greatly stepped up during the two-year period so as to beat the crop production targets set for the region.

During this season more than 20,000 tonnes of fertilizer will be sold to farmers. The carting of the fertilizers into the Region is not as speedy as we would wish but in this respect, I still commend the help being given by the Tamale Private Road Transport Union, and appeal to them for more vehicles to speed up the operation. I appeal to others also throughout the country to emulate this example and come forward to help. So far 15,000 cutlasses have been sold to farmers throughout the Region and 6,000 more have just been brought in.

The Ministry of Agriculture will continue to make inputs available to farmers and it is expected that they will reciprocate Government's gesture by selling their produce to recognized agencies for proper processing and storage in order to maintain steady supplies at reasonable market prices.

With the co-operation of the Ghana-German Agricultural Development Project, the Ministry of Agriculture will redouble its extension efforts throughout the Region. The impact of these efforts should be manifest in all the Districts.

I wish to place on record my appreciation of the excellent work being done by the Christian Churches in the field of agriculture in Northern Ghana. In the Northern Region alone, there are ten Church Agricultural Project Stations located mainly in the rural areas where they contribute immensely to the agricultural and economic development of small farmers.

The Government will continue to co-operate with these Church Agricultural Project Stations and, wherever necessary, strengthen their technical staff to enable them to perform even greater and better services to the people now and in the future.

Now, let me renew my warning to officials who have become part of our problems instead of helping to solve them. They should now wake up and live up to our rising expectations. If they feel themselves inadequate they should make way for others who can face the present urgent challenges. The Advisory Committee, the Regional Agricultural

Co-ordinators and all disciplinary authorities being set up under the Agricultural programme should ensure that all defaulting officials are brought to book.

It is our collective responsibility as citizens to produce enough food to feed ourselves. Let us therefore all work hard and make efficient use of our scarce resources so that this Agricultural Development Programme attains total success.

And now, I have the pleasure to declare the first phase of the Northern Region Agricultural Development Programme duly launched.

3

Mafi-Kumasi Cassava-Gari Processing Centre

Cassava-gari processing is not new to the rural community that lives around Mafi-Kumasi. The historic importance of the occasion which the President travelled up-country to grace with his presence lay in the novel application of intermediate technology in labour-and-time-saving to the task of grinding and pressing the raw cassava into gari. The Mafi-Kumasi project was sponsored and supervised by the National Council on Women and Development, mobilizing international aid in the form of USAID funding, technical assistance on the part of the Indian High Commissioner in Ghana and the University of Science and Technology, Kumasi. The project showed a way of helping village women to join a co-operative and thus to enhance their earning capacity and independence. The date was 11 July 1980.

I feel gratified indeed to attend this memorable occasion to celebrate with the Ghana National Council on Women and Development, especially, its achievements here at Mafi-Kumasi.

My presence here at this function demonstrates not only my personal conviction but also that of my Government and the People's National Party that our rural areas constitute the mainstay of our economy and that no area of Ghana will be neglected, on account of its size, remoteness or political affiliation. Our mandate is to salvage our economy and rescue our country from any further decline and shame. To succeed in this task we have to mobilize all our people.

Another significant aspect of this ceremony lies not only in the pomp and pageantry we have just witnessed but also in the attempt by the National Council on Women and Development, in line with Government's policy, through training, the acceptance of new ideas, innovations and skills, to narrow the gap between the incomes of rural and urban dwellers.

This ceremony also marks a significant stage in the search for the means of raising the standard of living of our women who are noted for their resourcefulness in trading, farming and cottage industries. The simple tools and technology demonstrated here have always been what they have needed most in their efforts to improve upon their skills and

20

earning capacities. The ability of the National Council on women and Development in translating these needs into reality, must be highly commended. Since it is by dint of hard work that the women of Mafi-Kumasi have succeeded in siting this Factory here, I wish to congratulate them also on this noble achievement. I hope that their shining example will inspire other women in other parts of the country.

Women should not concentrate on selling cloth, essential commodities, flour and other finished items alone but also engage in productive industries like tie-and-dye, poultry, pottery and soap-making.

You are all aware of our precarious economic situation. However, most of us do not seem to realize that this situation poses a serious threat to our survival and self-respect. As I have often said, no problem is too intractable to defy solution. The safest and surest road to our economic recovery and social upliftment is dependence on our own efforts since no one else owes us a living.

The agricultural potentialities of this Region are very well known. Government is prepared to offer the needed assistance to exploit them as evidenced by the fact that we have attracted a $28 millions' worth credit from the International Development Association (IDA), for agricultural projects in this region. Agricultural centres, extension and farming services, research and infrastructural facilities would be established to help farmers to be more efficient in their practices and land usages. In this connection, I wish to appeal to you, the Chiefs and people of this Region to put such facilities to good use thereby increasing your output and incomes.

Government also sees rural development as one of the keys to the economic emancipation and salvation of our country. We recognize the urgency of accelerating the improvement and growth of small-scale industries as a necessary step to stimulate and sustain the growth of the total national economy. We shall therefore encourage and emphasize small-scale industries, especially in the rural areas, while promoting large-scale, capital-intensive agricultural and manufacturing activities as well.

To ensure the efficient exploitation and utilization of the great potential of the rural areas, Government is currently studying proposals for the establishment of a National Board for small-scale industries under the Ministry of Industries, Science and Technology to help promote rural industries throughout the country.

Kindly permit me now to make a few other remarks at this point. No nation has ever achieved any meaningful progress in lawlessness and anarchy. Peace and stability are imperative needs in our efforts to implement successfully the numerous programmes designed to improve upon our performance and living standards.

Indeed, this need is also felt throughout the world and particularly in our continent with its fragile economies and unstable political systems. If we have peace and stability and are also willing to work hard and step up large-scale farming in addition to small-scale operations, we can easily produce enough to feed ourselves and even have surpluses for export. Our recovery and healthy development is contingent on peace, security and stability.

As a matter of urgency, our traditional rulers should release farming lands on easy terms to all prospective investors in our efforts to accelerate the attainment of self-sufficiency in food production. The payment of compensation on acquired lands is being streamlined in order to avoid numerous unpleasant disputes, destoolment charges and in-fighting which have been provoked by such payments in the past.

I wish to take this opportunity to highlight the baneful effects on the economy of the needless wave of industrial strikes, lock-outs and wanton destruction that has recently given this country a very bad name at home and abroad. My Government does not blame workers since we understand their plight and are working hard to find solutions to their problems.

However, those who mislead workers cannot, and will eventually not be able to, avoid blame. In the long run it is the workers and the nation as a whole and not the People's National Party Government that lose when our cocoa, gold and timber fail to reach foreign markets to fetch the foreign exchange, so badly needed for imports such as drugs for our hospitals, or machinery for constructing our roads and bridges. Worse still, when many urgently needed imports are prevented from being landed, unloaded and applied to our wants, then those who mislead others to cause such harm to the country are acting most irresponsibly, indeed, criminally.

We need the collective support and co-operation of all Ghanaians and therefore appeal to all workers to give the Government their support. We must be seen as partners in progress and not enemies in national destruction. My mandate as President is for national salvation, not destruction.

Kindly now permit me to render my sincere gratitude to the Governments of the United States of America and India for their valuable contributions towards the realization of this project and also to mention, specifically, officials of the USAID Mission and the former Indian High Commissioner, Miss Muthama who have provided the much needed technical and financial assistance. This is a unique example in international co-operation we much cherish. We look forward to more of such co-operation.

To our universities, research institutions and, in particular, the Consultancy Centre of the University of Science and Technology, I also render my sincere thanks. Government shall ever be prepared to assist them all to produce the simple tools, the simple but efficient technology that will revolutionize our economy. This is therefore the time for them to show their ingenuity and inventiveness.

As I have already indicated, the National Council on Women and Development deserves our greatest commendation. Their efforts in getting the project started and seeing to its ultimate completion has been a laudable achievement indeed. I hope that the Council will also turn its attention to other areas which will embrace more of our womenfolk in honest, honourable and productive activities.

My Government will provide the necessary support to help rehabilitate women who, for lack of gainful employment, have had to seek adventures in foreign lands. The Council should continue to fight against social disabilities which retard the progress of our women and the nation as a whole.

Honourable Ministers, Your Excellencies, distinguished guests, ladies and gentlemen, may what is produced by this Centre be satisfying; may the efforts of those who supply the raw materials for the factory be amply rewarding. In this hope, I have the pleasure to commission this Cassava Processing Centre.

4

Constitutional Institutions

The 1979 Constitution of Ghana required the establishment of a number of commissions among which were the National Development Commission, the Fisheries Commission and the Lands Commission. The President inaugurated these on 20 August 1980, at the State House.

It is my pleasure and honour to inauguarate today, the National Development Commission, the Fisheries Commission and the Lands Commission, three important Commissions established under the Constitution of the Third Republic to play effective roles in our march towards social justice and economic advancement.

Three weeks ago, I inaugurated three other Commissions in this very hall. This ceremony today therefore completes our obligation under the Constitution to set up such Commissions to aid and/or complement the efforts of Government in its plans and policies meant to promote sound and rapid socio-economic development.

The National Development Commission is, in particular, charged with the responsibility of advising the President on planning, development policy and strategies and therefore has a crucial and urgent role to play in our frantic attempts at resuscitating the economy and promoting all-round development. I therefore personally look upon the Commission as one of the most important support instruments of my Administration in our struggle for economic regeneration. In fact before I go any further, let me express the gratitude and also the congratulations of my Government to its members and also to the members of the two other Commissions for the prompt and positive way in which they have accepted to serve Ghana in their various capacities.

May I however emphasize the fact that these and similar Commissions established under the Constitution are not to be regarded as independent sovereign bodies which can opt out of the clearly expressed will of the people of the unitary state of Ghana of which I am the Executive as well as ceremonial Head. Even the President and Parliament are subject not only to the Constitution but ultimately to the sovereign electorate and the entire population of Ghana. Bigoted ideas and capricious interpretations of our various roles under the Constitution which embodies the collective wisdom, wishes and will of all the citizens of Ghana should therefore be very carefully avoided.

I know that the task before you is formidable but also that with your rich variety of backgrounds of intellect and wide experience in the running of affairs and the management of economies, the results of your efforts will provide government with workable and reliable blueprints for the salvation and eventual growth of our economy. I am therefore confident that you will rise equal to the challenges of your respective roles and functions in the general and permanent interests of Ghana as a whole.

It was the unsatisfactory economic situation of the last decade which brought into sharp focus the urgent need to take steps to arrest the deplorable and precipitous drift of our economy into the chaos which has caused the intolerable living conditions of the majority of our people. And it was this situation that led the makers of the Third Republic to fashion these and similar Commissions and Councils so that they can help recreate conditions to alleviate, not worsen, the tribulations of all Ghanaians.

Currently, the supply of food and other basic necessities is seriously in deficit in the cities and other parts of the country. Our industrial establishments are either completely out of production or working at very low capacities. There are growing signs of massive unemployment if this trend persists, yet our efforts to revive idle factories and increase the capacity utilization of those which had been tenuously working, are still being frustrated by unbelievable bottlenecks both at home and abroad.

I feel particularly concerned with and worried over the continued slide in the production and exports of cocoa, wood products, gold and other minerals which has been taking place over the past six years. The services provided by our educational and health institutions have also steeply deteriorated over the years and our other infrastructural facilities, especially our roads and bridges, have fallen into such a bad state of disrepair that, as I have been saying since April 1979, they have become death traps, hazards to life and property or mere apologies for what they once were only a decade or so ago. Our communications channels of all forms have long been clogged. In short it was because of these and for many other reasons that the Constitution-makers had to design these Commissions and Councils to play supporting, not obstructionist or destructive roles, in any efforts to reintroduce sanity into our society and our economy.

In addition to these past production and supply problems, or largely because of them, mounting pressures of demand have been worsened with our new birth of freedom in the midst of massive deficit public financing, excessive wage demands unrelated to any productivity, and outmodedly rigid labour laws which have blocked structural changes and adjustments on the labour market.

High rates of galloping inflation had also helped to disrupt productive

25

economic activity, drastically reduce the standard of living of workers and foster unproductive and anti-social speculative activities, all of which are detrimental to the interests of all citizens, particularly the lower income groups and those who, such as peasants and the urban unemployed, earn no regular incomes at all.

Our increasingly intractable domestic problems have also been exacerbated by unfavourable international developments. The single international issue for quite some time now which has been our major national concern has been the energy problem. Oil price increases have, since 1973, greatly speeded up domestic inflation, reduced growth prospects and further burdened our already worsening external payments problems.

Yet key indicators of the health of the international economy continue to point to a worsening situation which would further tighten and harden the already severe balance of payments problems under which we have been operating. It is therefore clear that the inherent strength of our economy will be compromised beyond repair and our weaknesses heightened unless appropriate measures can be taken to contain the production problems and demand pressures plagueing the economy. This is the nature of some of the problems to which members of the National Development Commission, for instance, will be required to help find solutions.

In discharging your respective responsibilities you should all be guided by the policy directives which formed the theme and the keynote of my Sessional Address to the nation assembled in Parliament last year and which have been re-emphasized and expounded in the last two budget statements. Broadly speaking, we want to rehabilitate our existing stock of productive and infrastructural facilities which are economically viable and also to redirect our efforts and resources into realistic productive activities.

It has been all too obvious for all our nationals that the spread of investment in the recent past has been rather too thin and disorderly with the result that the necessary care has not been taken to ensure that the installations are appropriate or maintained in reasonably good conditions so that they can support or justify the foreign exchange expended on them. Consequently, we have recently had to make huge allocations for spare parts even for newly acquired but poorly maintained machinery and equipment. Believe it or not but it is true that quite a lot of equipment imported before 1966 is still in the crates in which it landed in Ghana at that time. Naturally, these consignments have become unusuable now while the debts on them have also remained unpaid.

Then again, industrial promotion has been pursued without any agricultural development to increase productivity while releasing farm labour and also without due cognizance of the lack of suitable local raw materials or the suitability of local conditions. In brief, there has been an over-expanded industrial capacity and mostly in the wrong directions, hence the urgent need now for the PNP Administration to make painful but unavoidable readjustments in both the agricultural and industrial sectors. We have to rehabilitate what we can out of the basic industries and redirect our efforts and resources into areas where they can be economically sustained without unduly heavy outlays on fresh imported inputs.

To this end, we have to place particular emphasis on the development of agriculture and agro-based industries. Indeed, I have emphasized time and again the total commitment of my Administration to the development of a strong agricultural base. Even in its present state of relative neglect we all still derive our sustenance from agriculture and must therefore ensure that in the allocation of resources, pride of place is given to the needs of this sector.

The overriding commitment of my Government is to the achievement of self-sufficiency in food production, the improvement of cocoa production and the cultivation of industrial raw materials. An agricultural revolution is our long-term objective and we believe that the present agricultural programme will arouse the necessary new awareness which will generate momentum and sustain such aspects of our development endeavours which can become permanent features of an eventual sound revolution in both sectors.

Apart from agriculture and industry the improvement of the mining and timber sectors must equally be accorded high priority in the planning process. At the present levels of prices of minerals, particularly for gold, we can turn our perennial payments deficits into surpluses in a relatively short time if we can adequately invest in and fully tap our mineral resources.

Our ability to pay our way on the international market depends on our export capacity. In the face of continuing oil price increases, we must spare no efforts in exploiting to the full our export potential. I therefore urge you to pay particular attention to mineral exploitation and also the development and the processing of our forest products for export. Without the full and effective utilization of these natural and basic resources, our development efforts will be seriously hampered.

Mr Chairman, the success of planning requires the identification of problems and the design of policies and, even more importantly, the careful and efficient management of resources and the sustained and effective implementation of programmes drawn up. For far too long, Governments have pursued makeshift and frequently changing policies and have also carried a disproportionately large share of investment and employment in this country. Some of these investments, such as those in education, health, road infrastructures, water supplies and other basic services rightly belong to the public sector. But Government involvement in the productive sector, in agriculture and in industry has proved too expensive and inefficient.

The time has therefore now arrived for us to take stock of government performance in its pioneering role in industry, agriculture and distribution with a view to taking bold steps to change course, if necessary, without creating conditions for the exploitation of the masses by a few privileged indigenous and foreign groups within our national community. Some nationals have declared that they are capitalists and cannot work with us of the PNP. Well, we are Ghanaians and can work with all citizens in all capacities provided they care about the economic recovery, safety and progress of our country. As I have often said, no positive contribution towards these can be considered too little; no sacrifice on our part shall be too great.

We should be able to minimize the ever increasing and unrelenting pressures on government to spend beyond its means through inflationary financing. We should also aim at devising and implementing efficient manpower policies which will place more emphasis on the development of individual initiative, responsibility and self-reliance as well as financial policies which will ensure that resources are efficiently applied to promote sound economic recovery, eventual real growth and take-off.

I believe that we can attract domestic and foreign investment of the right type, on terms mutually beneficial to all sides, particularly in the production sectors, if we pursue sound, equitable and realistic plans and policies rather than continue to see and appreciate things in beggar-your-neighbour terms.

The preparation of some new guidelines on investment has been in progress for some time now and these will be made available to you to assist and start you off in your work. We should work towards creating a framework which will provide ample scope for investment, productive incentives and protection for the commitment of domestic and foreign private capital to the economy.

In the sector of utility services, our poor quality of work and inadequate maintenance have resulted in the rapid erosion or even total disappearance of past huge investments in roads, railways, ports and public buildings. While we aim at rehabilitating these past investments and services, we must also strive to improve increasingly on our living conditions and higher standards of work so as to minimize fixed over-head and maintenance costs in such social services as education and health which we must continue to provide for all citizens. However, these objectives should not be subordinated to the financial viability of or the maintenance of minimum standards in our utility services which seek to promote social justice.

I do not personally believe that there are any hard and fast doctrinaire prescriptions for planning in its technical scope and ideological orientations. What we urgently need at present is a set of realistic and implementable plans and policies which will restore life to our economy and restart us on a course of sustained growth and eventual developmental take-off.

Ladies and gentlemen, our country has produced many brilliant economic managers and administrators who have set enviable records at home and in other parts of the world. I therefore believe that you here present have the same capabilities and can produce similar results. I hope that you will give of your best in finding solutions to our myriad problems. To this end, I can assure you of my active and unstinted co-operation and support at all times. In any case, your roles and functions have been so designed as to make your efforts very useful props to those of Government.

Mr Chairman, distinguished guests, ladies and gentlemen, kindly permit me briefly to refer specifically to the Fisheries Commission.

In recent times we have been beset with problems in the fishing industry which are similar to the other problems I have mentioned already. The Fisheries Commission has therefore been established to be responsible, among other things, for the regulation, management and utilization of our national natural fisheries resources and also to co-ordinate Government policies relating thereto. To this end the Commission is expected to produce sound programmes for the orderly development of our fishing industry.

The Commission should formulate fish production plans, guidelines and programmes for the promotion, co-ordination, control and development of fisheries and fish utilization for human consumption as well as for animal and poultry feed. It should also initiate programmes for the promotion and exploitation of our tuna fisheries resources and establish bilateral arrangements with sister African states for fishing rights so as to offset the present difficulties facing our distant water fleet fishermen. Even more importantly, it should produce plans to encourage and promote State and private initiative in fish farming, and advise on fisheries research and co-ordinate research findings in the fishing industry in order to promote interest which will lead to improvements in fish production generally in Ghana. Admittedly, its functions as briefly summarized here will not be easy to accomplish. However, with dedication, singleness of purpose and a genuine desire to help feed our fast-growing population, it should be able to discharge them creditably.

The most pressing problem areas of the fishing industry include those of our distant water fleet created by the establishment of the exclusive economic zones by coastal states and those confronting Ghanaians desirous of entering into tuna fishing, which is a potentially great foreign exchange earner.

Ladies and gentlemen, if the Ghana Fisheries Commission pursues its objectives and functions assiduously and successfully it should be possible for the country to derive much benefit from the fishing industries. I am confident that with the interplay of the expertise of the members of the Commission as constituted, steady and durable progress will be made towards the realization of the objectives we have set for our fish requirements and for salvaging our economy.

Our priorities in the industry include the provision of inputs to canoe fishermen, who still form the backbone of the industry since they produce approximately 60–70 per cent of total fish landings in the country.

Government is pursuing plans to conclude arrangements for tuna deliveries to Ghana by vessels registered to fly our national flag and also to provide inputs for our inshore and distant water fleets. I expect the Commission to pursue these plans vigorously so as to achieve rapid increases in fish production for the benefit of our people. We shall endeavour to make the necessary resources available for the supply of adequate supplies of inputs, especially fishing nets, mending twines, outboard motors and the spare parts needed by our canoes and fishing vessels.

Mr Chairman, the Lands Commission has been made responsible to the Constitution thus clearly demonstrating the great importance our people attach to land matters. In effect, members of the Commission are being made custodians of the most important and cherished heritage of every Ghanaian, that is, the land. I am confident that they will take good and responsible care of it in the collective interest of our national community of today and of the future. Land everywhere should be held in trust and used judicously and equitably from generation to generation.

As you may have observed, there are major differences between the new Lands Commission and the previous one. The new Commission provides for the representation of such important institutions as the Ghana Institution of Surveyors, the National House of Chiefs and the Ghana Bar Association. The object of such representations is to enable the Commission to derive maximum benefit from these institutions. It is also to make sure that officials do not constitute themselves into landowners under the pretext of modernism, public interest and development, as had tended to happen in the past.

The old Lands Commission was responsible for the final processing of all documents on land, centred in Accra. The Minister, acting as Chairman, had to sign all documents pertaining to land in the country. This burden has been reduced by the Constitution to the extent that most of these documents will now be processed and signed at regional branch offices. This change is intended to streamline the administration of land and ensure rapid processing of documents relating to land. Accordingly, I hope that you will do all you can to ensure that this objective is achieved to enable Government's plans for agricultural and other developments to succeed at a desirable and honest pace, unhampered by inflated compensation, conflicting claims and fratricidal disputes.

Ladies and gentlemen, I need not emphasize that one of the causes of numerous cases of unrest in many parts of the country can be traced to land disputes. The administration of land in the country has, in the past, also been bedevilled with corruption. It is therefore absolutely necessary for you to discharge your duties with transparent honesty and impartiality so as to bring about peace in the sphere of land matters.

In the discharge of your onerous duties you may find that some of your responsibilities overlap those of other institutions such as the Ghana Forestry Commission. In such cases, I expect you to co-operate fully with the institutions concerned as to ensure that the overall objective of national interests and development is achieved. I look forward to seeing all of us march forward together from all directions in mutual understanding, co-operation, dedication, discipline, public spiritedness and a common desire to save and to serve Ghana disinterestedly and impartially.

Mr Chairman, distinguished guests, ladies and gentlemen, we have established these important Commissions as required by the Constitution, but the real and greater task is before the members of the Commissions themselves. Many well intentioned institutions of this nature have been established before but have become serious liabilities to the State because those charged with running them have failed to live up to expectation or have not grasped the spirit behind their conception, and have tended to regard them as their private properties, often operating even against the collective and permanent interests of our society. The Third Republic can no longer afford the luxury of such attitudes and failures. I trust that all the members of these Commissions will uphold the confidence the country has reposed in them and discharge their duties honestly, responsibly, diligently, sensitively, cost-effectively and humanely within the framework of the economic mess that is Ghana today.

Now, Mr Chairman, I have the greatest pleasure to declare the National Development Commission, the Fisheries Commission and the Lands Commission inaugurated.

5

Gold Endowment Conference and the Ghana Investment Code Act

There can be no more important matters to engage the personal attention of the President, than those embodied in his address at the opening of the International Seminar on Ghana's Gold Endowment, held at the Kwame Nkrumah Conference Centre, Accra, on 6 January 1981. Subsequently, the President inaugurated the Board of the Ghana Investment Centre on 1 September 1981, which followed after. The policy statements made in these two addresses state the Government's liberal policy on investment in Ghana. The follow-up action on the Gold Endowment Conference was the Investment Code 1981 which incorporated in one legal document a number of earlier laws and included the up-dating of investment legislation in Ghana.

The special merit of the Ghana Investment Centre is that it embodies under a single administration various institutions which have to do with applications, granting of approvals, issuing of manufacturing licences for new industries and expansion of existing ones, the granting of immigrant quotas, guarantees and fiscal incentives, and the lot.

The potentialities for Ghana's mineral and other natural resources are indeed vast.

It is my honour and, indeed, happy duty to deliver the opening address of this unique International Seminar on Ghana's Gold Endowment. The Seminar is indeed unique since this is the first time ever that representatives of most of the major international companies engaged in the prospecting of the mining, processing, production and marketing of gold have come together under one roof to deliberate on Ghana's gold mines and potentialities and the economic benefits that would be derived from them, for Ghana and the rest of the world. I shall therefore use the opportunity to sketch the official policy objectives of my Administration on this and other related matters.

But first of all, kindly permit me, Mr Chairman, to extend to all our foreign guests, in my own name and on behalf of the Government and people of Ghana, a very sincere, warm and friendly welcome to our country. I fervently hope that they will enjoy their brief stay with us, get to know and understand our country and people better and acquire a deeper appreciation of our present socio-economic situation.

I also wish all participants a very Happy and Peaceful New Year and many golden investment opportunities in Ghana in the years ahead. May 1981 and the future bring each and everyone of you success in your personal endeavours. I wish you true and lasting happiness.

Mr Chairman, although the greatest single asset of any nation is its people or its human resources, it is the resourcefulness of this human asset, endowed with intellect, which makes any nation great or small. Hence in the past it has been possible to speak of the smallest of the small and the greatest of the great among the comity of nations.

Natural resource endowments, when available, are additional assets which boost the efforts of the people but these are by no means the only prerequisite for national greatness, strength and healthy national economy, as evidenced by the shining example of a country such as the Swiss Confederation which has not been richly endowed with natural resources, apart from beautiful scenery, but which can yet justifiably and proudly boast of her strong economy and currency.

In contrast, Ghana abounds not only in human resources but also in varied and enormous natural resources. Her people can pride themselves in being very resourceful, and having a rich history. Ghana did initiate and spearhead the independence struggle and in so doing, greatly helped to place the African continent on the world map, with many new dimensions.

We can also say with pride that Ghana is among the developing countries with large numbers of personnel serving in high positions of trust in international institutions, establishments and organizations. Some of our nationals are also serving in advisory capacities in a number of developing countries.

This is a clear example of the human endowment of our country, the resourcefulness of our people and our contribution to the development of the international community. When we have, we give generously and freely to others. When we lack, we beg for alms from others. We are grateful for genuine assistance which we are prepared to repay.

Ghana is more richly endowed with natural resources than her present small population can exploit and consume alone. It was not a mere fairy tale that the country was called the Gold Coast from the fifteenth century up to 1957. The first point of contact with the outside world in 1381 was described as 'The Mine' and is still called Elmina. Ghana still probably abounds in richer and larger deposits of gold ore than many leading gold-producing countries in the world. In addition, we have large quantities of bauxite, some manganese, diamonds, iron ore, limestone and columbite-tantalite.

Nor is this all. Recent research and indications strongly suggest that we may be richly blessed with large oil deposits both off-shore and inland.

We have quietly but intensively been investigating the extent and spread of this 'black gold' only since my administration assumed office in September 1979, but already we have every reason to be happy at what is emerging from such investigations and exploration. Our actual and potential hydro sources of renewable energy are also enormous and we are working hard to develop them so as to cut down our present high crude oil import bills.

We have some of the finest timber and wood products in the world and our virgin forest is still substantial. We are blessed with vast stretches of fertile and arable land suitable for varied agricultural production. Our large man-made lake and rivers abound in a rich variety of fishes. Mr Chairman, and participants in this Seminar, what more can any country the size of Ghana ask for from nature? You name it and we may, perhaps, soon add it to the foregoing list. Could it therefore be that our wealth has partly been the cause of our present unenviable state of affairs? Personally, I have always been very much inclined to think so.

Mr Chairman, Ghana speaks today only of her prostrate economy struggling for recovery: a sad situation brought about by causes which can be summarized under two main heads. First, we seem to have become victims of the very generosity of nature to which I have already alluded. For instance, because of the abundant riches of our forest resources we appear to have become over-complacent with our cocoa industry, especially, while the golden pod and bean enjoyed high prices.

This industry should have been the major unrelenting preoccupation of our production endeavours but due to our complacency it was, with the other forest resources such as timber and wood products, neglected. Although uncertainties caused by widely fluctuating cocoa prices over the years were the first to shake us out of our complacency, the lessons do not seem to have been drawn and applied in a consistent and sustained manner.

Even after it had been clearly realized that our other natural resources should have started to be explored and developed, previous Ghana governments, to varying degrees of neglect or guilt, failed to provide the right climate and conditions for putting these enormous natural resources and comparative advantages to good use in the interest of all and for social justice. Lack of sensitivity and proper direction, mismanagement and bureaucratic callousness have also added their contribution to this sad situation.

Thus, those in permanent positions of trust and responsibility have not developed any real concern for or responsiveness to the needs of their fellow citizens. Ghanaians, therefore, progressively became, over the years, rather disillusioned, bewildered at their sorry plight in the midst of abundant natural resources, and cynical. They are ingenious only in cheating their fellows or the public in order to survive at all.

Ghana's economy has also been plagued by factors outside her immediate control. These have included galloping, imported as well as locally induced, inflation and, especially, the rapidly increasing cost of fossil fuel as well as the inflated cost of imported equipment and other manufactured goods.

Given our actual and potential wealth in enormous water resources, rich variety of fertile soils and minerals of all sorts, the outside world naturally failed, until recently, to appreciate our difficulties or sympathize with us. They even tended wilfully to misinterpret events happening here or to write us off. In this regard, while we berate ourselves in self-analysis, we can also blame the outside world, particularly our friends and well-wishers for their insensitivity to our genuine needs or their lack of quick and positive response to our urgent appeals for help. But can we really blame our own faults also on them since they can say that they do not owe us our living? I still think so because the world has now become too interdependent for the plight of any part of it to be long ignored by its other parts.

The People's National Party has sought and been given the mandate by the electorate to bring the past state of affairs to an end by arresting any further decline of our economy, rekindling the resourcefulness of our people and showing the world that Ghana can never be lightly written off. In fact, Ghana will forever remain a very strategic country in Africa and the entire world. Indeed, I have no doubt that we shall rise again sooner than can be imagined and that therefore our friends and well-wishers should come to our aid now without any more hesitation.

Mr Chairman, since assuming office, my Administration has laboured painstakingly to bring sanity back into our economy. We have already gone to great lengths in reordering our priorities. Thus, even within our limited resources we have been modestly repaying part of our external debts to reassure our creditors of our good faith and thereby to reopen our credit-worthiness. We have caused some modest repatriation of profits accumulated over long periods of time. We have also laid the foundations for the rehabilitation of our infrastructure and our industries for steady and sustained economic recovery and growth and for sound, balanced national development.

You will therefore agree, Mr Chairman and distinguished participants, that given our dwindling foreign exchange earnings and the limitless demands being urgently made on them to alleviate the hardships of our long suffering people, Ghanaians can give no better demonstration of profitable and mutually beneficial investment opportunities for ourselves and our friends at home and abroad.

One of the major obstacles which has retarded our past national progress has, admittedly, been our reliance on mono-crop economy. Thus, we have, for far too long, largely depended on our declining cocoa

35

industry alone. This situation has only been greatly compounded and confounded by the increasingly crippling oil import bills since 1974.

Our fast-growing population had long demanded the diversification of our mono-crop economy since we cannot continue forever to depend solely on the one commodity of cocoa for our growing national imports, and basic domestic consumption requirements such as rice. We have therefore now resolved to develop the vast, untapped natural resources I have already briefly enumerated.

My Government has also embarked on the determination of the exact extent of our hidden natural resources and on the creation of the necessary climate and conditions which will increasingly attract potential overseas investors and thus enable us to diversify our present cocoa-based or mono-crop economy.

Mr Chairman, but for the Akosombo Hydro-electric, renewable source of energy, thanks to the foresight of the late Osagyefo Dr Kwame Nkrumah of blessed memory, our economy would long have been totally destroyed by our fuel import bills alone. The Seminar which you are starting this morning is therefore one example of the many efforts we are making to diversify our sources of foreign exchange earnings and for solving the numerous problems facing us at home.

Being experts and entrepreneurs in the field of gold prospecting, mining and production, most of you participating in this Seminar know only too well that ten viable gold mines were still operating at the end of the Second World War but that this number had dwindled to only four long before 1979. Thus, from a peak output of over 900,000 fine ounces of gold in 1960, our present production has dropped to the level of only 380,000 fine ounces by 1979. In terms of percentages which are, perhaps, more precise, Ghana produced about 35 per cent of the world's gold output at one time, but could hardly produce 2 per cent by 1978.

We endeavoured last year to provide adequately for resuscitating the existing gold mines and hope to continue assisting the industry increasingly, within the limited resources available to us. We expect the existing gold mining companies quickly to expand their gold production activities, including winning, prospecting and determination of the extent of hitherto undiscovered gold deposits which litter the country, from the littoral to Nangodi in the Upper Region.

I am informed that our gold ore reserves fall under three categories, namely, banket, reef and alluvial gold and that they are zoned into 487 blocks of about sixty square miles each. I therefore sincerely hope that, during this Seminar, our overseas friends and participants will have the opportunity to examine closely some of this data, exchange ideas not only among themselves but also with their local counterparts and thus draw the appropriate conclusions from the nature and extent of the reserves.

Indeed, I hope that you will leave the Seminar better equipped to enable you to report accurately, faithfuly and favourably on your findings and also to make investment recommendations of mutual benefit to all of us. I even expect that by the end of this Seminar you would be firm converts to our cause, as determined to champion it within international business and financial circles as the Ambassadors accedited to us have already creditably done with their Governments throughout the last fifteen months.

For the advance information of our overseas friends, and interested participants in this Seminar, my Administration has decided to declare gold mining a High Growth Sector of our economy and will therefore make every effort to sustain the steady recovery, development and growth of this industry.

We shall progressively and steadily remove the bottlenecks and tardy procedures which have long bedevilled the system and thus create the necessary atmosphere and conditions favourable for investment in this and many other sectors of our economy. In particular, we hope to go further and provide special incentives to the gold mining sector in order to promote rapid overseas investment in it. In line with these policy objectives, new draft proposals will soon be placed before Parliament for enactment to give such proposals the necessary legal authority.

The new Bill will seek to revise guidelines on equity participation in joint mining ventures, management agreements, the repatriation of risk capital and dividends and improved conditions of service for technical expatriate personnel. We are also making efforts to review the present tax regime in order to bring it in line with those of other gold producing countries and thus make investment in this sector competitive.

Distinguished participants and guests, my Administration is well aware that national security and political stability are vital prerequisites for the inflow of investment capital. We therefore wish to reassure potential and friendly foreign investors that Government and the entire Ghanaian public will do everything in our power to ensure stability and the safety of investment in Ghana.

As I have already had the occasion to remark to the Diplomatic Corps in Ghana, we may not have reached the serene and rarefied mountain top of peace, security and stability yet, but considering the chaotic and anarchic security situation we met on assuming office, we have made considerable progress and the situation, which has now greatly improved, shall increasingly be consolidated. Our collective national achievement in re-establishing civilian democratic rule also speaks for itself.

I therefore wish to appeal once more to the international community to also translate their goodwill towards Ghana into concrete economic activities, for political stability has always been contingent on economic stability and progress everywhere in the world and Ghana should not be

37

expected to be an exception *ad infinitum.*

Mr Chairman, I wish to add and re-emphasize that the peace and political stability which some foreign investors often require of us as pre-conditions for investment can, in fact, not be re-established firmly and permanently if they all continue to sit on the fence or wait and see. Like all other peoples elsewhere, Ghanaians cannot wait indefinitely since, in the very long run, they will all be dead. They want their living conditions changed for the better in their lifetime since our enormous natural resources endowment is their fortunate birthright. Indeed, unlike Coleridge's Ancient Mariner, they cannot forever stand the tantalizing sight of:

Water, water, everywhere nor any drop to drink,
Water, water, everywhere and all the boards did shrink.

Let us remember always also that investment has been going on in other countries such as Italy, the UK, the Federal Republic of Germany, Japan, the USA, and so on, despite occasional frightful terrorist activities in those countries. They have also been investing in other areas less tension-free and stable than Ghana. Again, it is rather strange to us that while the super-powers and mature economies freely carry out substantial trade among themselves at need, they tend to frown upon smaller countries which only want to be 'friends to all and enemies to none'.

In brief, Mr Chairman, Ghanaians are not the first in the world to have an internal crisis or to be a restless and troublesome people. On the contrary, we are among the most generous, good-natured and warm-hearted and should therefore not be forced into feeling too bitter for possessing these virtues which most other peoples lack and for which mankind is the poorer.

Distinguished ladies and gentlemen, even though this Seminar has been organized to deal exclusively with Ghana's Gold Endowment, I wish to avail myself of this opportunity briefly to highlight for your study a few other important areas of our interest to which we have paid great attention throughout last year and which may also interest our foreign friends. We have large deposits of bauxite which can quickly be exploited and processed into alumina to feed our already existing smelting capacity.

The project alone also offers several other areas of investment for which we shall be prepared to provide the appropriate incentives. These include huge caustic soda facilities as inputs for the alumina production itself and a fairly well-developed salt industry which can provide the required brine for the caustic soda plant.

We also want to develop our enormous additional hydro-electric potentialities such as those of the Bui river and several other projects so as to provide the necessary power for many other industries which can all be more economically run on cheaper, renewable sources of energy than on fossil fuel. Our substantial iron ore deposits cry out for investment capital. Need I mention our diamond and columbite-tantalite deposits and other supporting projects too numerous to detail here?

In short, Mr Chairman, the sky can be the limit in Ghana to the far-sighted, honest and audacious investor. Indeed, the more you invest here the more you may discover that Ghana is really a geological miracle. Please, be forthcoming soonest and do not hesitate or delay any more.

Finally, distinguished participants and, especially, our overseas friends, I must thank you very sincerely for responding positively to our invitation to attend this unique, golden Seminar. I wish all of you a happy visit to Ghana, very frank exchange of ideas and information and therefore very fruitful deliberations during this Seminar which I now have the singular honour formally to declare open.

Dr Hilla Limann inaugurates the Investment Code Act
Tuesday, 11 August 1981

It is with a great sense of satisfaction that I give my assent to the Investment Code Act recently passed by Parliament. By this simple ceremony, the Investment Code has now become part of the law of the land.

I should like to express my deepest appreciation for a job well done and grateful thanks to all those who have worked relentlessly to bring this new Investment Code into being. In particular, I thank the Technical Committee which put the basic material together and the Drafting Committee which willingly gated itself for two weeks and elaborated the first meaningful draft bill for Cabinet's consideration. They did a yeoman's job by consulting many shades of opinion on my request. The whole nation is grateful to them. I also wish to record my deepest appreciation of and thanks to the Chairman and members of the Council of State who also subjected the Draft bill to careful scrutiny and made extremely useful comments and observations which were subsequently considered alongside numerous others we collated on the first draft bill. We are also grateful to many organizations and individuals within Ghana and abroad who made very useful contributions, comments and observations which have all been very carefuly considered in the Act as finally passed.

Last but not the least, I wish to record my profound appreciation to the Speaker, to the Chairman and members of the Finance Committee and, indeed, to all Members of Parliament for their very careful consideration of the numerous amendments submitted to them and also for their hard work in painstakingly debating the provisions of the bill until it was finally passed.

As it now stands, the New Investment Code, 1981, is the product of many minds and hands. It is the national document that my Administration set out to produce so as to meet the challenges and international business requirements of our times and thus pull Ghana out of the stagnant backwaters of modern economic development.

Indeed, since the advent of the Third Republic no single bill has provoked as much debate and genuine interest in all sections of our community as the Investment Code Act. This clearly shows the importance the whole nation has attached to the Code. This final Act also vindicates my Administration's conviction that there was a clear need for new legislation to replace the numerous old regulations governing or rather hampering, investment in Ghana.

As you are all well aware, Ghana had been starved of any meaningful and productive foreign investment long before the Third Republic came into existence. This had resulted mainly from maladministration, very slow and labyrinthine procedures and callous misuse of national resources, all of which led to the complete loss of confidence in us as a people. The final *coup de grâce* fell when Ghana was totally blockaded prior to 24 September 1979 and the trickle inflow of goods for which we were even prepared to pay completely dried up. It was a very grave situation indeed.

On assuming office, the prime and most urgent responsibility of the People's National Party Administration was therefore quickly to undo the blockade, reopen our supply lines, reverse the negative trends of the past, restore confidence in Ghana and create a congenial climate to attract foreign investment.

To this end, we had also to re-establish some discipline in the administration of the nation's resources by reconstructing a national budget which had not been done for several years past. We have since achieved some measure of success in our financial administration, having streamlined our import licence system and issued three national budgets already. We have also re-established confidence in the economy primarily by paying off our short-term debts, reordering our priorities and introducing bold measures designed to lift the economy out of the abyss. Those who do not know or wilfully ignore the depths of our economic degradation and chaos by September 1979 cannot easily understand or appreciate what we have done so far.

Ladies and gentlemen, as I have already indicated, the need to change the laws governing investment in Ghana had been long overdue. Our laws had been completely out of line with modern trends and the investment regulations of other countries competing for funds from the same sources while, moreover, investors needed to be reassured that they would not lose their investment funds but would rather have opportunities for repatriating their honestly earned profits. In short, it was absolutely necessary to change the whole investment climate in Ghana.

I am therefore glad that we have all had the courage of our convictions to do so in good time for the benefit of our people and in the face of wilful distortions and ludicrous arguments that we are selling out our birthrights. An economically dead Ghana will have no voice in the comity of nations to speak of rights at home or abroad. On the other hand, no investor can take out of Ghana such infrastructures as farm houses, factory buildings, hotels and tourist complexes, bridges and barrages. On the contrary, all these and many more by-products of investment can only enrich our birthright.

Having achieved some of our objectives in the Investment Code Act, 1981, it remains for our foreign friends and investors to take up the opportunities now open to them in Ghana, especially in the areas of exploration on-shore and off-shore for oil and natural gas and also in the gold, diamond and bauxite mining sectors. Other areas include our vast agricultural, timber and tourist potentialities which require investment for effective exploitation. Indeed, since agriculture is our top-most priority, our vast stretches of arable and fertile land and enormous water resources for irrigation offer great opportunities to potential investors in this field, especially in the light of the growing spectre of widespread annual food deficits facing the whole world.

Your Excellencies, members of the Diplomatic Corps, we appreciate the good work you have been doing by reporting faithfully to your governments and financial circles on the decisions and sacrifices we have been making to put our own house in order. We thank you for attending this small function in such large numbers. However, as I have often said, we urgently need large infusions of institutional and private investment since our own resources are at present woefully inadequate for resuscitating our economy and fulfilling the aspirations of our people as quickly as they expect us to do. As I have also had the occasion to emphasize in London last May, we are not asking for charity; we are offering investment opportunities for mutually beneficial economic interactions. You may therefore wish to complete a good job you have ably started by advising your governments, financial and business circles not to sit on the fence any longer.

My Administration is convinced that peace and economic stability are the best guarantees for political stability and investments. We are leaving no stone unturned to ensure the democratic way of life in Ghana. Our friends, well-wishers and the older democracies should therefore actively invest in this system as well, rather than look on passively while even some international organizations try to force socially impracticable recommendations down our throats. An anaemic patient can be helped back to life only by fresh and more blood transfusions, not by draining the body and leaving an empty, dry shell or skeleton.

Excellencies, besides the Investment Code Act, 1981, we have also taken certain measures designed to speed up the processing of investment enquiries. We have inaugurated four Promotion Councils to quicken investment activities in mining, in prospecting on-shore and off-shore for oil and in the implementation of the Kibi Bauxite Project. We hope to set up similar Councils for the Bui Dam and Opon Mansi Projects. The Investment Centre to be established under this Act will complete this process and I fervently hope that this will spare investors the ordeals of slow procedures and avoidable administrative inefficiencies. The activities of the Promotion Councils will be co-ordinated by the Board of the Investment Centre under the Vice-President who will not brook any delays and 'stop-go, stop-go' tactics.

Once again, Excellencies, ladies and gentlemen, I should like to express my profound gratitude to all those who have helped directly or indirectly to produce the Investment Code Act, 1981 which should usher in a new era of investment in industry, agriculture, mining and many other sectors for the mutual benefit of all Ghanaians and foreign investors.

Address at the inauguration of the Board of the Ghana Investment Centre Tuesday, 1 September 1981

It is a pleasant duty for me this morning to inaugurate the Board of the Ghana Investment Centre. This ceremony, though simple, is nonetheless very significant since this is probably the most important Board so far inaugurated under the present Administration.

Following the passage of the Investments Code Bill by Parliament into law and my formal assent to that Act, the inauguration of the governing body of the Investments Centre completes the long process started a year ago of establishing the new, high powered institution to replace the former Capital Investments Board of 1963 set up by the far-sighted late Osagyefo of blessed memory.

I warmly congratulate you on your appointment as Chairman and Members of the Governing Body of the new Ghana Investments Centre. The responsibilities I am now placing on you today are as heavy as the high hopes raised by the Investments Code and Centre which are high not only at home but also abroad. Indeed, you are being called upon to perform such intractable duties as simplifying our hitherto cumbersome procedures, nonchalant attitudes to work and attracting massive investment into Ghana after nearly one decade of capital depreciation, in the face of an unavowed and imperceptible economic boycott and a final total blockade of our country by our trading partners and investors. This was due largely to unstable and unattractive conditions as well as the past gross mismanagement of our economy. The combined effect of these negative and evil practices scared away investors one after the other until all sources open to us completely dried up by 1978.

Mr Chairman and members of the Centre, as I indicated recently no single Bill in the life of our present Parliament has provoked as much public interest as the Investment Code Bill. The public at home and abroad will therefore be carefully watching and analysing all your decisions, their effects on the nation's economy and on our well-being. I wish you great success in the discharge of your duties to the Centre and the nation and request you to be forever mindful of the permanent interests and true aspirations of our national community in your decision-making and policy implementation.

As the governing body of the Investment Centre, one of your cardinal duties will be to promote and regulate investments in all sectors of our economy. This will also embrace your honest advice on the priority sectors into which Government may have to attract and direct investments. To do this effectively, you may perhaps have to recommend further legislation to encourage investments in specific areas of the economy. Naturally your most elementary responsibility is to ensure that the provisions of the Investment Code Act are strictly and honestly interpreted and enforced. As I have often said, the public is watching all of us and we will make or unmake ourselves collectively or individually.

The major concerns of foreign investors in the past had been the cumbersome bureaucratic and slow procedures which they faced in Ghana, West Africa and the Third World generally. In fact to business people and investors, time is money and should therefore not be squandered. Long delays and frustrations cost not only money in hotel bills, transport and telephone charges, but also goodwill lost in the end.

I therefore charge you, Mr Chairman and members of the Centre, to take immediate steps towards streamlining and simplifying procedures that had hitherto hindered the easy inflow of investments into Ghana. Areas to be closely and quickly examined include immigration, licensing of industrial sites, land acquisition procedures, customs clearance, granting of concessions and many other related matters.

In this regard, I hope that the Centre will also closely monitor the type of reception accorded potential investors arriving in Ghana and help ensure that officials of Ministries and other Government Departments treat visitors and, indeed, the general public with courtesy, punctuality and honesty.

Lackadaisical or lukewarm attitudes to official duties should be eradicated so that the public and investors will not eventually become disillusioned and again divert their investment elsewhere as in the past.

Mr Chairman, you and all involved and concerned citizens are only too well aware that Ghana is competing with other countries for investment, whether it is in agriculture, mining or searching for crude oil. You should therefore not hesitate to deal severely with any official who uses his or her position to hamper and sabotage your efforts and the realization of the objectives of the Investment Centre.

Mr Chairman, it is also the responsibility of your Board jealously to guard and protect the natural resources of this nation from indiscriminate and unprofitable exploitation. To this end I must emphasize that although the new Investment Code seeks to improve upon the investment climate of our country for mutually beneficial economic interactions between Ghana and foreign investors, it is not a blank cheque for the easy plundering of our natural resources by a few nationals and foreigners. You should therefore ensure that projects approved by the Centre produce benefits for Ghana and all our people.

Ladies and gentlemen, Ghana is the only West African country which still possesses reserves of special species of timber at present. Attempts may therefore be made to exploit this fact to our disadvantage by excessive logging without reafforestation. While we will welcome large investments in this sector for efficient local processing of these special species and, indeed, for the very revival of the timber industry, we ought to ensure adequate replanting in these and other species in order to provide for future generations while plant and equipment which will be installed as part of new investment, are also fully and efficiently operated.

In this regard I should like to reiterate that the ban on the exportation of 14 special species has not yet been lifted as is being alleged in some quarters. Indeed, at the recent meeting with the Executive of the Ghana Timber association, I only requested that a Committee should be set up to collate proposals from all sections of the industry for its revival, including the effective utilization of the 14 special species. The Committee's recommendations will be jointly studied by Government and the Timber Associations and this will involve the Investment Centre and other Government Agencies in their efforts to attract investments into the timber and other industries.

Mr Chairman, the Investments Centre is expected to ensure that all projects approved will also introduce the appropriate technology which will benefit our people and the economy so that we can build up the necessary pool of skills and eventually make maximum use of our human resources. Projects approved should therefore satisfy this condition and also be export-oriented. We must increase our earnings in foreign exchange and correct the present sad situation of most of our industries depending on our imported raw materials, which is making unbearable demands on our foreign exchange earnings at a time when such earnings have been dwindling steeply. You should therefore encourage investors to use local materials already available or to take steps to produce such materials locally.

Distinguished guests, I wish to assure all potential investors once again that we are not merely putting new wine into old bottles and that the Board being inaugurated this morning is the governing body of a new institution statutorily established under the Investment Code 1981 (Act 437) designed to safeguard investment, ensure effecient and profitable operations and guarantee repatriation of honestly earned profits and that every effort will also be made to process investment enquiries quickly and implement approved projects speedily and efficiently.

I wish also to reiterate my call to both institutional and private investors not to sit on the fence any more but to come forward and take advantage of the many opportunities now open to them in Ghana.

In conclusion, I wish to repeat what I have already said in London and Bonn to would-be investors that we are not asking for charity but offering handsome investment opportunities for our mutual benefit.

Once again, I warmly congratulate you, Mr Chairman, Honourable Ministers and distinguished citizens who have accepted to serve on the governing body of the Ghana Investment Centre. In wishing you howling success in the discharge of your assignments, I have the pleasure and the honour to declare the new Ghana Investment Centre and its governing body formally inaugurated.

6

Timbod Metal Factory

The President went to Bibiani, a hitherto deserted mining zone up country, to out-door another economic venture on 18 June 1981.

Using the occasion of the commissioning ceremony the President referred to the rich potential of natural resources in the Western Region. The opening up of this rural location to economic development by the Polish-backed Timbod Metal Factory at Bibiani is a manifestation of the vast investment possibilities which the country offers.

The President declared that the country held the doors wide open to investors.

I am extremely happy to be back here today among the chiefs and people of the Bibiani Area first to renew and re-strengthen our association and to exchange ideas on local and national problems. The tour renews our determination to run an open and participatory government involving our rural folk in policy formulation and implementation. It is also a pleasure for me to take advantage of the opportunity to commission the Timbod Metal Factory.

We are deeply impressed by the rousing welcome and the friendly reception you have accorded us since our arrival. We thank you sincerely for the honour done us by this very impressive and colourful durbar.

Nananom, the establishment of this factory, the third industrial concern in this town, adds another positive dimension to the socio-economic development of the people and I am sure that you join me in expressing our profound gratitude to all those whose efforts, hard work and sacrifices have made this factory become a reality today. In particular, I wish to place on record Government's appreciation for the technical assistance of the Polish Government without which it may not have been possible to establish this complex.

This Timbod Metal Factory certainly stands as another fitting monument to the long-standing friendship and co-operation between Poland and Ghana. I therefore hope that these friendly and mutually beneficial relations will be expanded and further strengthened. Indeed, the factory clearly demonstrates the confidence which the Polish and other foreign governments and investors continue to repose in the economic recovery and development of our country.

I wish to emphasize my Administration's determination to encourage investors to invest in the exploitation of our enormous natural resources. It is fitting for us to talk about investment opportunities in the Western Region, since the Region is one of the richest parts of Ghana in natural resources. Great economic resources to be developed in the Region include timber, rubber, palm oil, gold, manganese and iron ore awaiting investment and exploitation for mutual benefit. To this end, we have taken a number of positive steps to create attractive investment conditions and ensure the continuous flow of capital into Ghana. In my recent tour of four European countries, I informed potential investors that their investment funds will be fully protected and that now is the time for them to invest in Ghana more than ever.

As we invite foreigners to invest in our country we must also brace ourselves up as a people for the disciplined, hard and honest work that will ensure efficient and effective use of funds to be invested in our country. I am aware of the useful role the Bibiani wood complex is playing in improving upon the quality of life in Bibiani after the closure of the gold mine here had rendered it a ghost town. The addition of this new industry should further improve upon these efforts, but it is also crucially important for the progress of the factory that Nananom, the local traditional rulers, and their people should give of their best to the management of these industries to enable them to achieve their goals in your collective interest. Since most of the workers predominantly hail from here, there is need for continual communication between management and the chiefs and elders of the area to reduce conflicts and frictions to the barest minimum. Naturally, the success of the companies will also be the success of the people here.

The Managing Director has requested adequate import licence for the complex. As you are well aware, due to the scarcity of foreign exchange and the numerous demands on Government, we have had to set ourselves very strict priorities. However, the timber industry is very high on our list of priorities and will therefore be adequately served.

You will remember that when I visited this area last year, I emphasized the need to maintain discussions and contacts with the people so that with a common understanding we can together rebuild our country and make it great and prosperous again. In renewing these contacts today again, I invite you to redouble your efforts towards the recovery of the economy and the reconstruction of our country. I wish also to renew our pledge to resuscitate the economy, restructure our society and improve upon the living conditions of our people. I therefore assure Nananom and the people here that with their co-operation, understanding and hard work, we shall succeed.

The problems of this area and the Western Region as a whole are not new to me. Having travelled several times on your roads, spent nights at places without electricity and seen things for myself, I can assure you

DG–E

47

that my Administration can never forget these things and is seriously committed to solving such problems. As a matter of urgency, the major roads of the Western Region have been given priority attention. On the local scene, I am happy to announce that the Bibiani Water Project will soon be commissioned. The new Ministry of Youth and Rural Development is also undertaking a major exercise to ensure that your feeder roads are kept motorable at all times.

Nananom, let me now advert our minds and attention to a matter of crucial national importance. The Voters' Register has been opened for all who qualify to register and thus enable them to vote at elections. After a long and tortuous journey, Ghana has finally returned to the path of democracy as the only rational form of Government in which all our people can take part in shaping our destiny. We have a duty therefore to defend this hard-won democracy by registering in our numbers as voters to ensure that our freedom to select or elect our leaders is not sacrificed on the altar of anarchy and vandalism. Like the wise farmer who reads the weather and prepares his farm in readiness for the rainy season, let us all register to enable us to have a say in electing our own leaders thus ensuring the true processes of democracy.

In conclusion, I would like once again to thank the Government and the people of Poland for their technical assistance in establishing this factory, the Ghanaian partners for their perseverance and the chiefs and people of Bibiani for their wonderful reception.

And now, Nananom, ladies, gentlemen and fellow citizens, I have the greatest pleasure in declaring the Timbod Metal Factory formally commissioned.

7

Commissioning of the Birim River Bridge

Like the blood in the human system, roads and bridges are the arteries of economic activity. In full appreciation of this fact the Limann Administration paid priority of attention to re-activation of broken down roads and bridges. The following address by the President was on the occasion of his visit to Ghana Consolidated Dimaond Limited and the site of the Birim River Bridge on 25 July 1981

I wish to express my sincere thanks to all of you gathered here for the warm reception accorded me and my entourage. I believe that this gathering is an indication of your continued support and confidence in my Administration. I am also very thankful to Ghana Consolidated Diamond Limited for having made it possible for me to be associated with the official commissioning of this magnificent bridge. The occasion offers us a welcome opportunity to become more closely acquainted with the operations and problems of the company.

Barely two weeks ago, I had the honour to declare open for public use a new bridge built across the Black Volta at Bamboi. That bridge now provides a very important link between the Northern and Southern sectors of Ghana. Such bridges, including the one we are about to open today are, for very obvious reasons, of great importance for all of us. My Administration's conviction is that the rehabilitation and construction of our road network for econmic and other development projects would be meaningless without well-built, reliable and durable bridges which are the essential links connecting all parts of the country, particularly the productive areas to our consuming urban centres. Bridges are therefore very important parts of our road reconstruction programmes. The Birim Bridge will provide dependable facilities for both pedestrians and motorists who can now transport goods quickly across the Birim River in both directions.

I am told that the bridge which spans forty-six metres and is seven metres wide was erected in 1980 at the cost of ₵1.7 million by Messrs Seltrust Engineering of the United Kingdom, with the support of the management and personnel of Ghana Consolidated Diamond Limited and that the steelwork was designed and supplied by Messrs Thomas Storey Limited, also of the United Kingdom. Designed to carry a load of 200 tonnes, the total time for its erection was only two and a half months. We must therefore thank the designers and contractors for this engineering feat and the speedy completion of the construction works.

Your Excellencies and Nananom, this bridge is of special significance, besides the general advantages I have already mentioned. Just as the structure of ownership and basis of this Company's operation themselves, the erection of the bridge provides a shining example of the type of co-operation which can be developed between Ghanaian and foreign companies for our mutual benefit and advantage. It also represents an excellent example of the technology transfer and the pooling of local and foreign resources which we very urgently require and wish greatly to encourage for our national development. The excellence of the construction work and the very short time within which the project was completed provide an eloquent testimony to the resourcefulness of Ghanaians working with good supervisors. For these and many other reasons, I do sincerely thank our foreign partners in this company, Messrs Consolidated African Select Trust, for their long standing commitment, dedication and continued co-operation with us in Ghana. It is my fervent hope that the co-operation and excellent relations which existed between us for the past fifty-seven years will be expanded, sustained and further strengthened to our mutual benefit.

Turning to the Company's operations properly so called, I wish to re-emphasize what the Minister of Lands and Natural Resources has said on his recent visit, namely, that Government is fully aware of the Company's problems which are mainly financial and the depletion of ore deposits which provided the basis for economic operations. As regards the financial problems, the Company is a net foreign exchange earner but its operational costs have risen far above your earnings, over which the Company virtually has no control. In this connection I wish to assure you that in view of the Company's enormous contributions over the years to the country's economy in employment, in foreign exchange earnings and in its future prospects, we are determined to ensure that you are given maximum assistance to minimize the hardships you are now experiencing. Already, Government's determination to help boost the mining industry and the export sector of the economy as a whole has been made evident in the various measures taken and proposals contained in the Investment Code which Parliament has just passed into law.

Besides helping to find solutions to other operational problems, in the particular case of the mining sector, my Administration is also determined to intensify and sustain mineral exploration in all parts of the country. It is partly in furtherance of this policy that I have personally come to commission this bridge today which will make an important and indispensable contribution to the Birim diamond exploration and prospecting work in progress. Information available at present from the prospecting work indicates that deposits are available to extend the life of this mine for many more years.

Since we have the mineral deposits, we are determined to provide the necessary encouraging and competitive framework for interested local and foreign agencies who are prepared to co-operate with us to exploit them for our mutual benefit. It is, however, my view that the framework being provided by Government, particularly in the new Investment Code, will achieve very little if our counterparts and local work-force do not fully reciprocate with hard work. The enactment of the Code demands maximum productivity and an absolute sense of discipline and dedication from all sides. The Code is, in fact, a challenge to all Companies and Ghanaians. Foreign and local investment would also be of little use, if our work force is also indisciplined, unproductive, dishonest and unstable. We would do well to eschew all such lapses and vices, if any, so as to improve upon the investment climate of our country and also greatly step up our productivity. We must all appreciate that it would be unrealistic and morally wrong for us to demand higher and higher renumeration and improve conditions of service which bear no relation to or are commensurate with productivity and output. As workers it is very important for us to avoid these tendencies in our efforts to rebuild our economy. You can count on Government's protection but you must also help Government to realize its objectives which are all in your interest.

Managements are also expected to be more resourceful, innovative and flexible, particularly in its cost-saving and revenue-earning measures. In the typical case of this company, I am happy to learn that you have a Special Projects Division to which you have already deployed some of your excess labour. While awaiting the outcome of the Birim prospecting work, I urge management to continue to diversify its operations into other viable areas. For example, by involving yourselves in road construction works and farming you will be helping all and sundry, particularly, in the locality you are operating. I have no doubt that a mining company such as Ghana Consolidated Diamonds with its several years of experience has the necessary expertise and resourcefulness to cope with meaningful diversification programmes. Besides being innovative and resourceful, Management should always bear in mind that the interests of their shareholders and workers are of equal supreme importance. The index of a successful management is high productivity, equitable returns on investment and peaceful labour relations. In this connection, I am confident that Ghana Consolidated Diamonds will not be found wanting.

Ladies and gentlemen, since it is Government's determination to help the mining sector out of the woods, as I have already indicated, I am requesting the management of this Company to submit to me as early as possible, realistic mining plans for the Birim-Supon Confluence Area which already forms part of the Company's concessions and also on the

UNDP proved grounds in the Takrowasi South and Takrowasi Bend areas. The plans should include the number and types of equipment required to start the operations. This done, my Administration will be in a position to start negotiations for loans to acquire equipment and expertise to begin the phasing-out of operations on the depleted Akwatia Concessions and a smooth transfer into the Birim area. Let us work candidly, honestly, sincerely and hard together so as to ensure the success of the Birim Project and the smooth cross-over from Akwatia to Birim. I am confident that this bridge we are now ready to commission will bear us across and lead us from Akwatia to a brighter future in the new areas of diamond mining.

Your Excellencies, Nananom, ladies and gentlemen, once again I wish to express my gratitude to you for this ceremony. I have no doubt that Government can continue to count on the support of the Chiefs, people, workers and management in this area in our task of rebuilding the national economy for a better life for all.

I now have great pleasure in declaring this magnificent bridge duly commissioned.

8

Inauguration of the Earth Satellite

The inauguration of the Earth Satellite on 12 August 1981, marked the historic occasion when Ghana joined the space communications club. The President himself at a colourful ceremony switched on the system at Nkuntunse, a few kilometres away from Accra on the Nsawam Road. Among the efforts currently being made to revive the economy, the coming into operation of the satellite station signified a major technological up-dating of the country's communications system.

I deem it a great honour indeed to be associated with this historic event marking Ghana's entry into the world of satellite communications which should revolutionize our telecommunications system.

The completion of this first satellite station, though behind schedule, has brought me back to Nkuntunse today for the second time within one year. But even more importantly, it has finally brought high speed communication facilities from such distant countries as Britain, France, Italy, West Germany, America and many other parts of the world to the doorsteps of many of our urban dwellers.

In particular, it will enable businessmen in Ghana to call their principals direct in these and many other countries without going through the despair which used to be their unfortunate lot. Similarly, overseas business enterprises can now dial and speak to their partners in Ghana direct. Nor should the social benefits of this be overlooked since hearing, even if once in a while, the voice of dear ones several thousands of miles away may be enough to keep busy people well posted and reassured that all is well at home which will thus improve upon efficiency and reduce travelling and over-all operational costs of business enterprises.

Today's event is a far cry from a similar occasion which took place exactly 100 years ago in 1881, when the first telegram lines were installed between Cape Coast and Elmina. Indeed, this function celebrates not only the leap into satellite communications but also the centenary commemoration of the introduction of telecommunications in Ghana which began with the installation of that simple two-way device linking the eight kilometre Cape Coast–Elmina stretch.

Developments in this field since 1881 progressed steadily but were slowed down by the First and Second World Wars and were definitely stalled by the 1966 *coup d'état* with the result that the 68,848 telephone stations in Ghana today hardly function at all. This $14.6 million earth satellite station will now provide large capacity, high quality and reliable external telecommunications services on a 24-hour basis, in great contrast to the old system which lacked high and medium frequencies with its low capacity, poor circuit quality and varying adverse atmospheric and ionospheric conditions.

However, the PNP Administration will not remain satisified with this satellite station since it is not complete in the present poor state of our internal telephone system. Our ultimate objective is easy and quick communication at home and direct links with all member states of the Organization of African Unity, and in fact, with every corner of the world.

To this end, plans are already far advanced for us to join the Pan African Telecommunications Network (PANAFTEL). Indeed, I am happy to announce that the African Development Bank has granted the Posts and Telecommunications Corporation, under Government guarantee, a loan of $6 million which represents 64 per cent of the total cost of the project with the remaining 36 per cent to be financed from the Posts and Telecommunications Corporation's own resources. Work on the project which is expected to be completed by the end of 1983, is already in progress.

As far back as 1965, the need for PANAFTEL has been of great concern to the OAU. This concern has been made increasingly more acute by the extreme difficulties facing external communications in our continent which still invariably pass through former colonial capitals. Thus, we cannot at present speak to our brothers and sisters in nearby Lomé by telephone without passing through both London and Paris. This greatly slows down business at both the private and public sectors levels, to the detriment of all concerned.

I wish to re-emphasize that we cannot lay claim to any achievement in the upliftment of our communications system, if the internal telephone network remains in its present appalling state. In our efforts to modernize our internal communication system, an amount of over ₡344 million will be spent on an expansion and rehabilitation programme so that the system may cope with the internal and external influx of communications. The programme shall be executed in phases, and contracts have already been awarded for the first phase which is estimated to cost about ₡50 million, being provided by the World Bank.

The first phase of the modernization programme includes a National Telephone Switching Centre in Accra and also the replacement of the existing local automatic exchanges in Accra Central and Cantonments with new and larger capacity exchanges. Among many innovations in the programme is the automatization of some of the existing manual exchanges.

Microwave radio links are also being installed in the Western, Central, Eastern, Volta and Ashanti Regions between Takoradi, Tarkwa, Obuasi, Dunkwa, Bekwai and Kumasi. Other places which will benefit from this facility are Enchi, Koforidua, Mpraeso, Ho and Hohoe. The links will provide additional trunk lines to reduce to the barest minimum traffic congestion on these routes and thus make telephone contacts between those towns and their district and regional centres quicker and more reliable.

The second phase will comprise the construction of entirely new automatic exchanges in Kumasi, Oda, Winneba, Nsawam, Mampong-Akwapim, Saltpond, Nkawkaw, Hohoe, Berekum and Axim.

It is needless for me to narrate all the economic and social benefits, which will flow from the completion of these projects. Suffice it to say that the investments being made and yet to be made in our telecommunications sector will be sound, worthwhile and more than justified. Indeed, all Ghanaians should be proud of such investments when the programme is completed and they should protect them jealously.

The worst evil which has long afflicted Ghana's telecommunications has been cable cutting, destruction and stealing. Let us all therefore check those who are determined to live off the backs of their fellow citizens, who care little how destructive their actions may be. In fact, all these plans and even this Earth Satellite station will come to nought, if the public does not help to protect and maintain them.

We must all therefore be on the alert and continually check such evil practices until they disappear from our society.

I need therefore not remind all citizens that it is their duty to check anyone destroying or stealing cables. It is the responsibility of all of us to protect our collective property and national assets.

We must do exactly what we should do when we see any one carrying away a piece of our personal and private property acquired through our hard work, sweat, toil and sacrifices. We should all assist in putting an end to this and other evil practices which ruin our economy and greatly tarnish our national image.

The birth of this Earth Satellite Station greatly boosts the expansion and technological transformation of telecommunication services in Ghana which had lagged far behind our national requirements, both quantitatively and qualitatively. Telephone demand has built up substantially over the years despite a ten-fold increase in telephones in the last two decades. Similarly, heavy congestions have developed in telephone traffic in both local systems and trunk networks. These shortcomings and avoidable inefficiencies have provoked the justifiable dissatisfaction and indignation of the public with the services provided by the Posts and Telecommunications Corporation. The Corporation is duty bound to maintain, service and run the facilities with care, and not neglect them until they break down altogether, as has happened to many of our infrastructures over the last decade.

Just two weeks ago, we were able to see the live broadcast of an event which took place several thousands of kilometres away through the medium of this satellite station—we were able to see the royal wedding ceremony of Prince Charles and Lady Diana, just as anyone in London would watch a local television set.

I wish on our collective behalf to commend all those who have directly contributed towards bringing this project to fruition, particularly the personnel of SPAR Technology of Canada, the main contractors, and the Ghanaians who have worked side by side with our Canadian friends. Above all, I must express my Administration's gratitude and that of the people of Ghana to the Government and people of Canada whose efforts have greatly helped us in raising the funds needed for the implementation of this project which has so happily coincided with Parliament's passage of our New Investment Code 1981. I hope that, taken together, these two important events will greatly contribute towards our economic recovery, growth and take-off.

9

Inauguration of the Petroleum Promotion Council

Address on the inauguration of the Petroleum Promotion Council (PPC) at the Castle, Osu, on 7 August 1981.

Economic development can only flourish when the infrastructure of physical and organizational facilities back it up. The Council being inaugurated, was such an organizational back-up.

Barely one and a half weeks ago, I had the pleasure and honour formally to inaugurate the Kibi Bauxite Promotion Council and requested it to ensure the early implementation of that much awaited project. Today, it is the turn of the Petroleum Promotion Council, the third of such Councils planned by the Administration of the People's National Party aimed at injecting additional dynamism into project appraisals and implementation for our national economic recovery, growth and take-off. The first was the Gold Promotion Council established under the Vice-President earlier in the year.

The search for oil in Ghana started as early as the turn of the century in the Tano Basin areas of the Western Region which had for a long time been noted for the occurrence of oil seepages, gas and tar sands. However, from 1903 to the 1970s only shallow boreholes and a few wells were drilled by a number of foreign companies without much else being done about drilling to prove the existence of oil in commercial quantities in that basin.

In 1977, Philips Petroleum Company took over the Tano Basin concession and has since drilled eight wells, several of which showed signs of crude oil deposits and even proved commercial quantities of natural gas. I am reliably informed that Philips Petroleum has just commenced the drilling of the ninth well in the northern sector of their concession where prospects are said to be quite high. Only one out of the first eight wells had been promising but was later found to contain sand at its lowest reaches which does not allow high rates of flow to the surface as initially expected.

Since recorded time there has never been any smoke without some fire. Philips Petroleum Company has therefore justifiably intensified its drilling efforts, but perhaps, the less said at the moment about this the

57

better since 'discretion is the better part of valour'. In any case, our detractors were barefaced enough to deny what the whole world knows about Ghana's Gold Endowment when, after much research into, and reassessment of, our gold ore reserves, we organized an International Seminar and highlighted our potentialities in the field. Some of our fellow nationals have always seemed to derive a perverse sort of pleasure in running down their own country since our attainment of political independence.

Members of this Promotion Council are perhaps already aware that apart from Agri-Petco which is producing some oil offshore near Saltpond, a number of reputable French, Italian, Canadian and American companies are also now ready to start geophysical or drilling activities in other offshore blocks. One of these, Texas Pacific of the United States of America, completed geophysical survey in the Keta Basin just last week and is expected to start drilling their first well towards the end of this year or early next year. The Romanians, and lately the Brazilians, have also expressed interest and readiness to take part in exploring for oil in Ghana. Perhaps, I should mention that Romania is one of the oldest oil-prospecting and producing countries in the world.

Members of the Petroleum Promotion Council, I have briefly highlighted recent developments so as to indicate the changing investment climate Ghana already enjoys today. Those who criticize merely for the sake of criticism, and those who fly the kite of the multinational bogey before the people of Ghana should realize that no nation has ever been able to exploit its hidden wealth without first marshalling the necessary resources, equipment and skills which are available outside. We must therefore encourage and promote increased exploration and prospecting activities in our gold and hydro-carbon zones.

Given our rapidly growing population and the ever-rising expectations of our people, the task before you, members of the Petroleum Promotion Council, is crucial and urgent indeed. Nevertheless, I am confident that you will all rise to the occasion and deserve before long the thanks and praises of all Ghanaians.

The increased activities we are anticipating in the field of oil exploration has also to be matched by the rapid development of the local expertise needed to man the industry in the future. I am happy to reveal that a number of scholarship offers from several friendly European countries for courses in Petroleum Engineering Geophysics and Geology have recently been accepted for deserving young Ghanaians to study abroad. At the beginning of the next academic year, two Ghanaians will start courses in Petroleum on Algerian Government scholarships while Philips Petroleum has also offered some training facilities to other young Ghanaians overseas.

I, therefore, expect this Council to assist in closely monitoring our efforts in this all-important aspect of the development of our national petroleum industry, in order to ensure that these students are trained to return to Ghana in time, properly equipped, to assume their vital roles in our national, and perhaps our sub-regional economic development.

A year ago I directed that a National Petroleum Company should be formed to handle the problem of our ultimate objective of achieving self-sufficiency in our oil and other energy requirements as early as practicable. The Company will embrace all the different wings in the industry from exploration and well-drilling through refining to distribution and marketing.

It is encouraging that three recent studies concluded by technicians from Algeria, a World Bank team and the United Nations Centre on Transnational Corporations have all endorsed the idea of forming such a National Petroleum Company since I mooted it a year ago.

As I hinted to you awhile ago, we lack trained Ghanaian personnel to handle the various highly technical assignments in exploration. The Minstry of Fuel and Power has therefore been directed to examine all the possibilities open to us, and, where necessary, it should obtain the services of qualified foreign technicians under the various technical and cultural agreements we have concluded with friendly countries.

Members of the Petroleum Promotion Council, it is said that there is an oil glut on the world market at present. This has, however, not had much effect on the cost of petroleum to many non-oil producing countries of the Third World and we are still too over-dependent on petroleum imports.

Many experts in the oil industry have even predicted world-wide short supplies again by the end of this decade and warned that several non-oil producing economies will come under even severer strains than now before the end of the 1980s. We are already experiencing the effects in Ghana.

Barely two years ago, crude oil prices were less than half their present cost and yet the so-called glut has not reduced our present high crude oil import bills even one cent. We must therefore sit up and plan ahead, as the late Osagyefo did with great foresight, with regard to the development of our hydro-electric resources in the 60s.

We must also continue to intensify our efforts in the areas of hydro, solar, wind and mini-hydros sources of renewable energy. It is precisely for this reason that my Administration has made substantial resources available to our research institutions this year to enable them to intensify their research work in these fields.

The application of solar pumps, heaters and dryers, instead of diesel-generated machines, has begun to have a great impact on irrigated agriculture and on the economies of several countries. Being so strategically located on the equator, Ghana enjoys the direct intensity of the sun all the year round and should therefore take full advantage of this source of renewable energy, in addition to our substantial reserve in hydro sources such as the Bui Dam Project which we are feverishly trying to implement.

For the moment, while we still depend so heavily on petrol and petroleum products we should all develop a clearer understanding and appreciation of the fuel conservation measures being adopted in order to be able to continue providing for our basic needs from our greatly diminished foreign currency earnings. Let us jointly combat all antagonistic forces in our society, including those who smuggle or divert petroleum product meant for specific areas of the country.

This unpatriotic and selfish conduct does a lot of harm to most of our hardworking farming population whose sweat and toil earns us the foreign exchange with which we import crude oil. In fact, the whole economy suffers since many farming activities now depend on petroleum products to increase production and output without which we shall continue to import such food items as rice and maize which can easily be grown locally in large quantities for our own use and even for export.

Members of the Council, as you settle down to your tasks, I expect you to bring your devoted attention and enthusiasm to bear fully on your duties. You will have to work closely with the Technical Action Committee under the Minister of Fuel and Power which, as its name suggests, will handle the preliminary technical work before submission to the full Council.

I have faith in you and trust that by the time your tenure of office on the Promotion Council and the Action Committee comes to an end, Ghana would have attained that coveted aspiration and joined the club of oil-producing countries.

10

Kibi Bauxite Project

The pouring of libation for field work to begin on the Kibi Bauxite Project on that fateful Saturday 26 September 1981, may be taken to represent removal of a possibility from fable to fact. The ceremony marked the beginning of work on phase one of a four-phase development programme for the Kibi Bauxite Deposits. For too long had the people of Ghana waited for that day when work was to begin for the development of Ghana's enormous bauxite resources.

When I received an invitation to attend this durbar here today, I at first assumed that it was related to the countrywide celebrations marking the Second Anniversary of the Third Republic and the People's National Party Administration. On closer examination of the programme, however, I was very delighted to find one item of great significance, with a new dimension and even of a very special attraction to open the way for the entry to the Kibi Hills of the first group of personnel from the Consortium engaged for the Phase One field work of the Kibi Bauxite/Alumina Project.

It therefore gives me particular pleasure to be here again with you today not only to attend this colourful durbar but also to partake in the impending symbolic ceremony of libation-pouring for a project which is very close to my heart as one of the top priorities of the PNP Manifesto. Indeed, Nananom and people may recall my frequent assurances that the PNP Administration is deeply and irrevocably committed to the speedy development of the Kibi Bauxite/Alumina Project and my indication during your last annual festival that field activities would soon start here on it.

The brief ceremony about to be performed is one further testimony of that commitment not only for the benefit of our fellow citizens of this area but also in the vital and permanent interests of the nation as a whole. This simple but important customary rite is to mark the beginning of work on Phase One of a four-phased development programme for the Kibi Bauxite deposits. A lot of hard work had to be done since our assuming office in preparing for today's function; as usual, we have preferred working to merely talking. We shall continue to resist the temptation of allowing publicity to overshoot development plans and their implementation which has caused far too many disappointments

61

and disillusionments in the past.

The Project comprises an open bauxite mining, the design and construction of plant to extract about 800,000 metric tonnes per year of alumina from the Bauxite ore and the designing and construction of such vital infrastructural facilities as housing, hospitals, schools and so on. This stage of the project will therefore lead to the elaboration of a Project Development Plan and a Report.

The reputation and names of the companies which have entered into agreement with us to start this phase of the project are very well known. I therefore wish to make special public mention of them on this occasion. They are:

(i) Messrs Brown & Root Incorporated of the USA.

(ii) Bankers Trust International Limited of the United Kingdom.

(iii) Granges International Mining, A.B. of Sweden.

Last, but not the least is,

(iv) Swiss Aluminium Limited or Alusuisse of Switzerland, which is providing the consortium with process technology.

The Project Development Plan and Report will include the establishment of ore reserves and mining methods, selection of process and design criteria, site investigations, personnel skills, survey and training programmes, preliminary engineering, capital cost estimates, economic analysis and a sales plan as well as a development plan for the three subsequent phases of the project.

Phases Two, Three and Four consist of the commercial, financial and technical implementation of the development plan and plant operations as well as Ghanaian personnel training.

As many of you may be aware already, my Administration wants to develop Ghana's enormous bauxite resources and process them into that all-important metal, aluminium. This plan is not new since it was first conceived by the late Osagyefo, Dr Kwame Nkrumah of blessed memory, who would have implemented it long ago if the clock of our history and economic development had not been set back since 1966. The new element and dimension is the political will and determination which the People's National Party Administration has again brought to bear on it.

Indeed, the construction of the Akosombo Dam was meant to be the first step towards the realization of the objective of the total integration of the aluminium industry in Ghana. The completion of this Project will therefore provide the necessary and next major link in the chain for achieving that fully integrated industry planned during the First Republic. My own political will and commitment for its implementation is therefore total since the PNP Manifesto demands it.

The benefits that will accrue to the nation with the integration of this industry, that is, from the mining stage to the metal and fabrication stages will be invaluable. Indeed, the benefits will be far-reaching and wide-ranging and will include the social aspects of opening up this relatively rural area of Ghana and providing many job opportunities resulting from processing our bauxite ore locally. Another important aspect of this project is that it falls squarely and fittingly into the People's National Party Administration's rural development plans which can hardly be over-emphasized.

In this regard, I am happy to announce that despite our present critical financial situation, we have already committed over ₵12 million to the project even at this Phase One stage. The foreign exchange component of this amount will be US$4.75 million. In addition to this, we have promptly provided three VW cars and one Range Rover to the Team so as to speed up their activities on this all-important project. It is our strong resolve and ardent hope that this project should be implemented with the minimum of delay. Indeed, I can assure you, Osagyefo, Nananom, elders and fellow citizens that this project will engage my personal attention and will thus be accorded the highest priority in our public capital expenditure disbursements as on similar projects of national importance.

To accelerate the pace of this project's development, we have already accepted a recommendation for the formation of an entity to be known as the Kibi Bauxite Development Company (KBDC). Final discussions and arrangements for the formation of the Company have reached an advanced stage already and we hope to ensure that it is floated as soon as practicable, possibly by the end of October this year. To this end, Mr Kwesi Baning, Deputy Director of the Geological Survey in charge of the Ashanti Region, has already been appointed Project Co-ordinator to expedite preliminary preparations for the Company. I hope that he will live up to my expectations as Chairman of the recently inaugurated Kibi Bauxite Development Promotion Council.

Your Excellencies, Members of the Diplomatic Corps, we appreciate the good work you have been doing by reporting faithfully to your governments and financial circles on the hard decisions and sacrifices we have been making to put our own house in order. We thank you for attending this small function in such large numbers. However, as I have often said, we urgently need large infusions of institutional and private investment since our own resources are at present woefully inadequate for resuscitating our economy and fulfil the aspirations of our people as quickly as they expect us to do. As I have also had the occasion to emphasize in London last May, we are not asking for charity; we are offering investment opportunities for mutually beneficial economic interactions. You may therefore wish to complete a good job you have ably started by advising your governments, and financial and business circles not to sit on the fence any longer.

DG-F

63

My Administration is convinced that peace and economic stability are best guarantees for political stability and investments. We are leaving no stone unturned to ensure the democratic way of life in Ghana. Our friends, well-wishers and the older democracies should therefore actively invest in this system as well rather than look on passively while even some international organizations try to force socially impracticable recommendations down our throats. An anaemic patient can be helped back to life only by flesh and more blood transfusions, not by draining the body and leaving an empty, dry shell or skeleton.

Excellencies, besides the Investment Code Act, 1981, we have also taken certain measures designed to speed up the processing of investment enquiries. We have inaugurated four Promotion Councils to quicken investment activities in Mining in prospecting on-shore and off-shore for oil and in the implementation of the Kibi Bauxite Project. We hope to set up similar Councils for the Bui Dam and Opon Manso Projects. The Investment Centre to be established under this Act will complete this process and I fervently hope that this will spare investors the ordeals of slow procedures and avoidable administrative inefficiencies. The activities of the Promotion Councils will be co-ordinated by the Board of the Investment Centre under the Vice-President who will not brook any delays and 'stop-go stop-go' tactics.

Once again, Excellencies, ladies and gentlemen, I should like to express my profound gratitude to all those who have helped directly or indirectly to produce the Code Act, 1981 which should usher in a new era of investments in industry, agriculture, mining and many other sectors for the mutual benefit of all Ghanaians and foreign investors.

11

At Tamale in the Northern Region

In this his first visit to Tamale, in the Northern Region, the President stressed the necessity for step by step reconstruction of the shattered economy of Ghana speaking to Nanime, the Traditional Leaders, and a large concourse of people. The occasion was a special durbar at Tamale on 10 November 1979, to do honour to the new Head of State Dr Hilla Limann. He foreshadowed the shape of development projects which his People's National Party has in store for the Northern Region and the Country.

I am extremely happy to be honoured with such a colourful durbar organized by the Chiefs and people of the Northern Region. This is an indication of your spontaneous support and goodwill for me and my Government. For this we are most grateful.

I am also happy to revisit this promising Region so soon after the electioneering campaign. I normally used to come up here only once a year, at about this time, to spend my annual leave. This time, I have come, not to visit a few friends and relatives, but to share my thoughts with you on the problems facing this Region and the country at large and, if possible, to find the ways and means of solving them. This, you will agree, is an indication of my Government's interest in your rapid socio-economic development.

Nanime, fellow Ghanaians, as a nation, we are passing through the most difficult moments of our history after several years of secretive government and bare-faced mismanagement which have shattered our once buoyant economy.

Although the damage has been done already, it is not beyond repair. My Government having been given the mandate, is determined to rescue the economy of and eventually to put it back once more on a self sustaining course. This can the more easily and rapidly be done with the type of understanding and goodwill you, the Chiefs and people have displayed this morning and elsewhere across the country since the last week-end.

The problems facing us all are so numerous that unless we tackle them systematically as a united people we cannot hope to solve them. The said problems are not of my making or of any one party. Nevertheless, it is our duty, as a popularly elected government, to find equitable solutions to them. We are determined to do this. We can do it all the more effectively with the co-operation of every Ghanaian. We trust that all our countrymen will contribute their quota towards the total eradication of those evils from our society which have repeatedly made progress and prosperity elusive to us collectively. The solutions I want us to seek and apply must be lasting, permanent or final.

I know that many of us are impatient. We all want to see concrete evidence of what my Government has done or is doing for the nation. After years of deceit, irresponsibility, disorder and mismanagement, which have all combined to deprive us of our birthrights, the outburst of expectations is very powerful. I can sympathize with these feelings. I am more dissatisfied with the present state of affairs than most Ghanaians, particularly, the comfortable and cheap, not to say, uninformed critics.

I can therefore assure you that my administration is working hard to alleviate the sufferings we have all experienced in the past several years but we must all also realize and accept the fact that it is not as easy to rebuild our country to take its rightful place in the comity of nations. Let us not yield to the over-hasty critics who, for thirteen years were tongue-tied or who might have contributed, in many incontrovertible ways, to our present plight.

I, my Government and my Party promised, during the campaign in April, May, June and July, that we would save this country from further decline and national disgrace, according to certain stated time schedules. Let the critics remember, not only this, but also the circumstances in which we came into office. In short, they should do their homework seriously; they have no moral or even legal right to dictate new time scales for me and my Government.

So far, serious measures have been taken to rehabilitate broken-down vehicles so as to ensure a more efficient distribution and transportation system. Our import programme is being vigorously streamlined and certain vital needs, including foodstuffs and drugs, have already been ordered. The fuel problem has been tackled with a large measure of sucess, indeed queues have disappeared.

We are also working day and night on the problem of increased agricultural production, general rehabilitation, the re-utilization of existing idle factories and the procurement of equipment to restrain and redirect labour into more useful areas of priority and ventures.

Agriculture is at the top of our priority list. The Northern Region has a key role to play in any efforts to attain self-sufficiency in food production. Indeed, for some time now, this Region has been recognized as the 'granary of the nation'. Yet nothing was done to make it so; inputs were always lacking at the times they were required or when the weather was favourable.

This has led to the decline in rice production, even before un-seasonable rains could worsen the situation still further. The pity of it is that rice has now come to be one of the leading staple foods in many homes. My administration is determined to change this sad state of affairs through the adequate provision of inputs at the times they are most needed. We shall also mobilize our resources in the field of irrigation to help offset the problems caused by natural forces.

Next on our priority list is the development of our rural areas. The country people in these areas produce the greater part of our national wealth and yet the vast majority of them have remained neglected and under-privileged. The development of our rural areas demands, as a pre-condition, that the basic tools like hatchets, cutlasses, hand-saws, hoes which the farmers require, and the other human necessities such as soap, kerosene, salt, tinned fish, cotton piece goods and the like, must be made available for them to buy at reasonable prices.

Nanime, as traditional rulers, you command the respect of your people, you enjoy their affection. It is you who serve as the spokesman of their needs and also of the needs of Government. You have therefore a great role to play in the difficult task of rebuilding the nation. In this regard, it is rather sad to observe that the slow development of the rural areas has been due partly to destructive chieftaincy and land disputes.

Acrimony and disunity often make it impossible for your people to undertake development projects together which will improve their living standards. Land ownership and tenure problems militate even more gravely against modernization and economic development.

I wish therefore to appeal to you to endeavour to settle your disputes amicably, within the framework of the Constitution, in order to create a congenial atmosphere for economic development, to the benefit of the hard-pressed people. I also appeal to you to mobilize your people to provide communal labour to supplement the efforts of Government.

My administration will adopt and implement policies which will provide the overall development of the country. However, not much can be achieved unless the people are prepared to work harder in order to improve upon their lot.

As you are all aware, I am not a stranger to these parts. I am fully aware of problems facing the people in the Region, such as perennial water shortages, long distances and deplorable roads, poor education and health facilities and general peasant problems. My Government is committed to tackle these problems within the national framework and our present scarce resources. the Dalun Water Works, the Regional Hospital and other establishments shall receive the necessary attention.

As a long term solution to some of these problems, my Government intends to tackle the Bui Dam Project which when completed will supply power to the Brong Ahafo, Northern and Upper Regions.

My Government will also continue to develop Tamale as the industrial hub of the Northern part of the country and improve upon the physical outlook of the municipality to befit its status as the gateway to the North. These developments include the construction of dual carriageway, the redevelopment of the central area, road and traffic improvement and the provision of street lights and drains. Some people have to be moved to make way for construction works. I concede that nobody wants to move from his ancestral home in this part of the country but we have to choose between ancestral graves and a modern town.

I am happy to announce that the Canadian International Development Agency (CIDA) has agreed to co-operate with my Government to effect the social and economic changes required and to raise the standard of living of the rural population through the provision and expansion of physical infra-structural social services.

The programme involves the rehabilitation and expansion of water and power supply facilities in Tamale and District Capitals and also the provision of dams, dug-outs and bore holes for selected villages. Farmers will be provided with farm equipment and materials to increase food and cash crop production. Basic health and other social facilities will also be provided in an integrated development programme. The relevant letters of protocol have been signed and the project will soon be started. Indeed, I personally approved the appointment of the Project Manager even before I was sworn in. I therefore appeal to you, the Chiefs and people in the Region, to co-operate fully with the Canadian and Ghanaian staff who will work on this project.

In conclusion, I wish to urge all and sundry to place their hope and confidence in the future. All nations have encountered trials, tribulations and difficulties before achieving success. Let us lift up our hearts in the knowledge that however low we may have fallen, it is always possible for us to rise again. This is the time for us to wake up from our deep slumber. We must move forward together in unity so that we can build a better Ghana. In our endeavour to build a prosperous nation, my Government will need your support and encouragement. I am hopeful that you will give of your best.

I wish, once again, to thank you all for this singular honour done me and the members of my Government. We shall always cherish the memories of this colourful durbar.

12

At Bolgatanga in the Upper Region

From Tamale, the gateway to the north of Ghana and Capital of the Northern Region, the President arrived the following day at Bolgatanga, Upper Regional Capital, to be overwhelmed by another durbar of Chiefs and people, unrestrained in enthusiasm and welcome. He referred to preceding years of abandon and mismanagement and promised that his Government would keep faith with them in town, village and farmstead and would be attentive to the needs of small-scale farmers and craftsmen.

It is a great pleasure for me this morning to be among you to exchange greetings, thoughts and ideas with you on some of the many problems now facing our country.

For me this official durbar, the first since I took office, also marks a homecoming. I therefore avail myself of the opportunity to thank you very sincerely for helping others to put me in my present unenviable position and also the wonderful reception accorded me and my entourage. I am sure that this impressive durbar organized in my honour is a practical manifestation of the confidence that the chiefs and people of the Upper Region repose in me and my government. Permit me then, Nanima, to congratulate you and your people for the massive support you gave the People's National Party in the Parliamentary and Presidential elections. Now that we are all set on the thorny road to economic recovery and moral upliftment, all of us, irrespective of belief or creed must put our shoulders to the wheel and push on confidently, forward, never looking back, in a united resolve to build a better and meaningful future for ourselves and generations yet unborn.

I can assure you that my government, conscious of its obligations to the people and ever ready to chart new pathways to progress and prosperity will offer the kind of honest, disciplined and effective leadership that has been lacking over the last thirteen years and which is so desperately needed today.

Nanima, distinguished guests, ladies and gentlemen, it is an undeniable fact that the economy of Ghana has been destroyed in the past by a long period of drift, disorder, make-shift decisions and general mismanagement. We call to mind the most recent soul-destroying instances of our economic decline. For four successive years, from 1975, to be precise, agricultural production suffered severe set-backs partly as a result of poor weather and more as a result of inefficient planning and criminal mismanagement. The result, as we are all aware, has been sharp decreases not only in the supplies of domestic foodstuffs but more importantly, in the output and export products such as cocoa, timber and minerals. Added to this has been the reckless handling of the import programme and the import licensing system with the result that precious foreign exchange was wantonly dissipated, thus creating acute foreign exchange shortages.

The problems now facing the Government can briefly be described in terms of our immediate national needs which demand the alleviation, within the shortest possible time, of the hardships imposed on the bulk of our people by reason of the acute shortages of such consumer items as tinned fish, soap, milk, sugar and the high cost of other food items. The medium and long term solution include the restructuring of vital sectors of the economy which directly affect agriculture, rural development and the rehabilitation of roads.

The immediate pre-occupation of Government is to make it possible for the ordinary citizen to be able to buy the commodities he needs for his day-to-day survival. In the pursuit of this objective, we are faced with the problem of our diminished foreign exchange earnings and worse still, the blockade of our credit facilities and supply lines due to the uncertain and unstable atmosphere in the recent past and now the blissful and self-righteous bickering and bigotry of some of those who have helped to create our present mess.

Yet despite these problems Government is exploring all avenues to ensure that some relief comes to the people. I wish to assure you that the needed relief will soon reach our shores if we are lucky to get shipping space, and suppliers honour delivery dates. If there are any stocks being held back from the markets now, then this is without our knowledge and such economic saboteurs and enemies of the masses should be exposed for the action they deserve. As a people we should strive to look beyond immediate personal relief if we are to build a more dignified and stable society. My Government is determined to lead this country on to producing most of the food we eat. I would like to emphasize that while Government will not relent in its efforts to make available to every Ghanaian the goods and services needed for him to lead a decent life, it will be in the larger national interest for us to broaden our horizons beyond bread and butter preoccupations alone.

We need these commodities now and we will get them, but beyond them are the much more serious problems of dangerously bad roads, lack of drugs, soaring unemployment, rural economic and social stagnation and a souring of our national psyche.

Nanima, distinguished guests, ladies and gentlemen, these are some of the challenging problems facing us but I have no doubt that with understanding, patience, goodwill and co-operation from all of you, my government will solve them much more rapidly than the threatening situation suggests. It was the development strategy of past governments which had increasingly worsened the plight of the rural dweller. The several efforts made in the past to develop the rural sectors failed mainly because the planning had urban bias and preoccupation.

My Government also believes that our over-centralized administrative structure, with initiative and decision-making concentrated only in Accra, should give way to a flexible, decentralized system which will take into consideration local resources in policy planning, formation and implementation. We will therefore involve local participation in the initiation, planning and implementation of rural development projects.

Because the rural areas had been neglected, rural people have drifted to urban centres. This in turn resulted in stagnation of farm output.

Since more exhortations to return to the land, without the accompanying tools and incentives, have never yielded the desired responses and results, my administration will provide the appropriate equipment and concrete assistance to small-scale farmers. What can a person do without ever a hoe, cutlass, a matchet or a lantern and kerosene. Since our rural people produce the bulk of the food we all eat, our agricultural programme must of necessity employ labour-intensive techniques, and low capital costs, backed by the provision of effective and intensive extension services aimed at assisting farmers to obtain higher yields. We are also reviewing existing credit facilities to small-scale farmers so that sufficient funds can be made available to them.

Nanima, I would like to re-emphasize what I have said elsewhere. The bedrock of our rural industrialization policy will be the development of simple home industries such as traditional indigenous handicrafts and small-scale agriculturally oriented enterprises. In countries such as India, tremendous advances have been made in home-made clothing industries which greatly contribute to the stability of the national economy. I would like to see the development of such viable home industries in this country contributing effectively to our industrial growth. I therefore urge all Ghanaian craftsmen to take up this challenge now.

I know that the craftsmen of the Northern and Upper Regions, like their counterparts in the South, have skills that few can match elsewhere. Our smock, kente and other handicraft products are admired all over the world. Thus, even our so-called advanced textile industries can use the skills of our many craftsmen even in designing new clothing for commercial purposes. Howbeit, it is my government's intention to help develop local products in exportable quantities and I shall take a personal interest in the matter.

As a first step, I suggest that craftsmen in various fields should pool their resources together in strong co-operative organization so as to make representations for assistance. This is the challenge I am throwing to our craftsmen which I hope they will take up.

Nanima, distinguished guests, ladies and gentlemen, permit me now to dwell briefly on the problems facing this Region. It is a source of great pain for me to realize the extent of depression that has engulfed our people as a result of the many deprivations they have had to endure. In the last few weeks, I have been to parts of the country visiting the Eastern, Volta, Western, Central and now the Northern and Upper Regions, as I had earlier done from April to July. In all these travels, I have heard the same tales of woe, namely broken-down schools, lack of school equipment, bad roads, lack of electricity, lack of good drinking water, lack of drugs in hospitals and a host of others. I have been deeply saddened at this neglect and destruction. What I have seen and experienced has strengthened my resolve to take effective measures to introduce some order and discipline into this economic malaise. I want to assure you that my commitment to the underprivileged people of this country is irrevocable and in the years ahead the solution of their problems shall be my personal concern.

In conclusion, I would like to thank you, Nanima and your people for organizing this colourful durbar and allowing me this opportunity to address you.

13

At Sunyani in the Brong Ahafo Region

This address was in response to the hearty welcome of chiefs and people at a durbar to meet and honour the President in his post-election tour of the Regions. The venue was Sunyani, Brong-Ahafo Region, the date was 17 November 1979. He paid tribute to Ghana's rich and diverse culture, the colourful display of which was on show.

Permit me to express to you, chiefs and people of the Brong Ahafo Region, my profound gratitude for honouring me with this colourful durbar.

My presence here today, like visits I have made to other parts of the country, gives me the opportunity to get in touch with you all, to gain more insight into your problems which are necessarily my problems also and to discuss with you how best we may solve them in peace, harmony and understanding, in the best interests of all our peoples.

I am highly impressed not only by the colourful display of our rich cultural heritage, but also and more significantly by the warm and enthusiastic reception at this durbar. This expression of assurance that the people of Brong Ahafo will throw their full weight behind my Government in the solution of our multifarious problems steels my determination and strengthens my belief that, no matter what our individual political inclinations may be, we are united as fellow citizens by common purpose and a common desire to heal the nation's wounds, reconcile and unify the nation and salvage our economy from total destruction. Indeed, this durbar clearly demonstrates that we can all put away or suspend our party differences and work together to exorcise the evil spirits haunting us in the common national interest.

Confident of and buoyed by this spirit of unity and co-operation, I appeal to you all to join me to eradicate from our society all the dehumanizing experiences we have patiently tolerated for far too long.

Nananom, I wish to pay a glowing tribute to you and the people of this Region for your immense past contribution to the economy of our country. You have served the country immeasurably in the production of food-stuffs for our sustenance and, even more importantly, the production of such exportable items as cocoa, timber and cola nuts which contribute to make our economy prosper. In this regard, it is regrettable that this substantial contribution had generally not been sufficiently appreciated in the past as evidenced by the nonchalant manner you have been treated in the fields of transportation, water supply and electricity. I shall strive, with your support, to rectify this situation not merely testifying to the importance of your contribution to our national evolution.

My Government also recognizes the important role the people in this, as in other Regions, have played in the past in making Ghana great. I acknowledge their indispensability to our future progress. For their well-being and progress, we shall offer more than mere words and pious promises during our tenure of office. We shall endeavour to defend and protect their interests, as in other Regions, particularly those of the under-privileged.

Indeed, it is my wish that, with time and patience, the difference between my administration and previous governments must manifest itself not in speeches and resolutions but in such deeds and positive results as often speak even more eloquently than words.

That is why I and my team have been quietly toiling methodically, and insisting on the need to evolve lasting or permanent solutions to our perennial problems so as to ease or even wipe out the attendant sufferings. You should therefore pay no heed to those who derive profit from the disorder and confusion that hasty, erratic and ill-conceived decisions have inevitably caused in the past.

Nananom, distinguished guests, ladies and gentlemen, for many years our economic fortunes have been worsened more and more by such antics, impatience and personal greed, particularly to the detriment of the vast majority of our national community.

The economy is now in such a very critical condition that the Government is working day and night in a delicate surgical operation. In the weeks ahead, we shall announce some of the results of our toils since assuming office.

In the Sessional Address shortly to be presented to Parliament, I hope to lay bare the facts about the state of the nation, the steps so far taken and what will be done in the short, intermediate and medium term and in the future to restore sanity and health to the drowning economy.

The excesses and waste that have characterized our national life are already being systematically checked and shall continue to be drastically controlled. I therefore appeal to you all to rise to the challenge now and accept the necessary measures needed to check the confusion, disorder, indiscipline and mismanagement which have, in the past, blocked the way to decent and better living conditions for the vast majority of our people.

For my part, I wish to emphasize that no effort shall be spared, no sacrifice be too great for me and my Government in our determination to reverse the imbalances which have increasingly accentuated the ordinary disadavantages of the masses of our people, particularly in the country-side. In this earnest endeavour, Government needs the patience, tolerance, understanding, co-operation and support of all Ghanaians. Indeed, the problems now confronting us must be faced squarely and tackled by all of us in that atmosphere of peace, stability and harmony that demonstrates confidence and trust at home and abroad and without which we cannot recover, still less progress.

Yet, the stability we need in the country has continued to be threatened by a few irresponsible people, diversionary tactics and sad events such as social unrest, intra-ethnic and institutional conflicts and criminal ac-tivities which have led to the escape from prison of convicts in Accra earlier this week and which has left such a bitter taste in the mouths of all decent Ghanaians. These despicable events have provoked a number of very serious questions in my mind. Have lives been sacrificed for nothing? Have we all been hypnotized by a few self-righteous and self-opinionated people for their selfish ends?

My Government condemns recent criminal activities and the other events immediately preceding the jail break as deliberate attempts to subvert the spirit and letter of the Constitution which we all publicly pledged on 24 September, to respect, uphold and defend. Henceforth we must all honour this pledge faithfully, and refrain from dishonouring ourselves any more.

My Government has repeatedly emphasized its commitment to the rule of law. We have also pledged not only to respect the decisions of the erstwhile Armed Forces Revolutionary Council (AFRC) as guaranteed by the Transitional Provisions of the Constitution, but also to continue with cleaning up our public life. We shall therefore resist, with all the power at our disposal, attempts by any individual or groups of in-dividuals, no matter what their status, to place their personal interests and ambitions above those of the national community.

Having obtained the mandate to reorder the affairs of this country, my Government will not allow a few self-opinionated people to undermine our efforts. We are determined to let the new civilian experiment suc-ceed. We shall also not shirk our responsibility towards all our people, particularly the under-privileged rural folk and labouring masses. I must therefore warn that those who want to foment trouble at this crucial time of our national life shall be firmly dealt with, according to the laws of the land and without fear or favour.

I must reiterate that peace and stability are necessary prerequisites of survival, success, progress and social justice and that therefore there is absolute need for all of us, both at home and abroad, not only to exercise patience but also to develop confidence in our ability to observe and

75

promote the rule of law and that delicate balance upon which rests both democracy and our last chance to pacify and unify our nation in its ethnic and cultural diversity. I shall do my duty to the nation. I hope that you will also discharge your duties to save our country from any more humiliations, indignities and national disgrace and shame.

Nananom, distinguished guests, ladies and gentlement, may I now turn, briefly, to some of the problems that the Government wants to solve in this Region. I have already paid tribute to the industry of the people producing foodstuffs and other crops to sustain the country. However, I must also remark that a large quantity of some of these goods are smuggled outside the country through our western borders, as elsewhere. This smuggling out of the country helps to strengthen the economies of other countries, as against ours. This is particularly so with the cocoa industry in which we have been suffering heavy losses. As a result, we lost our place as the world's leading producer of this crop. Is it not disgraceful that by our own irresponsible and unpatriotic acts we should contribute to our nation's decline?

I warmly appreciate the efforts of those vigilant and patriotic citizens who have been fighting against odds to check cocoa smuggling and other evil practices in this Region. To them I say well done and bravo! I invite others to emulate their good example.

I should also like to seize this opportunity to appeal to the chiefs and people of this Region, the Police and Border Guards and all other establishments in this Region to help check smuggling in order to boost our cocoa production and consequently our economy.

As I have said already, our rural peoples, as elsewhere, have tended, always, to be at a disadvantage. That is why my Government is determined to inject a measure of social justice into our national life. We must all therefore develop the necessary conscience and feeling for others. To this end, I hope that you will contribute your quota to our economic recovery by refraining from acts that tend to undermine these efforts and our economic recovery and progress. I also appeal to you all to step up production in all the economic activities for which this Region is so well known.

I am aware of some of the problems facing this promising Region; bad roads, lack of electricity, good drinking water, poor transportation facilities, lack of drugs for hospitals and clinics and many others. Government has demanded a comprehensive report on the immediate problems facing all the Regions and I can assure you that we are feverishly analysing and identifying the ways and means for solving some of these problems, within the shortest tolerable time.

Government has placed, as a matter or urgency, firm orders for agricultural inputs like matchets, fishing nets, drugs and other vitally needed consumer items, particularly by our rural communities. I hope that when these goods begin to arrive there will be that fair measure of relief for all of us as we have already achieved in the area of our fuel needs.

Our short-term and intermediate measures are being designed to produce spill-over and multiplier effects on the productive sectors of the economy so that we can progressively reduce our over-dependence on the importation of goods that can be produced within this country. This Region can expect to benefit greatly from those measures. You will benefit even more from our long-term projects and programmes as the economy revives and gains momentum.

Let me reiterate that I appreciate your contribution to the growth of our national economy and that I shall therefore do all I can to provide for your needs and promote the implementation of such nationally vital projects as the Bui Dam.

Nananom, may I, in conclusion, thank you very sincerely for this honour done me, my entourage and my administration.

14

Meeting of the National House of Chiefs at Kumasi

The place was the Hall of Chiefs, Kumasi. The occasion was a meeting of the National House of Chiefs on 17 January 1980. Assembled were some Heads of Traditional Rulers from all parts of Ghana, robed in their elegant regalia of colourful robes, gold and silver ornaments under giant umbrellas. That was Dr Hilla Limann's first meeting with the assembled natural leaders upon his assumption of office as President of Ghana.

He pleaded for collective rally of all in meeting the changed and changing order.

It is with the deep reverence, respect and pride that I address you today, the first since I assumed office. Under the circumstances kindly permit me belatedly to express to all of you, on my own behalf and on behalf of the Government felicitations and best wishes for the New Year.

This occasion is also particularly significant in other ways. Thus, I am speaking to the custodians of our rich cultural heritage. Even more important, I am also addressing some of the most influential opinion leaders whose contribution to the socio-economic and political development and progress of our country for good or evil, cannot be underestimated. I hope that you will bend your efforts towards the former rather than the latter. If you do not, then woe betide us all.

As chiefs, you are the presumed embodiment of the soul of our people. You therefore have an invaluable role to play in helping to reshape the course which will assure for Ghanaians a well-ordered, equitable, socially just and prosperous society in which feudalistic and unprofitable privileges and anachronisms can no longer hold sway. Indeed, you are under pressure to adapt and change in order to meet the imperatives and demands of a new social conscience. This task is all the more urgent today because of the ever-pressing need to pool our resources together in the current efforts at seeking solutions to the problems which have persistently militated against our rapid development and prosperity.

Nananom, as I have said on several occasions, the problems facing this country are numerous, difficult and challenging. I have also always added that the only way we can successfully overcome these problems is to tackle them collectively with singleness of purpose. It is precisely for this reason that I shall never be tired of appealing to all Ghanaians, irrespective of Party affiliations and sectional interests, to ensure the success of this third attempt at civilian rule, since what is on trial is not the PNP Government alone but the whole civilian experiment. Failure in this third attempt will spell the doom of our nation. In this regard, our role as a Government is to provide direction and leadership in this challenging task of restructuring our economy, reviving our social and cultural values and raising our national image and prestige at home and abroad.

Nanima, I firmly believe that, collectively as an institution and individually as leaders, chiefs have a great role to play in rescuing Mother Ghana. Most of you have been leaders in your traditional areas ever since the very birth of the Republic of Ghana or even earlier. You have thus lived through the changing fortunes of our nation. I have no doubt that you lament the sorry state in which we now find ourselves, a position which is the product of our own making. Indeed, some of us have actively participated in taking decisions that have brought us the present regrettable results. Others have stood by unconcerned or felt impotent to react to decisions that adversely affected our collective well-being. We must forever be grateful to the few who have always fought fearlessly for what they believe to be in the interest of Ghana.

Niimei, my appeal to you this morning is that you ought to realize and accept the fact that the times have changed and that all of us must regard our problems as a collective responsibility and must therefore rise up like one people to find solutions that will bring lasting peace to our nation, and greater welfare to all our people.

Togbuiwe, in my efforts to involve all sections of our national community, especially our chiefs, in our struggle to restructure our economy, I decided to visit each Region to confide in the chiefs on vital national issues which often cloud easy explanation or understanding from a distance. I started this exercise in October last year when I visited the Upper, Northern and Brong Ahafo Regions. I had to postpone my visit to other Regions in order to prepare and present my Sessional Address to Parliament and then work out our Budget proposals for the rest of the 1979–80 financial year. With these major issues now out of the way, I am happy to resume the visits. My presence here today is therefore part of my visit to the Ashanti Region. I shall follow this up with visits to the other remaining Regions in the ensuing weeks.

Important as these individual visits are, I am still very happy to meet all of you here under one roof during one visit. I therefore take this opportunity to raise one major issue that affects our economy and to which all of you are competent to make meaningful contributions.

As you are all aware already, agriculture is the bedrock of all the Government's present policies. It is precisely in this very area also that

DG–G

you, as chiefs, controlling vast acres of land and as leaders of our rural folk who constitute the bulk of our farmers, can assist the Government in mounting the programme for growing more food to feed ourselves and also for cultivating other crops to keep our industries fully at work. Indeed, Nananom, is it not shameful that a country with such a rich variety of fertile, arable lands should suffer from food shortages or import basic raw materials for our factories which can be produced locally? We must take immediate steps to remedy this unacceptable situation and get out of it, if possible for ever.

That is why the Government has initiated bold agricultural programmes to augment our production in these two vital fields. As custodians of stool and other lands, I strongly appeal to you to contribute your quota to the national effort by willingly releasing land on easy terms for agricltural and other purposes. We cannot want development and yet deny ourselves the means for its successful realization. I therefore appeal to you seriously to review your present land tenure systems and ensure the prompt release of land whenever this is needed by both Government and private entrepreneurs for the smooth implementation of our 'Grow More Food' campaign. It will be short-sighted and even dangerous for us to indulge in costly litigation and land disputes while continuing to experience food shortages in the midst of vast acres of fallow land yearning for cultivation. I therefore call on you to help change these attitudes. I am sure that the nation can count on your goodwill and understanding in this as in other respects.

Nanima, permit me now to turn to Chieftaincy itself which is one of our most important institutions. Our cultural practices and beliefs have been faithfully preserved by our chiefs throughout our history. These have always provided the guiding principles which determine our way of life as a nation. Indeed, the institution is a very valuable asset and should rightly be preserved and cherished. But in order that the importance of this institution should not be diminished in any way, it should itself strive to be a symbol of incorruptibility, justice, fairness, respect and dignity, yes, the sort of dignity that we all want regained in this country. It must therefore be capable of identifying the needs and aspirations of all our people and of responding to them adequately and in good time. In short, it must offer the expected leadership in transforming our society in such a way that what it retains will not be wholly absolete and irrelevant; and what it innovates will not be wholly strange and destabilizing.

Regrettably, in recent times the institution has opened itself to certain activities that have marred the reputation of a number of chiefs so much so that many people have now lost sentimental or historical attachment to their chiefs. Some of these activities have included the easy way in which some wealthy people have all too easily and suddenly laid claim to stools, thus setting aside all the traditional procedures for selecting chiefs. The most unfortunate aspect of this is that such attempts have always succeeded with the help of some traditional ruler or other who should have jealously guarded these procedures. It therefore seems as if the institutions, which should be sacred, are being undermined from within.

As the highest institution in this area of our national life, perhaps, this august House may wish to direct its serious attention to this and the other points which I shall refer to below. Another unfortunate aspect is the alarming rate at which chiefs have become involved in the reckless dissipation of monies paid to them as royalties and/or compensations for stool lands and as funds for developmental projects within their traditional areas. A number of chiefs also suddenly became contractors in the recent past, directly or through front men, with no expertise or knowledge for undertaking the projects awarded them. No wonder they could therefore not complete such projects. Such practices have only tended to diminish the importance of your dignified institution within our society. I therefore appeal to you, Nana President of the National House of Chiefs and your colleagues, to institute measures to ensure that the House can collectively apply sanctions against the acts of individual chiefs which may attract adverse comments or even bring the institution of chieftaincy into disrepute.

Within the institution itself, I appeal to all of you to try to avoid delays in the determination of chieftaincy cases. Lackadaisical attitudes on the part of panel members in the determination of chieftaincy suits only help to prolong litigation in the areas involved thus perpetuating tensions and wasting valuable scarce human and material resources.

I hope that as required by the Constitution, the House will initiate steps to provide a comprehensive list of all categories of chiefs throughout the country in order to maintain public confidence in the institution. Let me also repeat calls made to you in the past to review the unprogressive customs that affect marriages and burials in our society.

On the part of the Government, I firmly assure you that we shall not interfere in chieftaincy matters. We will however be ever ready to come to the assistance of the institution whenever you collectively require us to do so. You may also wish to learn that I have already instituted measures to ensure that the expansion programme of your office accommodation and meeting hall here in Kumasi is speeded up. The question of your present monthly allowances is being actively studied but some time is required to streamline the economy and to ensure that the cost of living is brought down to reasonable levels before any concrete action can be taken.

Nana President of the National House of Chiefs, Nananom, Nanima, Niimei, Tegbuiwo, Honourable Ministers, distinguished guests, ladies and gentlemen, no nation can turn its back on its cultural heritage. I therefore appeal to you always to be conscious that, as custodians of all that we hold dear, you ought yourselves to be shining examples for others to emulate. You may wish seriously to consider the need to adapt our sacred traditional norms and rich cultural practices to suit the challenging times so as to benefit all Ghanaians, both young and old

Finally, I wish to thank you again for this golden opportunity afforded me to share my views with you on national affairs in general and on chieftaincy matters in particular.

15
At Kumasi in the Ashanti Region

The President was paying his respects to the Asantehene and his chiefs and people two days after addressing the National House of Chiefs at the same venue, Kumasi, the capital of the Ashanti Region and the heart-centre of Ghana. At such a durbar of chiefs and people under Otumfuo the Asantehene, there can hardly be a greater display of the nation's culture, whether in the royal splendour of the chiefs, linguists, asafo people and elders or in the art and craft treasures, of drums, stools, jewellery and the like. The drums and horns, the castanets in concert under the clear Ghana sunshine—nothing can surpass this animated scene.

I wish to express my deep appreciation to you, Asantehene and to the Chiefs and people of Ashanti for this colourful traditional welcome accorded me and my entourage in this ancient, renowned, 'garden' city of Kumasi.

Since assuming office, I have officially visited three Regional Capitals and parts of the Eastern, Volta, Central and Western Regions to meet the chiefs and people and discuss with them face to face some of the problems facing our country and also to identify, with their help, some of the solutions to such problems. Your own absence, from Kumasi, Otumfuo, when you were away in the Upper Volta, compelled me to put forward my visit to your Region at the time.

My attendance at this durbar will be seen as a fulfilment of the pledge I made to practice 'open government', to consult the people at all levels of our national society and to promote 'participatory democracy'. These are some of the ways in which to make Government less remote and also to let us know in time whether things are going well or badly. It is also, in this regard, that I have appealed to the public at large to take its destiny into its own hands and not deny ourselves our heritage. Hence I have endorsed and officially supported the voluntary vigilance activities of our youth and other patriotic citizens who have taken such appeals seriously in the national interest. I shall support and defend that idea to the hilt. Meantime, as a start in my public consultations, I have already met and discussed some of our national problems with some farmers, industrial workers and students. I hope that this durbar which marks the climax of my three days' visit to the great Ashanti Region, the largest in the country, will heighten the resolve of all of us to work closely together in peace, harmony and understanding in the larger interests of all our people. Nananom, the number of days I have devoted to visiting your Region is indicative of the importance I attach to you and your central and cardinal position in our country.

I must confess that I am overwhelmed not only by this impressive display of our cultural heritage but more importantly by the spontaneous turn-out, warmth and receptivity of the people.

This only further strengthens my conviction in the inherent capacity of the Ghanaian to rise above petty and sectional considerations in the supreme interests of the country as a whole. Indeed, we may have our individual and regional differences, but this should make for national unity in diversity. The sense of oneness which has characterized this durbar, as on other occasions elsewhere in the country, further convince me of a bright future for our country despite our past and present tribulations. We can tackle our problems as one determined people in search of economic recovery and national dignity.

Let me reiterate and emphasize what I have repeatedly stated elsewhere already. This third attempt at civilian rule is a crucial test of our ability as a people to rule ourselves through our own elected representatives and also to solve our problems by ourselves. For our own sake as adults and for the sake of our children, we must succeed. However, in order to succeed, we must close our ranks, mobilize our resources and work selflessly and single-mindedly. This is the only way in which we can quickly overcome our present economic difficulties. Sterile disputes, overweening bickering and carping criticism can only fritter away our already very scarce financial resources and worsen our economic decline. I certainly welcome fair comment, and appreciate and will defend the right to criticize the issues at stake. I have done this all my life. However, I do not have much respect for loud-sounding, uninformed or wilfully distorted presentation of facts masquerading as criticism. The out-pourings of windbags and empty barrels are out of place and in very bad taste in our present national plight.

Otumfuo, Nananom, distinguished guests, ladies and gentlemen, due to our present critical, almost desperate economic situation, in line with my campaign of discipline and rejection of indignities and the status of a beggar nation in the midst of enormous human and material resources, my government has had to adopt tough fiscal measures to attack our problems at their roots and eliminate the canker that has afflicted us.

These measures will undoubtedly cause displeasure in some sections of the easy-going, privileged and over-subsidized sections of our society. The Government is very much aware of the reality and importance of this aspect of the Budget since it is meant to curb the insatiable appetite of the few who derive the benefits of subsidies initially meant to alleviate the hardships of the rural folks and workers.

For years Governments have kept bad faith with the people by not telling them the truth, the plain truth, about our economy. Worse still, they resorted to deceptively cosmetic measures which only provided temporary reliefs leaving basic problems untouched. All political parties were and are still aware of this situation. None of them was however fully aware of the depth of destruction and the size of our public indebtedness, domestically and externally.

During the election campaign we consciously asked for a mandate to arrest any further decline, national disgrace and shame. We have been given this mandate. We can therefore not gloss over our problems as in the past. Moreover, we have promised open Government which means absolute candour in diagnosing our problems and finding lasting solutions to them. Indeed, since desperate diseases demand desperate cures, no elected Government can shirk its responsibility in this regard, hence our realistic proposals for solving the most bewildering of our economic problems as revealed in the present six months' budgetary measures. This must be emphasized. A start has to be made to prevent total national disgrace and shame. That start is now and cannot be postponed any longer.

One of our past national weaknesses has been the habit of passing the buck. Thus, our leaders either lacked the courage or shirked the responsibility to take measures which were necessary for our economic health and advancement.

The PNP Government will not pass the buck precisely because we have asked for a mandate to put an end to indiscipline in our public life. We have therefore instituted measures which we sincerely and honestly believe will save our country from further decline, disgrace and shame. We are convinced that this will be to the benefit of our people in the long run.

I urge all Ghanaians to realize that we will clamour for deliverance from our woes in vain if we are not prepared to accept the realities and facts of our desperate economic situation. We cannot live cheaper, more lazily, more ostentatiously and glamorously than people in rich, powerful and developed economies of the world.

I do not agree with the view of our detractors that the present economic recovery measures should have been introduced gradually. That will solve nothing. The rest of the world is not waiting for us but moving ahead. For instance crude oil prices have gone up already since the Sessional and Budget Statements were made. We must be prepared either to face our problems and make up our minds to solve them now, no matter how hard this will be for us or else allow them to become more compounded and insoluble later. In this regard, better now than never.

85

That is why my government has decided to honour our election promises and make a frontal attack on our problems. I assure you that given the goodwill and understanding of all our people, we will solve the problems which have proved intractable in the past. Ghana cannot rise again by continuing to be an undisciplined beggar nation still wedded to over-sophisticated tastes and demands for which she refuses to work and pay. No country can take us seriously, if we continue to beg for loans only to buy food and fuel, only to sell it far cheaper than it costs the consumer in some oil-producing countries. Worst still, posterity will never forgive us, if we pawn the future so irresponsibly and heavily for our present selfish comforts.

Nananom, ladies and gentlemen, at this juncture, I wish to address myself to some of the specific issues raised in the Otumfuo's address.

Agriculture is the top priority of our policies. I am therefore encouraged to learn that Nananom fully support this basic concern of my Government and are ready to provide the framework for its success. We in turn will give you every encouragement and support.

The Ashanti Region has in the past immeasurably contributed to the economic development of this country through the production of food, cocoa, timber and mineral wealth; and through cultural activities and other achievements. I must commend you for this and urge you to greater efforts, particularly in the areas of rural developments and industries in which your ingenious weavers, goldsmiths and other artisans can hold their own against the best in the world. In this regard, I wish to add that in the years ahead your energies, resources and hard work will be needed more than ever before. I trust that just as Nananom have promised, we shall see more fruitful co-operation and giant strides in the national endeavour to put our country back on the road to recovery, progress and prosperity.

As I have indicated in my Sessional Address, the question of land reform still remains a vexed issue since we still cling to anachronistic beliefs in our various land tenure systems. For the Government's Agricultural Policy to become meaningful, there must be a socially just land tenure system to encourage agricultural production and sound economic planning and development. I am therefore greatly encouraged at the assurance that land will be readily made available for the cultivation of the various crops on which we want to concentrate our attention in the allocation of resources.

You may wish to hear, Nananom, that during the current financial year two seed processing plants will be established in Kumasi and Winneba for which ₵6.0 million has been provided. An amount of ₵0.80 million has also been allocated to the Sheep and Goats Projects at Ejura, Juaso and Pong-Tamale.

The positive contribution of minerals to our foreign exchange earnings has been recognized in the Budget. For the optimum development of our mineral resources, the sum of ₡1.07 million has been provided for gold prospecting in the Akrokorri Mampamhwe, Obenenasi and Pepe Akontanasi areas. It can therefore be seen that Government aims at stepping up the development of economic ventures in this Region of great economic potentialities.

I am aware of the concern of Otumfuo and Nananom and all other interested parties about the issues which led to the appointment of the Coussey Committee and also the anxiety about the publication of the report. Similar requests have been made from numerous quarters in spite of repeated public confessions of lack of newsprint in the country for a long time now. However, I wish to assure Nananom and all other parties that this matter shall receive appropriate attention in due course so that a solution based on justice, equity and fair play can be found.

I have taken note of all the other important points raised in your moving address for the attention that they so necessarily deserve. Let me assure you, Nananom, that I am personally and firmly committed to the successful completion of the Medical School in this most centrally placed city of our country. Kindly permit me to add at this crucial period of fighting for our national survival, Nananom should rather give that kind of leadership which will redirect the energies of the people into productive activities instead of being wasted on conflicts and pointless litigation as if we were warring peoples among ourselves within our national boundaries.

Otumfuo, the Asantehene, Nananom, distinguished guests, ladies and gentlemen, the fate of our country, the future of our children and of our very survival as a people rests on all of us and on our ability to rise up to the demanding challenges facing us.

The very enormity of the tasks should galvanize us into such a concerted action as will enable us to solve them with courage and determination. If we move together as one people, we shall succeed. If we drift apart we shall inevitably fail. We shall pay dearly, very dearly indeed, if we fail the youth and generations yet unborn. We have no right to pawn our country any more for our laziness, corruption, irresponsibility, and vain and ephemeral pleasures. We owe a duty to the present and future youth of our country to recreate what our generation has wantonly dissipated. The time to save our country from further decline, destruction, disgrace and shame is therefore now and not later. Our banner in our efforts to salvage our shattered economy should henceforth bear the inscription of 'Save Ghana Now'.

Once again, I must thank you very sincerely Otumfuo, The Asantehene, Nananom and indeed all of you who have listened to me, for this great honour done me at this very colourful, cultural and most impressive durbar.

16

At Koforidua in the Eastern Region

In his meet-the-chiefs-and-people rounds from Region to Region, the President, on 26 January 1980 now arrived at Koforidua in the Eastern Region. He aired his concern about past mismanagement in national and corporate affairs, party political disunity, dishonesty, indolence, shortages of all kinds and the blight which has overtaken the country's cocoa industry, the mainstay of the economy.

He raised hopes in major mining prospects in the Region upon which the Government had embarked, notably the Kibi Bauxite deposits which had begged too long for exploitation.

It is a privilege and an honour for me to meet and address you this morning on some of the burning issues of our country.

On my own behalf, and on behalf of the Government, I wish to thank Nananom and all those who have come here to participate in this grand and colourful durbar.

Your presence here this morning is, indeed, a flowing testimony of the support and co-operation which the chiefs and people of this Region extend to the Government. I am deeply inspired by this sincerity and spontaneity and also by the assurances we have just received. This, more than ever before steels my conviction that the broad masses of the people, to whose welfare we are also committed, are solidly united behind the Government's efforts at rebuilding the nation and improving the standard of living of all our people.

Nananom, for a long time, our country has been driven along the path of self destruction by reckless policies and irresponsible governments. This intolerable situation was compounded by antagonisms that rankled in the body politic, pushed it apart and led to chaos. It is against this background that my Government proposes the concept of open government and participatory democracy with the undoubted virtue of bringing government to the people; sharing ideas on our problems and evolving solutions to such problems at the grass roots level of our society. Our belief is that all must be involved in what touches us all. This magnificent durbar, like all the others should be seen as part of the beginning of this process of sharing and exchanging ideas on the state of our nation.

It is my firm belief that what the country needs today is the healing of wounds, reconciliation and unity, even if in diversity. The confrontational and antagonistic politics of the past drove wedges between us as a people and thus helped to create some of our present problems. Having been bitten once in the past, we should now be twice shy. Indeed, the elementary instinct of self-preservation leaves us no other choice. Ghanaians are disillusioned at present because of the many intolerable humiliations we have all silently endured from governments in the past which treated us as if we were children or as if they were occupying foreign powers.

Nananom, Government is very much aware of the anxious expectations of the people for relief not only from past evils and present deprivations but also from falsehoods, humiliations and indignities. We can all feel proud and dignified even in the face of our difficulties only when we are treated as intelligent and responsible adults not when we are patronizingly treated as morons incapable of understanding the realities of our country and the wider world of which we form a part.

Nananom, I believe that if we eschew cheating and irresponsibility, managerial incompetence and indifference and rather replace these with the virtues and principles of hard work, honesty and self-discipline we will set the pace for rapid progress in our efforts to rescue and rebuild the nation from her present sorry plight. Many nations have passed through similar, and in some cases even worse crises than we are experiencing at the moment but with self-discipline, determination and single-mindedness of purpose, they have always rescued their country and its people. I am sure that we can also do the same. It is now or never!

Fellow Ghanaians, very much alive to our election pledges and also conscious of our responsibilities, my Government is working relentlessly to resuscitate the economy, enforce public accountability, lead exemplary lives, restore public confidence in government and rebuild our society based on equity and social justice.

What is needed now to encourage and supplement this determination is the willingness of Nananom and all our people to contribute in a practical and meaningful way to our collective efforts towards the socio-economic regeneration we promised and for which confidence and trust were reposed in us by electing us to office. In this regard, perhaps we can all benefit from the words of the late President Kennedy of the United States of America when he appealed to his compatriots not to think only of what their nation could do for them but rather what they could do for their nation. I do here and now strongly make the same appeal to my fellow citizens of all levels and ages.

Nananom, distinguished guests, fellow Ghanaians, in our efforts to face the challenges of national reconstruction, we shall have to take and implement some bold and realistic decisions, as we have already done in my Sessional Address and the Budget statement which are now before Parliament. Some of us may find such decisions unpalatable because they attack our privileges. However, I appeal to you to stand solidly behind the Government in its efforts to save all of us from further degradation rather than encourage or promote the accumulation of private windfall fortunes any more by a few unproductive hangers-on in our society at the expense of those following honest pursuits to earn their living. This is the only way in which to revive our self-respect, self-confidence, pride and dignity and to enable us no more to bow down our heads in shame when we describe ourselves as Ghanaians at home and abroad.

As we clearly indicated in our Manifesto, in my Sessional Address and in the Budget Statement, our development strategy is based principally on raising agricultural production so as to provide more food for our people, more raw materials for our industries and increased export commodities to earn us more foreign exchange. The wealth of our own land, richly endowed as it is, contains the key to the door of our salvation and indeed honourable and lasting solutions to our problems.

As I have repeatedly indicated already elsewhere, we cannot continue to spend most of our scarce resources to import food to feed ourselves while we are so abundantly endowed with vast fertile tracts of arable land, crying for exploitation to produce our own more nourishing food stuffs locally. At best such imports should supplement and not replace our local stable foods which are not only more natural to us but are even healthier, more satisfying, appetizing and life-sustaining.

My Government shall therefore pursue a dynamic agricultural programme which will reduce and eventually eliminate our heavy dependence on imported foods with all their health and economic hazards.

Nananom, closely linked with the development of agriculture is the rehabilitation of our roads and also the construction of feeder roads, since without access roads to farms, product cannot be effectively gathered and distributed. Indeed until food-producing areas are linked up with good roads to enable food to reach markets, our campaign to grow more food can not succeed. In this connection, Government has allocated an initial ₡50 million towards the construction of feeder roads as a start in the current six months Budget.

Nananom, the cocoa farmer has admittedly contributed very much to the development of this nation and should therefore receive a fair return for his labours. Indeed, my Government greatly appreciates the great role which the farmers have played and will continue to play in sustaining the economic survival of this country. We are also very gravely concerned about the loss of our position as the leading cocoa producer country and are therefore seriously considering how best to improve upon our performance in cocoa production.

In this regard, the Cocoa Council soon to be set up will have the task of addressing itself vigorously to the improvement of the quality of life of the cocoa farmer as one of the necessary means of regaining our leading world position in the production of this commodity. In this regard and also as stated in our Manifesto, we shall work out a more national system of our cocoa pricing policy which will take account of the needs of the industry, the interest of the farmer, the welfare of the economy, the development of world prices for the crop and the welfare of its producers.

Nananom, my Government will in future not tolerate the reckless dissipation of funds meant for cocoa purchases. The Interim Management Committee of the Cocoa Industry has therefore been instructed to ensure that farmers receive prompt payment of their produce. The Committee has already sorted out the former system of bank transfer of funds it inherited and which caused the bottlenecks and delays of the October 1979 season. In future, you should promptly report those who may issue chits in the purchase of cocoa so that they can be appropriately dealt with.

Fellow citizens, on my tours around the country and in parts of this Region, I have met the same sad story of want and neglect, and everywhere these include the lack of drinking water, run-down schools, very bad roads, the need for electrification and many others. We are determined to solve these problems, even if in phases within the present economic constraints. You may therefore be pleased to learn that Government has provided nearly ₡4 million in the Budget to complete the Akwapim Ridge and Kwahu Ridge District Water Schemes. An amount of ₡2.2 million has been provided as part payment for a pilot plant research laboratory and other dispensary equipment for the Centre for Plant Medicine at Mampong-Akwapim.

Nananom will be pleased to hear that an amount of ₡530,000 has been allocated for diamond prospecting in the Birim, Bonsa, Ankobra and Pra Rivers. Even more importantly, we are feverishly negotiating for the exploitation of the huge Kibi Bauxite deposit project which we have found to be enmeshed in crippling local politics and a vicious circle of international intrigues all of which we condemn unreservedly.

Fellow citizens, several other projects, spread over this Region and the country at large shall also be taken up and eventually completed. We do not believe in abandoning projects on which public funds have been spent for political reasons. Our aim is to develop the country, not to play politics with projects. To this end, a comprehensive report is being compiled, and as resources become available the priority needs of the country will all be tackled. However, I wish to point out that the Government cannot alone meet all the developmental needs of our country.

The various District and Local Councils must undertake self-help projects to supplement Government efforts. I also appeal to Nananom to take the lead in the drive to encourage the people to pay their taxes so as to raise revenue for the development of their areas. The private sector can also help a lot as it has always done in the past in our overall Regional and National efforts. I therefore appeal to that sector also to step up its developmental activities, particularly in agriculture and the provision of communal amenities and facilities in their areas of operation. The Banks should take the lead in this regard.

Nene President of the Regional House of Chiefs, Nananom, Honourable Ministers, distinguished guests, ladies and gentlemen, as I have often said, the task of nation-building has become the collective responsibility of all of us. We must therefore move forward in a united resolve to work in co-operative efforts in our common interest.

The enormous amount of goodwill I have seen here and in other parts of the country convinces me that we shall succeed. Indeed, we cannot and must not fail. In this regard, my Government is determined to play its role effectively. Moving forward hand in hand with the public as we have set out to do, we can all expect a bright future.

Nananom, fellow Ghanaians, on behalf of my entourage and on my own behalf, I must thank you very much for this durbar, for your expressions of support for your views and for also affording me this opportunity to address and share my views with you.

17

At Ho in the Volta Region

The Volta Region is about the most heterogenous among the Regions of Ghana, in terms of ethnic diversity, language and past colonial history. Rather than being a link with the former Gold Coast the River Volta had been the barrier to social, economic and political intercourse between the two geographic regions. Happily, today, the smiling expanse of the Volta Lake, the largest man-made lake in the world, is open to development which unites and integrates the people of the entire land of Ghana.

The need for unity, then, was the major theme in the President's durbar address made to the Chiefs and people at Ho in this his official visit on 9 February 1980.

I wish, first of all, on my own behalf and on behalf of my Administration, to thank the Chiefs and people of the Volta Region for this colourful durbar organized to welcome me and my entourage to the Volta Regional Capital, Ho. I wish further to express my appreciation for the warmth of the reception I have continued to receive since starting my visit to this Region yesterday.

Last November, I had a taste of the unique hospitality of the people of this Region when I attended the Hogbetsotso Festival of the Chiefs and people of Anlo at Anloga. Little did I realize then that the grand spectacle I saw was only a foretaste of the grandeur of today's activities.

My colleagues and I are indeed privileged to be amongst the friendly people of the Volta Region to enjoy your hospitality, to witness your rich cultural traditions and to exchange views with you on the burning issues of our country. We feel particularly at home because we have been always aware of the active support and goodwill that the People's National Party and the Government enjoy among you. My administration considers this Region one of the most important, historically, economically and administratively. That is why I am determined that your rich human and material resources should be utilized to the fullest benefit of the Region and throughout the whole country where your influence is felt and indeed very much appreciated.

As I drove along on my inspection of projects, yesterday and today, I could not help but feel horrified at the extent of waste and destruction that have taken place in this part of your diverse Region. I can assure you that in our overall policy of rehabilitation we shall strive to repair the damage and move forward to positive development for your benefit and that of all our people.

Togbewo, in our efforts to resuscitate our economy and our degraded national image—a situation which makes us bow down our heads in shame—I have repeatedly emphasized that we need the co-operation of every Ghanaian. Without unity, hard work, sincerity, honest and devoted service to our country, we cannot carry out this rescue operation.

In the most trying times confronting us as a people only unity and singleness of purpose can give us the necessary courage to steel our will and determination to succeed. It is for this reason that I have strongly condemned recent attempts by certain individuals and groups of citizens to apportion blame for our national woes on tribalistic lines. We are one people. We are all Ghanaians and should therefore desist from seeing ourselves as Northerners, Akans, Ewes or Gas. Narrow ethnocentric tendencies cannot save us. They are pernicious and dangerous and must be eschewed at all costs. What unites us as a national community is stronger and more pervasive and should therefore transcend our local feelings and considerations. Consequently, I appeal to all our nationals to realize that our oneness, our collective destiny, overrides our regional, ethnic and cultural diversity. The latter should rather enrich and reinforce the former. We must all therefore together put our shoulders to the wheel and rescue our beloved country from any further decline, indignities, disgrace and mortification.

Consequently, I also unreservedly condemn all secessionist moves artificially fanned primarily by a few disgruntled persons for their own selfish interests masquerading as champions of long rejected causes. Curiously enough, such individuals were mute when they held official positions in previous governments, very clear proof that the development of the Region and the country and the welfare of the people have never been their concern. I appeal to you to ignore such selfish importunities. Indeed if we dissipate our energies on peripheral problems we will lose sight of our primary objective of bringing relief to all Ghanaians after so many years of neglect and deprivation.

'A house divided within itself shall crumble' as Dante has said. Indeed, a divided city or country can never progress. It can only disintegrate. We must all therefore eschew such dangerous tendencies. Consequently, I take this opportunity to appeal to all of you to use your positions as traditional leaders to ensure the restoration of peaceful and brotherly relations between the people of Ho-Bankoe and Ho-Dome. Unhealthy rivalry between these two communities in this city will only lead to retrogression.

Inter-tribal conflicts and unrest within the Region and, indeed, in the nation at large can also only sap our vital and useful energies that should otherwise be directed into development and progress. The people of this Region, indeed all Ghanaians, are looking forward to a period of respite, calm, and improvement in their living conditions. We must all therefore pay serious heed to this and refrain from fratricidal feuds. We need your help in our efforts to heal wounds, reconcile our people and unify the nation more than ever before. Please help us. I would not have been a politician now if I could not realize and share the aspirations of our people with whom I have lived very closely all my life. That is, indeed, why I believe that we should hasten carefully in order to avoid worsening our already critical and unenviable situation. As I have already said, great, almost irreparable damage has been done to our economy. In our anxiety to improve our sorry lot we should be wary of decisions which can only serve as palliatives now, but which shall certainly prove to be our total undoing in the long run.

That is why the present policies of my Government have been designed to correct the economic mismanagement and maladministration of the past several years. They also take into mature consideration such external developments as directly affect our domestic situation. One such external development is the recent announcement that the price of crude oil has again been increased by more than four dollars per barrel since January this year, that is, soon after we had prepared the Budget. Ladies and gentlemen, this will certainly have considerable repercussions on our budgetary proposals now before Parliament. More precisely, it means that we have to spend more of our scarce foreign exchange resources to pay for our fuel requirements.

Consequently, unless we take stringent measures to reduce fuel consumption we shall soon be spending more than 50 per cent of our foreign earnings on fuel alone, thus leaving nothing for even salvaging our economy much less to speak of development. Such a situation will be completely unacceptable to the vast majority of Ghanaians. I therefore appeal to all Ghanaians, especially the motoring community, to embark upon a nation-wide exercise of energy conservation. This is the only positive way in which to reduce our over-heavy expenditure on oil import bills. I must make it clear, very clear, that the only other alternative to this will be the total starvation of our factories and the cancellation of development projects for lack of funds to import the necessary inputs. This will also mean a lower standard of living for our people, especially the rural folk who do not enjoy the comforts of driving their own cars.

Nananom, kindly allow me to avail myself of this august platform to renew the assurance I have already made in previous broadcasts and speeches that my Government fully understands and appreciates the problems facing workers, farmers, fishermen and so on, and that we are earnestly working towards the solution of such problems. I should however like to point out and re-emphasize our view that the resort to

DG–H

threats or force as a means of seeking redress is not only wrong but also irresponsible and destructive. I therefore urge all involved to seek solutions to their grievances through peaceful means over the negotiating table. Indeed, it is worthless for us to torture ourselves to no end or cut our noses to spite our faces, for in the end we shall all be the losers, as has often happened in the past. I wish to direct the same appeal to all our youth and students for whose sake we are bending every nerve to save the country from any further decisions which will endanger their future. We pay heavily as a people for the loss of hundreds of thousands of man-hours of work because of irresponsible strikes and also for damage to public property, particularly in educational institutions.

As a responsive and sensitive Government we are prepared to listen to all grievances and find solutions to them but we need the peace and patience for which we have always pleaded. I wish to state that we shall not be found wanting if we are forced to take harsh decisions to curb lawlessness and anarchy. Let no one underestimate our determination to carry out our mandate obtained at free and fair elections in which we all exercise our franchise.

Togbewo, I would not like to mar this festive day by dwelling only on old wounds or treating you to a catalogue of economic woes. However, I wish to repeat and re-emphasize that we need a period of peace to stabilize our economic and social institutions, and as one people, with a collective goal, take our destiny into our own hands, get out of our plight, and reshape our future as a nation.

As I have had the opportunity to state elsewhere, my Government is totally committed to the development of every part of this country. During our electioneering campaign, we made specific promises to the people and shall stand by those pledges and not others being put into our mouths. Our avowed aim is to strive and make the life of the ordinary Ghanaian more bearable than it had been in the past. The policies outlined in my Sessional Address to Parliament and the consequential measures proposed in the recent Budget Statement have been directed towards this end.

Togbewo, I have stated in that Address that agriculture is the first priority of my Government. I want to re-emphasize that we are very serious about this and that our approach will be practical and responsive to the needs of that sector. Our efforts shall be directed towards providing individuals and organizations engaged in this field with the necessary inputs, incentives and encouragement to enable them to produce more food to feed us and also raw materials to resuscitate our industries. I therefore appeal to you all to mobilize all your energies in this campaign for more production in the agricultural sector.

Is it not untenable, fellow citizens, for a country with such vast tracts of land as ours to continue to spend large sums of foreign exchange on

96

food imports? As part of our two year agricultural programme my Government plans to develop more land for farming purposes. In furtherance of this we shall expand and utilize all the existing irrigation schemes and potential of this country.

Togbewo, we have provided an amount of ₵2.6 million for the Afife Project which involves the irrigation of vast tracts of land for rice production. We shall also exploit the full potential of the Volta Lake for irrigation purposes. To start the Lake Shore Irrigation Project, Kpandu Torkor and Kete Krachi and other areas in the Afram Plains. A sum of ₵2 million has already been allocated for infrastructural development.

The PNP Government will also provide for the importation of adequate inputs of small pumps for irrigation and for the benefit of small scale farmers along our rivers and streams. The giant Afife Rice Project and the multi-million-₵edi Sugar Project at Have are under active study for early implementation. My Government will take an active and keen interest in them. We have already provided an amount of ₵350,000 for the cost and maintenance of the Have Sugar Project.

Togbewo and fellow citizens, at long last the integrated agricultural scheme with financial support from the World Bank is about to start in this Region. You are aware, I am sure, that the Upper Region started such a project three years ago. This second project will definitely start by the next financial year. Indeed, the Project Manager has virtually been appointed. This project aims at developing and increasing our agricultural potential side by side with the provisions of infrastructural and social amenities. Thus, while thousands of acres of irrigable land are being prepared in any given area for allotment to local farmers, roads will also be built with water and electricity supplied to such areas. Similarly, schools and clinics would be provided for the farming community. This, ladies and gentlemen, is the only way in which we can attract and maintain the interest of the younger generation in farming. In short, it shall be an integrated and comprehensive programme aimed at improving upon our productive performance and raising our living standards. I therefore appeal to you to take full advantage of it as it gets going.

Togbewo, Nananom, ladies and gentlemen, we know that about sixty per cent of the annual fish catch in the country is produced by our canoe fishermen. For this reason, my Government is leaving no stone unturned to procure fishing nets, mending twine, outboard motors and the spare parts which should reach this category of fishermen at reasonable prices. Indeed, consignments of outboard motors have already arrived in the country and some are being sold at controlled prices to some fishermen. I hope that they will reciprocate by delivering the fish to the consuming public.

The projected development of the Volta Lake Transport will also be integrated with fishing to ensure that such facilities as landing sites and access roads serve the needs of the fishing community along the shores of the Lake.

Togbewo, my Government is fully committed to the infrastructural development of the rural areas of Ghana. I can therefore assure you that we will fulfil our obligations towards the hitherto neglected rural people who actually produce the bulk of the wealth of our country. I am happy to reiterate that plans are near completion for extending power from the Akosombo Hydro-Electric Power Grid to most parts of this Region. The Federal Republic of Germany has already released 28 million Deutschmarks to us for the implementation of the first phase of the project. We are very grateful to this friendly foreign Government for this assistance. In this connection I may also add that, thanks to the same Government, the perennial problem of very acute water shortages in Ho will be solved when the Kpeve Project is completed. To this end, I have personally appealed to the competent authorities I met on the site yesterday to so expedite action that the project could be inaugurated by the end of June this year. My Regional Minister and others concerned should ensure that whatever assistance may be required from Government is provided. I therefore hope that they will invite me to come and turn on the tap for your assured, uninterrupted and clean water supplies before the next Budget comes into effect in July this year.

Togbewo, the deterioration of health services in the rural areas is also a matter of great concern to my Government. One of our priority areas is therefore the rehabilitation of our existing health centres, clinics, and hospitals to make them functional again before new ones can then be built. We are however making efforts to give the necessary assistance to the work currently proceeding on your Regional Hospital.

And now Togbewo, Nananom, distinguished guests, ladies and gentlemen, I wish to express my deep appreciation for the enthusiasm and patriotic zeal with which the people of this Region have embraced the idea of the voluntary vigilance groups in response to my appeal to all Ghanaians to take their collective destiny into their hands and protect the nation's wealth from the activities of cheats and nation wreckers. You should make sure that goods meant for you remain in the Region or are not hoarded by a few selfish people.

The sum total of the foreign exchange we lose every year through the activities of smugglers runs into several millions, an indication of the stubbornness of some of our own brothers and sisters, fathers and mothers, who will dare even the devil himself to satisfy their own greed and avarice, at the cost of their soul and at the expense of the rest of our society. I must therefore once more appeal to all of you, Chiefs and people, to support the vigilantes to uproot the canker of greed and selfishness from our society. I thank you profoundly for the laudable work you have already done in this field. I assure you that my Government and all patriotic Ghanaians will support, uphold and defend your efforts. We shall emulate your example which you should therefore intensify.

Togbewo, Your Excellencies, distinguished guests, ladies and gentlemen, there is no doubt that our country is at present not what we expect it to be. The great Ghanaian dream of progress and prosperity has eluded us in the past. My Government's resolve is to realize this dream. We therefore renew our appeal to you for your continued understanding, active and unflinching support in our endeavours.

Due to past deceptions and failures, our people are understandably disappointed, frustrated and disillusioned now, but I believe in our collective capacity to rise to the challenges confronting us to salvage our economy to make our nation great and our people proud again as Ghanaians and Africans. Indeed, more than ever before, we are determined to ennoble the lives of all our people. With your co-operation and support, we shall attain this and other objectives so that before long, Ghana will recapture her lost image. Let the enthusiasm and general feeling of oneness that has characterized this durbar therefore prod us into intensified activities for greater service to our country. If we do not rise equal to these challenges in our time we shall surely bury our heads in more disgrace and deeper shame.

On this note, Togbewo, I once more thank you very sincerely for this wonderful durbar and for the opportunity it has afforded me to exchange views with you. Even more importantly, I must thank you all again for the massive vote you gave the PNP, my candidates and me at the June–July 1979 general elections. Without that unstinted and massive support, 'Dr Li-who' would not have been here to address you today.

18

At Cape Coast in the Central Region

Next to the Accra urban centre, Cape Coast in the Central Region is a centre of intensive political activity and interaction. With a long standing concentration of second and third cycle educational institutions the electorate is relatively more politically conscious. Little wonder that a spirited reception met the President at his entry to attend the durbar which had been arranged in his honour on 16 February 1980.

It is indeed a very important and happy occasion for me to attend this colourful durbar of Chiefs and people of the Central Region today at long last. This is my second visit since assuming office. The first was the invitation I accepted soon after my inauguration to come and commission the Twifu Oil Palm Plantation Project. My very first official engagement in office as Executive President and Head of State was therefore carried out in this very important Region.

Curiously enough, I was also first introduced to the country as the PNP Presidential Candidate on this very spot early in April last year. A scare campaign just prior to that warming-up rally was that we were going to be hooted at. This neither frightened the Party hierarchy, party supporters nor me and so we came. Those who came to scoff remained and rather cheered us. This was the very beginning of our irresistible march towards success. Victoria Park, Cape Coast and the Central Region therefore occupy a very special place in my memory, and in our hearts an emotional attachment which was powerfully reinforced when, again, curiously enough, fate and the Party decided that my running mate, now the Vice-President, should hail from this age-old, famous city of enlightenment. May Cape Coast and the Central Region continue to win more laurels in their educative and civilizing mission in the years ahead. The PNP administration stands ready to encourage and support you to the utmost in such a noble mission.

My present official visit to you, as to other Regions, was planned last October. Such visits are meant to enable me to meet and exchange views with the chiefs and a cross-section of the people of each Region, to see projects and problems at first hand, and, even more importantly, to discuss our present predicament and the future of our country.

The splendour of this durbar, your turn-out in such large numbers here and in other parts of the Region, amply demonstrates the essential unity of our national community and our determination collectively to rescue our country from further decline and total destruction and disgrace.

I feel highly honoured to be so enthusiastically and colourfully received, particularly in this most historic of all our cities; a city that has played such a great and acknowledged role in the politics, economics and administration of our country.

Cape Coast is justifiably recognized by all informed Ghanaians as the oldest educational centre of the country. The living proof and most eloquent evidence of this role is that the largest number of our scholars and experts trace their beginnings and subsequent achievements back to institutions in this city. Even the very beginnings of a systematic political education for the youth started here with the creation of the Ghana National College by the late Osagyefo Dr Kwame Nkrumah, of blessed memory, in the late 1940s for the nationalistically-inspired students then being victimized for daring to stand up and be counted among those raising uncomfortable questions about the invidious position of exploiters and morally decadent local stooges and accomplices of colonialists on the national issue of independence. These are, indeed, honours for which this city and the whole Region can justifiably be proud. I feel confident that you will continue to do everything jealously to guard and nurture this reputation.

Nananom, it is very sad, even sickening to note that our declining economy has caused our once enviable infrastructures such as educational institutions and facilities to deteriorate to such very low levels as to provoke unrest in all other Regions. This situation has manifested itself particularly in the distress within our society and the large exodus of staff and other professionals into other sectors of the local economy presumed to provide better service conditions and also farther afield, into foreign lands. Our medical doctors, university lecturers, school teachers, artisans and other skilled nationals trained at public expense go abroad in search of better working conditions and job satisfaction. This is understandable and should be admitted.

However, my Government also considers this to be a very sad situation indeed, hence our determination to arrest the trend and eventually reverse it. This was precisely part of the mandate the People's National Party sought from the electorate and has been accorded it. By this time last year, we knew that our dear country for which its founding fathers, dead or alive, had sacrificed so much was being degraded, disgraced and destroyed by a few conscienceless and naked plunderers, butterflies, hangers-on, latter-day stooges and saboteurs. We had a rough idea of the enormity of the task of the national reconstruction now before us. We now know much more than that, having trekked around the whole country. We shall therefore do our duty undaunted as we understand it.

We shall not be deterred or lose our calm by cheap political stunts, provocative rantings, ravings and fuming. We are determined to discharge our sacred duty towards the whole nation.

In this connection, we are taking steps to cool down the long overheated economy. We do not believe that doing everything at the same time but achieving nothing at any given time, can ever solve any of our numerous problems. Similarly, we do not believe that pumping more and more money into the system, by granting demands for higher and higher wages while nothing is being produced can ever solve anything. We know that we all want not only adequate material rewards but that like all other consumers, the goods on which to spend our earnings are more important than the mere money illusion and that therefore such goods should be made available. This is what our agricultural programme seeks to do. We also all want opportunities to practise our professions and skills to the best of our abilities with the satisfaction and pride that can be derived from a sense of achievement.

That is why we have decided to concentrate our present meagre resources and all our efforts and energies on rehabilitating our productive structures, re-equipping our hospitals, university, colleges, schools and providing other utility services. In short, after so many years of criminal neglect and destruction, we have no other choice but to effect all-round rehabilitation, even if in phases as we must, before we can surge forward again.

In this herculean task there is no room for anyone to sit on the fence or to 'wait and see' anymore. The public is watching all of us. We can make or unmake ourselves. If we do not live up to expectations but rather seek to play cheap politics with the fate of our country we shall be doomed forever as a national community.

Nananom, much of our existing machinery has become obsolete. Lack of spare parts and maintenance have rendered much more completely inoperative. Your own nondescript hospital, other neglected structures and projects I have seen littered throughout the Region are typical of this appalling, all-round destruction and national despair. Yet, we are faced with the problem of scarce foreign resources which are now being even more cruelly eroded by ever-increasing costs of fuel and imported manufactured goods. The stark and undeniable fact is that this damage, including our moral degeneration of the past fourteen years can simply not be repaired overnight, in our present economic confusion and public poverty. Nor can interminable bickering and disunity save us. The patience, understanding and co-operation of all of us are therefore needed in a collective determination to build our country, regain our human dignity, our confidence and pride in ourselves, before we can hope to retrieve our destiny and lost position as the *avant garde* nation in Africa.

I therefore appeal to all of you, including our professionals, experts and other skilled nationals at home and abroad to take up these challenges, help clean up our present mess and rescue our country from ruin. I am aware that 'in order to love our country, our country must be lovely'. But I also know that we all have to make it so. No one else will do it for us. The country needs all of us now, not later. As a Government, we shall consider no sacrifice on our part to be too great; no contribution from you shall be too little.

Nananom, kindly allow me to repeat my appeal also to all workers in the various sectors of our economy to realize that demands for higher and higher wages now cannot and will never solve our problems. Such demands can only overheat the economy the more. Whereas my administration shall not preside over or condone the denial or negation of anyone's justifiable earned rights, we must also caution that to insist on such rights now, at the expense of the honest performance of our duties and without corresponding higher production will spell the total destruction of our already dying economy.

It is necessary to stress the point. Part of the answer to our problems lies in our failure to produce more goods at reasonable prices. That is precisely why it is in this very area that Government is concentrating all its attention. Meanwhile, there is therefore no room now for wildcat strikes and other industrial action to back up demands for more and more money. Such action will lead us nowhere. Ironically enough, employees of many establishments now demanding higher and higher wages, and even bonuses, have been performing dismally over the years due, not necessarily to their own fault, but partly to the total lack of inputs; and a lack of public accountability has also made for poor performance.

In short, we must control inflation, that cruel economic phenomenon which plays havoc with our pockets, our logical reasoning and our patience. I must repeat that the present beggar-my-neighbour tactics and mutual torturing can only be self-defeating.

We are painfully aware that we have all too often been called upon to make sacrifices in the past; which sacrifices we have repeatedly made for nothing in return.

Hence my Government has refrained from making such appeals and have rather chosen the path of the truth and public accountability at all levels. The truth is that whilst our coffers are empty many of our people, particularly in the richer, private sector, are not honouring their tax obligations. As a Government, we have been taken to task or pilloried even for past wrongs we have not committed and for such we are not responsible we have fielded these blames without demur. We need a similar approach from all sincere, honest and patriotic nationals. Our society should realize and accept its collective guilt and responsibility for the causes, nightmares or bad dreams we have all passed through in the past. Cheap fault-finding and buck-passing will never save us as a people. The contrary can buoy us up and enable us to repair the almost irreparable damage done to our economy, our moral fibre and to the prestige of our beloved country.

I therefore again appeal to all of you and, particularly, employees in the public sector, to realize and accept the fact that only patience, coupled with honesty, sincerity and hard work can save all of us from total ruin and disgrace. In addition, only an atmosphere of peace, calm, understanding and stability can promote steady recovery from our present chaos.

Nananom, distinguished guests, ladies and gentlemen, the PNP Government is determined to explore and exploit all our rich natural resources, especially in the agricultural sector, a sector which can feed all of us and also provide our industries with raw materials and save the foreign exchange used on the food items which can easily be produced at home. That is why the Government is striving hard to provide the necessary inputs, encouragement and incentives in this sector, to individuals and organizations and groups of block farmers like properly reconstituted Workers' Brigades. In this sector we appeal to you to mobilize all your people for agricultural production.

Our heavy dependence on cocoa as the biggest foreign exchange earner is being examined so that while that industry is being rehabilitated, much diversification can also be done. Our population has been growing by leaps and bounds. We therefore have to make a break-through by paying adequate attention to the production of edible and commercial crops such as oil palm, sugar-cane, cereals and also fish. The Central Region is eminently suited for intensified efforts in these areas and should therefore take full advantage of our new policy orientations to contribute its quota to the national effort.

Since over sixty per cent of our fish requirements is produced by the small-scale fishermen, we are determined to improve upon their lot. Government is seriously engaged in the process of providing the necessary inputs and incentives for them. In this Region the small-scale fisherman operates all along the littoral from Nyanyano to Akatakyi. They should organize themselves into co-operatives to enable them to buy their inputs at controlled prices. It is gratifying to note that they have already taken a step forward by adopting in-board motors as evidenced by their efforts at Elmina and Mumford. We shall give them every encouragement, support and incentive in their efforts to acquire fishing gear and other inputs and also to dispose of their catches economically.

Ladies and gentlemen, in view of the severe constraints on our available resources, Government has had to map out our priorities in the recent budget so that adequate funds can be allocated for only the most vital areas of our economy and development. This explains why some on-going projects have had to be temporarily suspended.

However, having regard to the paramount health needs of the people we have had to include a few health projects among schemes we have allowed to continue. Thus the staff quarters for the proposed new hospital designed to serve the entire Awutu-Efutu-Gomoa Districts, which have reached an advanced stage of completion at Winneba, will be continued. These and similar works in the Region will cost ₵100 million.

The new hospital which will replace your present eyesore of a Regional Hospital and also befit the status of your capital is now under serious consideration. The five blocks of eight flats each started at the site to house some of the medical personnel should be completed soon.

We are also determined to pursue a vigorous feeder roads programme while continuing with the construction of the three major national roads in this Region. It is hoped that contractors engaged in road construction work in the Region would intensify their efforts and complete, within the shortest possible time, such vital projects as the Yamoransa-Takoradi Road which has been re-awarded to Carl Ploetner (Ghana) Limited. I have been to the site and I am happy to note that work on it has pro-ceeded vigorously since I last used it. I commend that Company.

Government also attaches great importance to the supply of good drinking water because cleanliness and good health can save us much expenditure on drugs and medical care. Accordingly, and as a matter of priority, an amount of ₵3 million had been allocated for the improve-ment of the Cape Coast District Water Scheme. We hope that the people of Cape Coast and its surrounding towns including Elmina and Salt-pond, will soon see improvements in the supply of good drinking water to their areas. The Senya Breku Water Scheme is also nearing completion while work is in progress on the Foso District Water Scheme. These are estimated to cost ₵4 million.

We have allocated over ₵6 million for the purchase of minimum essential equipment, including a Private Branch Exchange for Cape Coast and other hospitals and are also planning to build a regional medical store which is very much needed here.

The successful implementation of all these projects, and many others I have not mentioned, can best be carried out with your unflinching support, hard work, co-operation and, particularly, your understanding for the strict measures being taken and the re-ordering of priorities which are all necessary to reintroduce discipline and sanity into the economy.

Nananom, as the natural rulers of our people, Nananom should ensure peace and stability in your traditional areas. I also enjoin you to provide much needed exemplary leadership so that your people can come together and work for the common good. Above all, Nananom may wish to avoid too much chieftaincy, land- and time-consuming disputes and litigations in their traditional areas. Such activities only tend to sap our energies and fritter away scarce resources which should be harnessed towards greater production and the provision of the facilities and amenities needed to make the lives of our people more meaningful to them.

Distinguished guests, the amenities I have listed above is by no means exhaustive. Our dream, as your Government, is to put an end to want and frustrations and go on to realize self-fulfilment and satisfaction. Our collective desire and aim as a people should be to put our country back on the road to economic recovery and eventual prosperity and thus leave for our youth and generations yet unborn the legacy of a healthy economy, political stability, greatness and pride.

I believe that we can achieve these objectives provided we close our ranks now. We should all support the Government and refrain from social strife in this noble task of rebuilding a better future for our country. In short, with your understanding of our national problems, with your co-operation, with your support and goodwill, we shall succeed. As I have often said, we dare not fail again in our third attempt at civilian rule.

On behalf of the Government and on my own behalf, I wish to thank you most sincerely for this rich display of your culture, for the warm reception you have accorded us everywhere since Thursday afternoon and also for the opportunity you have availed us to exchange views on the problems of our country which cry out for solutions. I hope that this interchange and interplay of ideas and views will be an on-going process so that in the months and years ahead, we shall continually put our heads together in the search for a better way of life for our people and for the safety and destiny of our dear country. Let us all stand firmly together and give the Third Republic the chance to succeed.

Save Ghana Now! Serve Ghana Now!

19

At Sekondi/Takoradi in the Western Region

The Western Region has long been the political barometer of the country. It had been the nerve-centre of organization for the Railway Workers' Union, a strategic organized union since the days immediately preceding Ghana's independence.

Natural and man-made disasters in the form of floods and broken-down roads and bridges, political chicanery and humbug in a spate of industrial strife and strikes were among the set-backs to which the President referred. On the positive side, he announced integrating rural development with agriculture, beginning with foreign assistance.

It is always a pleasure for me to have the opportunity to meet a cross-section of chiefs and their peoples, as at this durbar today. You are well aware that I have already visited seven regional capitals and some of their adjacent areas since last November. In fact this durbar marks the climax of my first official visit to your Region. I had visited this Region earlier in a different capacity.

The first visit was prompted by a very serious disaster brought vividly to my attention by Archbishop Peter Dery who had received horrifying reports from a marooned hospital and many cut off areas in Western Nzema. At that time all my efforts by road to reach that disaster area in order to help in the on-going relief operations proved abortive and I ended at Tandan. However, I am happy to note today that those efforts had not been entirely wasted since I was able to reach Half Assini at long last yesterday, as a result of those efforts. The road has since then been made passable. I hope that it will continue to be maintained in that condition. I may add that when I made that dangerous and unsuccessful journey I was not soliciting votes; there were then no impending elections in Western Nzema. . . .

I shall take steps to correct this erroneous impression later, when the matter ceases to be *sub judice*. For the moment, it may be helpful for such individuals to try and learn the geography of their country, if they are genuine, sincere and patriotic citizens.

Fellow countrymen, I undertake these dangerous and fatiguing journeys, visiting chiefs and their peoples, exchanging views and discussing our national problems as a means of finding practical and quick solutions to such problems. Since 'two heads are better than one', I believe that we can all learn and enrich our understanding and experiences through such contacts and such exchange of views.

My presence here today forms part of this process of consultation and interchange of ideas. It is my firm belief that this process of moving the Government to the people and taking you and your people into confidence about the state of the nation at every stage will promote clearer understanding of the problems to which we should collectively find workable solutions. This approach will also put an end to the age-old habit of rather remote and patronizing attitudes which characterized past Government. The approach is in line and/or in conformity with our idea of 'participatory democracy' the people endorsed in the June–July 1979 general elections.

Ladies and gentlemen, I suspect that those who profit from secretive, paternalistic and avuncular attitudes of Government have found this latter-day style unpalatable to them, hence their insulting tactics, often in flagrant disregard of the mandate freely entrusted to me and my Government. Such individuals fear and despise the masses in whose name they pretend to speak. May it be that they are frightened by the principles of open Government and participatory democracy, hence their determination to turn me into a tongue-tied ceremonial Head of State? Their position does not exist in the constitution of the Third Republic which provides for an Executive President, Head of State, answerable only to the Constitution and the electorate.

Nananom, the very warm welcome you have accorded me and my entourage everywhere throughout your Region and at this colourful durbar has been so overwhelming that I can hardly find words with which adequately to thank you. We are impressed not only by the pomp and pageantry of the durbar, but more significantly, by your individual and collective spontaneous enthusiasm and reception. With this kind of goodwill and the sort of leadership my Government wants to provide, we feel that Ghana may be back on the road to economic recovery and a forward surge sooner than the cassandra voices will ever care to admit.

Fellow citizens, my Government's faith in agriculture as the motive force of our general economic recovery, industrialization and upliftment shall be firmly and vigorously pursued. As a nation, richly endowed with large stretches of fertile arable land, no one in his or her right senses, particularly abroad, can understand us if we ignore the utilization of this rich resource which Nature has so generously bestowed on us.

As a people, we have, in the past, often not matched our pronouncements with our practical efforts. My Government cannot afford this luxury any more. We take, and expect you to do the same, the declaration of the next two years as a period of agricultural production, very seriously indeed. We therefore earnestly appeal to you to mobilize your people to embrace and help make the programme a tremendous success. For our part we shall spare no effort in our physical and mental labours, day and night, to pursue the programme for its successful implementation. We are determined and shall set the example ourselves. We shall not sit back and exhort officials to leave their offices and go into the field. We shall not wait for them as a scribblers, theorists, analysts and armchair advisers. We expect them to adjust quickly and join us in work and sweat.

Technicians in particular, should go out into the field and impart their theoretical knowledge and practical experiences to peasant farmers and small-scale industrialists who have, over the years, been the backbone of our economy.

Nananom, some aspects of past policies have tended to give the impression that the peasant farmer, particularly in this Region shall be swallowed up by cash crop plantation farmers promoted by the Cocoa Marketing Board and Ministry of Agriculture. This is erroneous. My Government does not intend unjustifiably to dispossess small-scale farmers of their lands and farms. We know that sturdy small-scale farming communities are the backbone of the nation's economy and that they cannot be replaced while we look on and allow them to be destroyed. Consequently, the Minister of Agriculture shall exercise caution in the future in acquiring land for the development of plantations. Nananom, may also wish to examine the claims and interests of individual farmers carefully before allocating lands for such plantations.

My Government wants to integrate agriculture and rural development. In this connection, I am happy to announce that we have approved the establishment, in this Region, of such an integrated Development Programme, the Western Region Agricultural Development Programme (WREDEP) which, thanks to assistance from the French Government may be launched next month. It shall embrace:

(i)   Revival of coconut farms in the Region which have been attacked by Cape Three Points disease. Seed gardens covering eighty acres each have already been established for this purpose, again with the French Government supply seed nuts from the Ivory Coast.

(ii) Proper re-organization of Oil Palm Plantations which face problems of disease, improper siting and lack of adequate mills.

(iii) Revival of rubber plantations, with better species, to help smallholders who are now abandoning their farms due to poor prices offered by Firestone (Ghana) Limited.

(iv) Intensification of food production in rice, maize, cassava, plantain and other crops natural to the various areas within the Region.

(v) Preparation of a five-year master plan development programme by appropriate Ghanaian agencies with the assistance of the French Government.

(vi) Provision of vehicles—trucks, jeeps, motor-cycles and bicycles for extension officers and also for carting foodstuffs from the hinterland to urban markets in the Region and,

(vii) Construction, in collaboration with the appropriate agencies, of roads to all agricultural and food producing areas in the region.

Nananom, the greatest obstacle to the socio-economic development of this Region has been the extremely atrocious nature of roads, due, in part, to the incessant torrential rainfall and the thick forest vegetation which make road construction difficult and very costly. My Government is therefore determined to make, at least, the existing road network motorable throughout all seasons. It is for this reason that the Ministers involved in this and in other problems facing the Region have come round with me so that we can see things for ourselves together.

It is hoped that given fair weather, the all important Bogoso-Ayanfuri road will be completed before the end of this year. We also hope to see the commencement of the Axim-Mpataba-Elubo road by next August. Efforts are being made to resume work on the suspended Ankobra and Tano river bridges. Indeed, work has already started on the Tano Bridge, with the co-operation of the Ivory Coast Government. An amount of ₵3.5 million has also been allocated in the recent budget for the resumption of work on the Ankobra Bridge. Similarly, the desired impetus for rural industries and development, abandoned in the past shall be resuscitated as soon as practicable.

Fellow citizens, since the Integrated Iron and Steel Project at Opon Manso is one of the hopes of our early industrial take-off, my Government is actively working on it. Indeed, its implementation will also provide employment and skills for hundreds of our people and put Ghana on sound industrial foundations. The appropriate agencies have been asked to reappraise the project for an early decision to be taken on it. From results so far available to us, there is no doubt that it is likely to be an industrial breakthrough. I assure you that my Government has the mandate and is determined to take such decision.

Nananom, we also intend vigorously to pursue the policy of decentralization since it is only through this that the desired impact could be made and felt on national and, particularly, rural development. In any case, our political mandate and the constitution itself demand this. In this connection, the establishment of additional District Councils at Half Assini, Bibiani and Enchi can no more be ignored and/or set aside, especially in the light also of the vastness of this Region and its very poor communication, road and air networks. We are therefore collating all such demands and will soon make the necessary legislative proposals for their earliest possible legal creation.

Nananom, distinguished guests, fellow citizens, I wish now to address you on a number of matters of the gravest importance to our economic recovery and national survival. The numerous demands for increased wages, salaries and fringe benefits with which my Government has had to grapple since assuming office have been overwhelming and injurious to our economy. Industrial strife raises not only issues of serious immediacy but also of very far-reaching consequences for our socio-economic stability, national unity and security.

Current trends on our national labour front should necessarily therefore be matters of grave concern not only to Government but also to the entire citizenry. Since 24 September 1979, no less than twenty-eight strikes have taken place. These involved a total of 21,000 workers. 20,000 were from the public sector alone. Total man-days lost to industry from these strikes were 107,328. In monetary terms, this loss has been enormous at a time we can ill-afford it. As a nation we face a ruined economy. The rights and justifiable claims which my Government has vowed to grant and guarantee should therefore be suspended for a while to help salvage the economy. To give just one example, the Obuasi Mines strike alone cost the economy ₵6 million.

Yet we are still being inundated with more demands for wage increases. The total cost burden of such demands run into ₵235 million. Our present financial resources and the economy cannot bear this at the moment.

I must repeat and emphasize that, conscious of our responsibilities towards the citizens of this country, my Government would not and can never ignore the genuine demands of employees for improved salary and working conditions. However, we must all realize that the economy can at this time not absorb the full impact of these demands. I therefore, once more, appeal to all and sundry to exercise patience, understanding, maturity and responsibility in asserting their rights now at the expense of peace, stability and national survival.

The best answer to the present high cost of living is the provision of more goods at reasonable prices. Higher wages chasing fewer goods will only accelerate the already runaway inflation which is hurting us all.

The point I have just belaboured covers also the problems of security and instability. I have repeatedly drawn serious attention to the strains, stresses and distress of our society. I have even repeatedly called for the nation-wide pouring of libations by our chiefs and the prayers of our religious communities for God's guidance and peace on our land. I wish again to make this appeal from this platform for the same prayers by Muslim and Christian communities and the pouring of libations by all our chiefs for peace in our country. This should be done with effect from the twenty-ninth of this month.

DG-I

111

Nananom, Honourable Ministers, distinguished guests, fellow citizens, let me emphasize that Government fully understands the problems of the people and shares their desire for improved living conditions. We were voted into office on the promise that we shall improve the lot of our people; it is our determination to fulfil this promise. However, in pursuit of this objective, we need unity and singleness of purpose among all sections of our people. I exhort you to join us in our attempts to solve our national problems to enable us to meet our individual grievances. Please, help us to help you.

Nananom, I hope that the feeling of oneness that I have experienced and observed at this and other regional durbars will be applied at the national front to enable our country to achieve peace, stability, recovery and advancement. I wish to record my deepest appreciation for such a reception.

We are, indeed, deeply touched by your display of hospitality and friendliness to us throughout our stay with you over the last three days. We hope that it will be possible for us to meet again in various parts of your Region in the not-too-distant future.

20

At Accra in the Greater Accra Region

The Greater Accra Region was the one which rounded off the President's regional tours. As the seat of Government where the chief Executive and other government officials reside, it was just as well that the familiarization journey took in the farther locations first. The President invited his audience to raise their sights to the day when the Accra plains and the Weija dam out-reach will become the irrigation miracle of the country, producing grain and vegetables.

I deem it a special privilege and honour for me to take part in this durbar of chiefs and people of the Greater Accra Region which also hosts our national capital and therefore serves as the nerve centre of our communal and social life. When Accra sneezes, Ghana contracts a cold.

I have, since assuming office, visited eight regional capitals and met chiefs, cross sections of people, workers and officials. We have exchanged views and ideas on the pressing issues of our economy. In the process, I have also inspected numerous projects, industrial establishments and public institutions. This durbar today rounds off such official familiarization visits to the regional capitals and their outlying areas. The tours have proved very rewarding indeed. They have confirmed not only the common-place knowledge that our extensive economic infrastructure has been destroyed but also that the immeasurable hopes, expectations and aspirations of all Ghanaians at this critical stage of our history has been sharpened. Just at the very time that we lack many things, both material and spiritual, we want or long for all our material needs to be satisfied at once.

Niimei, the tours have taken Government to significant sectors of the public and made Ministers more aware of the burning problems of all our people. Having travelled on what are mere apologies of roads or even death traps, having seen neglected health, and educational institutions, industrial installations and totally abandoned agricultural projects which had once functioned efficiently, our sense of urgency as to what should be done has been greatly sharpened and enhanced.

We have also been impressed throughout our tours by spontaneous expressions of support for the Government. We have observed widening and deepening trends of understanding of our problems.

There is much sympathy for the sincere attempts which we are making and a desire for well-thought-out plans that can be evolved to revive our economy and give back to all of us a meaning to our lives.

Niimei, fellow citizens, the pleasures and glamours of city life have been systematically whittled away by many years of neglect and economic mismanagement. The problems confronting us as a nation inflict the same hardships on all Ghanaians. The peculiarities of urban life have therefore tended to magnify some of these problems and heightened the daily discomforts and inconveniences of our people. We have all suffered, if even unfairly, as a result of the deprivations that years of mismanagement have brought us.

Distinguished guests, we are now caught in a vicious circle of low morale, low investment and productivity and yet very great demands are being made for all sorts of goods and services which we lack the resources to provide immediately.

In the face of these problems it is only natural for the Government to view tendencies towards strife and instability with great concern; hence our repeated calls for patience, peace, stability and hard work. I should therefore like to appeal once again for industrial and social peace. All workers should exercise that restraint which will allow us time to improve upon the purchasing power of the Cedi through productivity and the provision of more goods and services. We shall eventually honour all legitimately earned rights and claims which had been denied and artificially held in check long before we resumed office.

In the field of agriculture and the programme announced in my Sessional Address to Parliament, I wish to stress that the Greater Accra Region has strategic advantages. In addition to its industrial potential it also faces the prospects of an agricultural revolution in the vast Accra Plains irrigation project. This offers great opportunities to both local and foreign investors.

The secret to the success of most countries lies in their approach to agriculture and its related industries. Blessed with vast tracts of arable land we must now turn our serious attention to this sector. I therefore appeal to local industrialists to direct some of their investment efforts to this area in which high dividends awaits them.

Work is progressing on the Weija Dam to increase the output of water supply to the western part of Accra and also for being tapped to irrigate large tracts of land. When completed by 1981 this Project will put about 15,000 hectares of land under irrigation for farming purposes. I appeal to Niimei to make land readily available in other areas for those willing to take advantage of our new policy orientations and particularly our agricultural programmes.

Steps are being initiated to provide the necessary inputs for both small scale and commercial farmers to enable both of them to contribute their quotas to a green revolution. Niimei should also deploy their influence to mobilize their people in voluntary efforts to start communal farms in order to increase food production. My Government stands ready to assist materially and otherwise in all such efforts.

Another area engaging Government's serious attention is our very poor communication system which greatly hampers efficient economic and social activities. We are therefore bending every nerve for an early implementation of the satellite earth station project to enable this country to have direct access to the Atlantic Ocean Satellite in the INTELSAT system, providing pre-assigned circuits for telephone, telex and telegraph to many parts of the world which have common interest with us. The station will also provide facilities for the reception and transmission of live television programmes to and from any part of the world.

Excellencies, ladies and gentlemen, as we have often emphasized, members of my government are fully committed to improving the condition of all Ghanaians, particularly our rural communities, through the provision of such necessities of life as good drinking water, electricity and health facilities. In these efforts, rural peoples in the Greater Accra Region are likely to receive their fair share of improvements and benefits.

A common complaint we have heard throughout the country has been that members of local communities have derived very little benefit from factories located in their areas. Instead, finished products are sold only to city dwellers, to the detriment of rural peoples.

To remedy this sad state of affairs, Government is taking steps, through the appropriate Ministries, to ensure that a certain percentage of finished products should be made available to the people in whose area any factory is located. Such measures shall be made to conform with the requirements of the constitution for decentralization to which effect a Bill will soon be placed before Parliament.

Fellow citizens, I must now appeal once more to Niimei to sink their differences and chieftaincy disputes and evolve a new type of leadership that will meet the challenges of our times. This will enhance their status and enable them to play a more dynamic role in the localities for our national recovery and development.

I have taken due note of the request of Niimei for evaluation, and their eventual phased implementation in line with our present resources, priorities and policies. I wish to reiterate that my government will not discriminate in the provision of amenities and economic project implementation. However, the spirit of self-help and local initiative is likely to receive more help. This should therefore be fully exploited. I have also taken due note of Niimei's request for the establishment of a Greater Accra Regional House of Chiefs, which, I believe can be considered alongside similar requests in line with the Constitutional requirements for decentralization.

Niimei, Your Excellencies, ladies and gentlemen, my Government had indicated the policy-framework for our economic rejuvenation taking account of our most pressing and immediate needs. We have laid the basis for a steady flow of essential goods needed to rehabilitate the economy and also provide relief for workers and the rural folk. Such a policy has been dictated by the need to make judicious use of our scarce financial resources so as to provide those basic inputs and incentives which will help step up all-round productivity. With the support, goodwill and co-operation of Niimei and their peoples, we feel confident that we shall succeed in carrying out our economic recovery programmes.

I should like to thank Niimei and their people for their loyalty and support and for the opportunity afforded me to address them at this durbar. On our part, we shall continue to involve you and all well-meaning citizens in the governmental process so that, in our collective efforts, we can recreate a better Ghana for ourselves, the youth and children yet unborn.

In conclusion, I wish to restate the solemn determination of the People's National Party Government to save this country from any further decline.

21

The State of the Nation Address by the President, September 1979

I am sure that you would want me to share my thoughts with you this evening on the historic occasion of the Inauguration of the Third Republic and on the stupendous tasks ahead of us.

I speak to you tonight conscious of the gloom that has long filled many hearts in our society whose fabric has been permeated with many and varied dark spots. After the events of the June Revolution, we stand at the crossroads of our history today.

The traumatic experiences of the past had left us destitute of ideas and courage. So desperate economically and so very low in public morale have we sunk, that we had to be rudely shaken up from our slumber of indifference and apathy.

Faced with monumental challenges and unimaginable problems, our country today faces crises of confidence which strike at the very core of our national will to survive. These crises were manifest in the mounting doubts about ourselves as a people, in the hopelessness of our lives and in the abdication of the principles and values that had once made our nation the envy of others.

Never before had our people been stretched to the limits of endurance and the future looked so bleak. Happily, a fresh start has now been made in the quest for moral regeneration and a new national identity.

As a people we had, before last June, become so self-indulgent that our values had been perverted. The capitulation to greed, graft and avarice so triumphed over our sense of proportion, decency and fellow-feeling that we have had to pay dearly for it. We must now admit, if even rather too late, that the inordinate pursuit of material wealth and its vulgar ostentation—the cause of our present woes—leads to general despair, personal tragedy and grief. Consequently, we must now redirect our energies towards the common good and eschew the temptations of personal aggrandisement.

The enormity of the problems facing us can easily crush us if we yield to despair. The state of the economy is hopeless. Inflation rose rapidly over the past thirteen years to the record level of 130 per cent per annum before sliding down to the present position of 89 per cent, which is still too high.

The tempo of economic activity over the last few years, as measured by the Gross Domestic Product, has been stagnating. In recent months, it has even ground to a halt in some fields.

Our external accounts are in such a precarious position that for the first time in our history, we are perilously close to bankruptcy. No wonder then that deepening pessimism gripped our people with the consequent souring of our national psyche.

Although looming internal and external dangers recently threatened to break our spirit and engulf us as a people, we have not succumbed to them. We must continue to resist not only such dangers but also the easy temptation to slide back into the control of reactionary forces lurking all around us. We cannot allow our country to sink since we must preserve and transmit our rich inheritance to posterity. The verdict of our children and our children's children will be pitiless if we wantonly fail.

We can and must turn the tide of our present adversity. We must therefore take the road into the future, conscious of the fact that we dare not fail. I must repeat that this is our last chance.

We are so conscious of our proud past that the present appals us. We must strive to rise up again so that this country can once more become a better place to live in. Indeed, in order to love our country, our country must be lovely. It is within our power and means to render it so. Although some may have lost hope, I am not convinced of the impossibility of building a new, stronger and more stable society.

Admittedly, the wounds we want to heal are deep, but they can be assuaged and healed. I and my Government are determined to work relentlessly to this end. Let me emphasize this determination by saying that as Leader of a Party committed to the welfare of the masses, I shall work tirelessly to meet our obligations to the hapless and helpless people of this country.

We may make mistakes, particularly in the eyes of carping critics. We may not be able to answer all questions or provide solutions to all problems at once, but we will strive hard to ease the burdens of the people. We will offer more than mere exhortations. We shall ourselves set the examples of discipline, hard work and honesty.

Our government will be responsive and responsible. The general welfare of the people shall be the guiding principle of our policies and order of priorities. But since low morals tend to kill high morals, we shall also constantly think big so that we shall not only feed ourselves adequately but also prosecute such great projects as can make Ghana great. You should therefore be prepared to stretch your wings and fly like the eagle rather than continually be longing to coop yourselves up and feed with chickens.

Thus, important projects vital for our national development and welfare should, in future, no longer be condemned as prestigious for in the long run they prove more necessary for our survival than so-callled essential commodities.

In the days and weeks ahead, my Government's comprehensive programme will be released and you will all be required to participate fully in its implementation.

Fellow countrymen, one major problem facing us as a nation has been the destruction of our moral values, resulting in selfishness, greed, avarice, irresponsibility, corruption, lack of public accountability and reckless dissipation of public funds which, as evidenced by recent revelations, had all been erected into the norms of the times. This is therefore the time for instilling not only a new spirit of consciousness and awareness in all of us, but an auspicious moment for deep reflection, both in and out of government and in other responsible positions.

Through the ballot box you have chosen and entrusted me with the great responsibility of charting a new national course to salvation. I hope that I shall be worthy of your trust. I do sincerely extend my gratitude to all Ghanaians for this opportunity to serve. I thank the leaders and members of the other parties for their willingness to co-operate with me in our common endeavour to save our country from disgrace.

As the President of the nation, I shall strive to serve all without fear or favour and with malice towards none.

I shall respect the Constitution and invoke it to deal ruthlessly with anyone who will misuse his position to plunder the nation.

Those who engage in trade malpractices, popularly known as 'kalabule' must refrain from these nefarious and anti-social activities. I must warn all those who may think that the departure of the Armed Forces Revolutionary Council opens the sluice-gates and provides an invitation to them to return to such anti-social activities. There is no place for such people in the new Ghana. I am determined to stamp out bribery and corruption, smuggling, indiscipline and to revive public spiritedness. I am sure that you will support me in this determination.

Let me repeat my appeal to you all to accept the realities of today and make the necessary adjustments. We must all resist the temptation to cheat, plunder and rob our country and our fellows.

Each one of us must be the instrument either for the success or for the failure of the Third Republic. In this, if in nothing else, we all share a common destiny. We must all therefore accept the need for common action and a sense of mission in the pursuit of our goals. We shall have to float together or sink separately.

Even a little sacrifice from every one, a little faith in each of us and in our abilities, will save us all.

Fellow countrymen, at this turning point in the history of our country, we have no option but to accept the duty to save ourselves as a nation and not just as individuals. We must look to the future with hope and no more; to take the easy path is to take the path to destruction and damnation. We must regain our self-respect and dignity as citizens, and our greatness and pride as a nation. Let us move forward as a united country, resolved never again to allow our birthright to be stolen away from us.

Speaking to you tonight as your President, humbled by the heavy tasks and responsibilities which now devolve on me, saddened by the intensity of our past sufferings, yet buoyed by your confidence and collective resolve to succeed, I invite you to join me in my determination and in all my endeavours to wipe out the tears of our people and bring back their smiles. I hope I can count on your total support.

22

Inauguration of the Third Republic, 24 September 1979

Not since the epoch-making day when the United Kingdom Parliament handed over the reins of responsibility to the people of Ghana was the national Parliament House so keyed up and so pregnant of meaning as when military handed over to civilian rule on the occasion of the inauguration of the Third Republic. The undertones of the following address were as fluent as the spoken text.

It is my special duty and pleasure to address you on this momentous occasion of the Inauguration of the Third Republic. I am most grateful for this honour.

We have convened at a most crucial time in our history which marks the end of the long period of blatant and shameless abuses which have so destroyed confidence in our people, in all our institutions and in our values that we are all yearning for a wholesome change for the better.

Never before, since independence, have the demands on government been greater, the tasks heavier and the fears, hopes and expectations therefore higher than now.

After many years of drift, of wandering in the political and economic wilderness, Ghana is about to find her feet and level again.

Through fair, free and democratic elections, the voice and power of the electorate have been expressed in the double victory of the People's National Party in the parliamentary and Presidential elections.

Overwhelmed by this show of confidence and trust I accept the high office of President with all humility. I solemnly declare my determination to work with all my heart and with all my strength, in the general and supreme interests of the nation.

I wish to avail myself of this opportunity to thank, not only the supporters of the People's National Party, but all Ghanaians for electing me to lead in the bleakest and most uncertain period of our lives as a people. I have accepted this choice as a challenge to take the lead in the crusade to retrieve and raise our sunken image and to regain the self-respect, confidence and pride of all Ghanaians.

This dawn of a new era of peace and hope for progress and stability affords me the pleasure to extend a special welcome to His Excellency

President Sékou Touré and other distinguished guests here as our brothers and friends to participate in the activities marking the formal inauguration of my Presidency and of the Third Republic. Your presence warms and ennobles our hearts. It is for obvious reasons that we have restrained ourselves from the glamour and panache which used to characterize your arrivals and stay in Ghana in the early days of our independence.

Your Excellency, distinguished guests, ladies and gentlemen, this is indeed history in the making; after years of inconclusive political experimentation, economic despair and moral degradation, Ghana is on the threshold of another epoch.

Twenty-two years ago, at the Old Polo Ground, the late Osagyefo, Dr Kwame Nkrumah of blessed memory, after years of sweat and tears, fulfilled a dream, the dream of independence.

He won independence for this country and thus ushered the new Ghana into unprecedented social, economic and political progress. Young, proud, buoyant and full of promise, Ghana led the way in the crusade for the total emancipation of Africa and the elimination of discrimination of all kinds. We gave everything we had, to help others throughout the African continent and far beyond. Even in our darkest moments we have never regretted this.

Today, Dr Nkrumah, Dr Danquah, Mr Casely-Hayford, Dr Busia, Mr Akufo-Addo and others of blessed memory are no more. That is, perhaps, why we are so much the poorer as a nation. In the name of Dr Nkrumah and the other founding fathers, we offer another dream again today: the dream of economic recovery and social fulfilment in the years ahead.

As we open this new chapter in our national history on this solemn occasion, I take the liberty to assert that we are all united as a people in our resolve to rehabilitate our economy, regenerate and rebuild the new Ghana.

Symbolizing the change long expected by the vast majority of our people, I call particularly on the younger generations, so fresh, bold, earnest and full of the uncompromising resolve to take up the task of putting Ghana back on the road to economic recovery and progress, the very ideals for which the late Osagyefo lived and died. I also appeal to the older generations to assit us in order to ensure that the rest of their lives may be brighter than now. The challenge is collective and total.

So is my commitment to these ideals and I must emphasize once more that there shall be no turning back from the just fight to provide for our people and our children, higher and decent living conditions. This inauguration therefore heralds a new beginning and the unshakable resolve of Government, and I hope, a new spirit among us all, to transform our country, so rich in human and natural resources, into a better place for all. This is the greatest monument we can erect to the memory of the late Osagyefo, Dr Kwame Nkrumah and his contemporaries who were dedicated to the proposition that 'only the best is good enough for Africa and for Ghana'.

We must all learn from the mistakes of the remote and recent past. The lessons drawn therefrom must bring a resurgent commitment to the basic principles of our nation and a firm desire to achieve our goals. The Ghanaian dream must not falter or fade again.

Your Excellency, ladies and gentlemen, these are grave times and I have no illusions about the enormity and complexity of the tasks ahead.

Abysmal economic chaos, awesome challenges and monumental responsibilities confront us in the face of measureless hope and ever rising expectations.

I am only too well aware, as I believe are Honourable Members of Parliament, that the vast majority of Ghanaians have, undeservedly, been reduced to such intolerable levels of poverty and degradation that their patience and fortitude can no longer hold, hence the imperative necessity to provide a new lease of hope and of life.

I am taking over the administration at a time when our fiscal resources have dismally diminished, and inflation has reduced the purchasing power of ordinary citizens almost to nothingness.

These are hard times which indeed we dare not deny and yet must face and remain undeterred. On the contrary, we must redouble our resolve to take our destiny into our own hands and save our country from total bankruptcy and disgrace. Mr Speaker, I call upon Honourable Members, and the entire public to be vigilant and offer no quarter to those denying us our birthright.

Founded out of a deep concern for the welfare of the people, the Government of the People's National Party, shall not shirk its responsibility to them. We cannot afford the luxury of failure.

Our systems, beliefs and values, indeed our very existence as a nation are on trial. The need to re-awaken faith in ourselves as a people and in our ability to tackle and solve our problems has never therefore been greater than now. I believe that out of our present wreck we can build anew.

I have a vision of Ghana in which the majority of our people shall not be reduced to grinding poverty again, a vision in which inequalities and inequities shall be minimized if not eliminated altogether, a vision of a new Ghana working selflessly together in unity.

You may think that I am promising the moon, well, science has even made it possible for mankind to reach the moon.

But, I am not promising the moon. What I promise is a Government that will work, a Government that will be open and honest, modest yet vigorous—one that will wage a relentless war on poverty and corruption, indiscipline, inefficiency and dishonesty while upholding the rule of law.

Your Excellencies, Members of Parliament, ladies and gentlemen, this is what I offer for our collective salvation. My ideals and goals shall however not bear any fruit if you in this august House and Ghanaians as a whole do not give me your support and encouragement. I am convinced that these will be forthcoming abundantly.

I shall work with and for the entire public. Indeed, the problems facing us are not for the PNP alone but for the whole nation. Thus, in our search for solutions to them, I expect all Ghanaians, irrespective of party affiliations, to pool their resources together for the common good.

That is why in proposing the ministerial appointments that I am submitting to the House today, I have studiously sought to ensure regional balance and national unity without sacrificing talent, experience and competence, in a quest to provide firmly-based national solutions to our problems. That is why I have also proposed non-PNP members to high office of State in Parliament, the Council of State and even in my own Administration.

Your Excellency, Chairman of the AFRC, I must now warmly congratulate you and your gallant colleagues for conducting the general elections and organizing the activities which have culminated in this solemn and memorable inaugural ceremony. The whole nation appreciates your efforts, selfless devotion and sincerity of purpose and says a big warm 'thank you'.

As we move into my administration, let me assure you and all Ghanaians that, guided by the lessons drawn from the events since 4 June 1979, firm in my own commitment to open and clean government based on participatory democracy at all levels, I shall not flinch from checking all forms of abuse and I hope that I can count on the support of Honourable Members of Parliament. Together we all want a peaceful and stable atmosphere which will enable us to tackle our onerous responsibilities relentlessly and without fear or favour.

Your Excellencies, distinguished guests, ladies and gentlemen, I wish finally to reiterate my appeal to all Ghanaians to join me in the national endeavour to salvage the honour and pride of our country. To this end, I pray for God's guidance and blessing to enable me to protect the most precious gift Ghanaians have given me their confidence—which I accept in all humility and which I shall treasure with all my mind and all my strength only for as long as I retain their trust.

23

The Chief Justice, Mr Justice F. K. Apaloo takes the Oath of Allegiance 3 October 1979

After this brief and impressive ceremony of swearing the Oath of Allegiance to me as the President of Ghana, I wish to assure you that you enjoy my total and warm confidence. You can therefore feel reassured that I expect you to feel confident in the discharge of the enormous responsibilities and burden which rest on your shoulders as the Chief Custodian of the judicial system of the country.

After thirteen years of deprivation, economic decline and individual humiliations and indignities, the vast majority of our people have become disillusioned with almost all our national institutions, including the Judiciary which I personally venerate and will try always to respect.

Aware of the extent to which our moral values have been destroyed and also of how the reputation of our governmental agencies have been tarnished, I have no doubt that you and the service you head also need to rededicate yourselves to the task of regenerating public confidence in yourselves. Please, feel free to modernize the Judiciary to meet the demands of the times. What you innovate need not be totally new, but what you retain should certainly not be obsolete. Bear in mind that the public now watches all of us and demands not only high standards of honesty and expeditiousness but also credibility.

We want to build a new nation, a new world of law and order in which the principles of human rights are preserved, in which the strong can be just, the weak secure and peace preserved, and where the scales of justice are held evenly, irrespective of wealth, social standing or influential connections. The rights of Ghanaians must, under no circumstances, be allowed to be trampled upon again. This means that you of the Judiciary, as the watchdogs of our legal system, have to live above suspicion and also maintain an absolute record of unblemished integrity. Cases brought before you should be dealt with expeditiously yet with fairness and without fear, favour or malice. The maxim that 'justice delayed is justice denied' is as pertinent today as it was hundreds of years ago.

Judging from numerous petitions I have seen in this very short time of my tenure of office, the public now resents double standards and the inexplicable or even conscienceless attitudes of some members of your Service.

My Lord, as I have said elsewhere, my Government has pledged to continue with the house-cleaning exercise. We shall do this from the unbiased belief and conviction that it is immoral to allow any individual or group of individuals to take advantage of the deplorable plight of the past few years to plunder and cheat any more with impunity. We rely heavily on the courts and not on guns as our instrument of ensuring that the guilty are punished and the innocent freed. I trust in your firmness and fairness in this exercise.

My Lord, this ceremony has been brief and I must also be brief. Let me therefore end by reiterating that my Government has full confidence in you and the Judiciary and recognize you as an indispensable arm in our efforts to build a clean and democratic society. Indeed, I believe that with concerted effort, we shall build this country again into a law-abiding, prosperous, dignified and happy nation. To you and members of your Service, I say, *quamdiu se bene gesserit*, but let us not fail the public at large. Let us live up to present and future expectations.

24

Swearing-in Ceremony of Members of the Council of State and Deputy Ministers

Members of the Council of State and Deputy Ministers of State are sworn in by the President, 7 February 1980.

After this brief but solemn ceremony it is my pleasure to congratulate you on your appointments to your respective high offices of State. As members of the Council of State and Deputy Ministers, you have today been called upon and you have accepted to play leading roles in the affairs of the nation. I hope that you will all find it honourable to serve your nation assiduously at this crucial period of our history. To this end, I implore you to discharge your duties creditably and to the best of your ability, without fear or favour.

It is exactly four months today since the first batch of Ministers were sworn in. Most of them have been working very hard to find solutions to our numerous problems. All of them have discovered that the problems facing us are difficult and complex and that there is no room for laxity on their part. I hope that they will share their experiences with you as you discharge your functions.

The Government has been drawing on the wisdom and rich experience of members of the Council of State for over three months now in the administration of the country and I am happy to inform you that the executive is benefiting a great deal from their counsel.

This only means that all of you bear a heavy burden in the collective responsibility entrusted to us to rescue our nation from further decline and total ruin. You must not relax in your efforts to contribute your quota towards this task of national revival.

Ghana stands very much in need of salvation after the traumatic experiences we have gone through during the last few years. You are all living witnesses to the damage which has been done to the economy. Morale in the body politic has sunk very low. The pride we all had in our nation at independence has disappeared and what remains of us today as a nation is deprivation and despair.

After many years of mismanagement and maladministration Ghanaians are looking to us as their last hope for deliverance from deprivations, indignities and humiliations. We therefore dare not fail them.

I must also remind you that for the third time in our existence as a nation we have had the opportunity freely to choose our own government. Most of our present woes can justifiably be blamed on the way governments have been forcibly changed in the past. We should therefore be prepared to be accountable to the public at all times so that our third attempt at civilian rule shall succeed. Woe betide us as a nation if we fail again.

To overcome our problems we need a sustained period of peace and stability yet parts of our society are in turmoil while some of our institutions also no longer command implicit respect. We can only ensure success through hard work, sincere, honest and dedicated service to our country. I therefore exhort you to work diligently and be fair in all your dealings with those you have been called upon to serve. The nation will judge us by our performance in the discharge of our duties. We can therefore make or unmake ourselves.

Once more, I warmly congratulate you on your appointments and trust that you will live up to expectation. I wish you success in all your endeavours.

25

Pope John Paul II's Visit to Ghana
10 May 1980

The President welcomes His Holiness on the unprecedented papal goodwill visit. The President is understandably moved to quote from the eighteenth century English poet, Thomas Gray's Elegy Written in a Country Churchyard. *The President is, of course, referring to the humble circumstances from which the Pope had worked his way to the papacy.*

It is with infinite pleasure that on behalf of the Government and people of Ghana and on my own behalf I heartily welcome His Holiness Pope John Paul II to Ghana. Our pleasure is the more inexpressible since the visit of His Holiness, the first ever by a Pope to Ghana, is one of goodwill connected with the centenary celebrations of the Catholic Church of Ghana which, I am happy to observe, continues to inculcate in the faithful, the Christian values of love, peace and brotherhood, and has been intimately and constructively associated with the spiritual and socio-economic development of Ghana.

In welcoming your Holiness, we note with particular admiration and renewed inspiration, your own humble origins and steady rise to the very top by dint of hard work and innate talents. We pay tribute to your many outstanding qualities as author, scholar, poet, dramatist and spiritual excellence. Your position in the world is unique; you are not only the spiritual leader of devoted Catholic Christians the world over but also an outstanding World Statesman. Your simplicity, friendly and charming manners have endeared you to millions all over the world. Your origins bear eloquent testimony to the vision of the poet who wrote:

> Full many a gem of purest ray serene,
> The dark unfathom'd caves of ocean bear:
> Full many a flower is born to blush unseen,
> And waste its sweetness on the desert air.

Your Holiness, we pay the highest tribute to the Catholic Church, that for the first time ever, these lines have been proved right in all respects in your own particular case. Your own record of achievement is unique in another, rather more remote way, namely, that self-discipline, initiative and hard work within the framework of a properly regulated freedom overcame the licence and indiscipline as characterized by the 'Liberum Veto' which eventually destroyed the country of your origin, a country which was once the largest and, perhaps, even the most powerful in all Europe.

We in Ghana have been following with keen interest the pastoral visits by Your Holiness to various parts of the world and deeply appreciate the message of peace and love which you have consistently delivered at a time when our world is drifting towards increasing tensions, instability and even anarchy. Everywhere complex problems, bewildering in their magnitude, continue to arise, leading to confrontations and violence which are prejudicial to international peace and security.

Your Holiness, the peaceful settlement of problems and disputes presupposes a readiness on the part of all countries, both big and small, to collaborate on the basis of goodwill and understanding, and above all, of the recognition that we are one another's keeper. A world divided into two unequal hemispheres with the people of the larger living in poverty, disease and hunger and those of the smaller in affluence is a sad indictment not only of the sense of social justice of mankind but also a veritable threat to world peace and security.

Your Holiness highlighted this problem when you appealed to the industrialized northern nations in your address at the United Nations General Assembly to put an end to the draining of the resources of the poorer southern countries and help in the equal distribution of the world's wealth. As Your Holiness rightly cautioned, the Third World cannot continue indefinitely to be the 'hewers of wood and drawers of water'.

It is in this context that we have also been earnestly appealing to all developed countries to co-operate fully in the implementation of the Action Programme of the New International Economic Order which alone provides a firm basis for one world based on justice, equality, peace and security. This message, Your Holiness, is of particular importance and moment to us in Ghana and has been embraced by both Christians and non-Christians.

Your Holiness, it is with measureless elation that we also recall the 'Pastoral Constitution on the Church in the Modern World' to which Your Holiness has made significant contributions. This key document has declared, *inter alia*, that the Church must be committed to a deep involvement in social development and world affairs because of her concern for human dignity. In keeping with this progressive and unifying policy, the Catholic Church of Ghana has made contributions of lasting value to Ghana's development in the educational, health and social fields and in many other areas of primary interest and concern to Government.

With over two thousand Catholic schools of various levels in the country, the Catholic Church, because of the quality and discipline of its education, has produced men and women of quality and ability in the arts, sciences and in politics who have made and are continuing to make invaluable contributions to the development of the country.

Nor is this all. Mindful of the health needs of the people, the Catholic Church has built twenty-four hospitals, eight clinics and an Orthopaedic Training Centre. Lately, the Health Service of the Church has been turning its attention more and more to preventive medicine and primary health care, another area of great interest to Government. These services which have been voluntarily forthcoming fill a significant void and have substantially supplemented Government's efforts at assuring a healthy and sound population.

It is also to the credit and foresight of the Catholic Church that it has increasingly become deeply and enthusiastically involved in agriculture. This involvement includes the sinking of wells, the construction of small dams and the instruction of small-scale farmers in the proper use of available inputs like fertilizers and improved seedlings. As agriculture is central to my Government's economic policy, the increasing contribution of the Catholic Church to this sector will be of vital encouragement and assistance to us. We therefore deeply appreciate and count on the continuing understanding, goodwill and support of your numerous flock in our agricultural activities, particularly, in the rural areas where our efforts are meant to improve upon the living conditions of the people.

On the occasion of the centenary of the Catholic Church in Ghana we warmly congratulate the faithful and are happy to share with them their proud and solid achievements. From the humble beginning of the Church in the year 1880 with the arrival in Elmina of two pioneer priests, it has grown from strength to strength and greatly expanded in its scope, through the firm foundations laid and the positive contributions made by Bishop de Bresilac, founder of the Society of African Missions, and his successors. The sense of fulfilment and maturity which the Church has now acquired owes much to their collective vision and dedicated pioneering work.

Today, the Catholic Church constitutes almost thirteen per cent of Ghana's population, by far the biggest single Christian denomination. All the various Archdioceses and Dioceses are manned by Ghanaian prelates which attests to the abiding faith of the Church in the ability of the Ghanaian to reach and take care of the spiritual needs of their compatriots. No wonder that the Church has achieved so much since its inception a hundred years ago.

The faith of the Church has been amply justified; its impact on Ghanaian society has been profoundly pervasive and beneficial. If the faith was established in difficulties and in tears, it is now rich in blessings and is thus reaping its accomplishments with deserving joy.

131

Finally, Your Holiness, I wish to express the fond hope that throughout your visit to Africa, you would continue to bring home to all of us, including leaders, both Christian and non-Christian, the need and, indeed, the necessity of good example particularly by leadership. I sincerely and unreservedly wish you a happy and memorable stay in Ghana and a fulfilling reunion with your numerous flock and admirers throughout the country.

26

Inauguration of the Press Commission, the Local Government Grants Commission and the Forestry Commission 25 July 1980

The Press Commission, which was to mother the press 'in an atmosphere of responsible freedom' was enjoined to develop true independence by being financially independent. The other Commissions were constitutional requirements, like the Press Commission.

I have the greatest pleasure and honour personally to inaugurate today, at long last, the Local Government Grants, the Press and the Forestry Commissions which have been designed under the Constitution of the Third Republic to play nationally important roles in the life of our country.

I had hoped that this solemn occasion should have taken place very much earlier than today. However, in this, as in similar other matters, it is always better late than never and this tardy inauguration would have served a very useful purpose if the delay has ensured that really new important steps are being taken to enable our democratic experiment to be based on firm and commonly acceptable foundations. At least, I personally take consolation in such a prospect.

I also hope that the deeper meaning and significance of this event shall never be lost on Ghanaians. Its importance lies in several important facts, including, particularly, our collective belief in and commitment to the pursuit and maintenance of an effective system of Local Government and decentralization, our belief in a free press and our concern over the conservation and responsible utilization of our natural resource inheritance. The first two of the three Commissions are among the necessary ingredients for constitutional rule, participatory democracy, open government and accountability to the sovereign electorate, just as the third one will ensure that while we enjoy our inheritance, we also invest in it and/or husband it well for posterity. Indeed, we must all endeavour to ensure that these commitments will be irreversible, that they will take deep roots and that they will be passed on from generation

133

to generation of Ghanaians.

Our aspirations in this regard can be realized but only if we refrain from rationalizing our private, transitory and often selfish interests into principles, to the detriment of the permanent interests of our country and the need to be credible in the eyes of the public at all times. For instance running down one's country through the press at home and abroad will do a great disservice to the true conception of freedom of the press. Similarly, pilfering District Council funds and mismanaging the administration of our natural resource endowment or of our Local Councils, can greatly undermine civilian rule.

Mr Chairman, the establishment of these three Commissions would not merely provide us with the psychological satisfaction of having satisfied our constitutional obligations. In themselves they are all very important institutions whose contribution to the socio-economic development of our country is expected to be very crucial indeed.

The constitution-makers have created them in the hope that the frustrations and abuses suffered by our people at various times in the past may no longer have free reign. Members of the three Commissions therefore bear the particularly heavy responsibility of providing a new sense of direction and competence in open, local or self-government, participatory democracy and in safeguarding the interests of the masses of our people, particularly taxpayers or those who bear the brunt of both the successes and failures of our country.

Excellencies, ladies and gentlemen, all organized civil societies are dynamic and organic entities which adapt and change imperceptibly, improving upon their past, present and future experiences and performances. Without this adaptability they tend to decay and disappear as has happened to many ancient civilizations, including those of our own sub-region of Africa, such as the Mali, Ghana and Songhai Empires of old.

To my mind, these three commissions, are eminently suited to promote not only the orderly evolution of our society but also the development of our country in a more honest and efficient manner than in the past.

The establishment of the Press Commission has fulfilled a great longing of many Ghanaians for an independent institutional framework within which the Press will operate in an atmosphere of responsible freedom. Its inauguration, perhaps the first in Africa, therefore marks a very significant milestone in the history and development of the Press in Ghana.

Opinions might have differed in the past as to whether it should be a Trust or a Commission but the idea behind it, as well as its purpose, has always been clear enough to its older defenders and proponents except, of course perhaps those now cashing in for their private and selfish interests. I earnestly implore such 'arrivistes', if there are any, to re-read

John Stuart Mill's Essay and other books on Liberty and also remember to look up the record on Mr Hansard and how they advanced various freedoms, including that of the Press whose modern defenders and practitioners are too numerous to be mentioned here. We all know contemporary press freedom fighters through their reports and articles in the world's press and should therefore emulate their good example.

Having briefly indicated the basis of my own conception and belief in press freedom, I must add that I shall, as the elected President, Head of State of Ghana, be forever prepared to submit to the acid test of public judgment the claims of those who may think that they represent the public more than me or any other political leader.

Bluff, snobbery and arrogance on all sides must now cease, so that the Press Commission can function in the way that it has long been envisaged by those who have never had any personal axe to grind—I have long been one of the protagonists myself.

Since the functions of the Press Commission have been clearly spelt out in the Constitution, I can do no more than reassure its members and our journalists that my Government will respect, uphold and defend the Constitution and thus do everything in our power to help the Press Commission discharge its obligations, in the overall interest of the public to which we are all to varying degrees accountable. In this regard it is necessary for the media, the Government and the public to reassess their respective relations in order to avoid needless bickering and much waste of time and money, at the expense of the permanent and collective interests of our country.

In my view, no truly free and respected newspaper or journal has ever subsisted on the taxpayer's money. This is the deeper reason for my appeal through Parliament in my last Sessional Address, for ways and means to be found for ensuring a really free Press in every sense of the term. Now that the Press Commission has been set up, I hope that its members will very seriously and quickly direct their attention to this most vital point in the fulfilment of their role and functions.

As you are all very well aware, the wilful suppression of nationally important information in favour of distortions, can be harmful to a free Press, particularly at the period of its early development when the reach of newspapers is still rather limited. I must therefore draw your most serious attention to this point as well. Similarly, fighting for positions and misusing public property in the process, as we tend to do in our country can also be harmful to the type of free press for which we have all been yearning. We must all behave and discharge our functions in such a way that we can honestly justify ourselves to the public. Our conduct must be able to stand the test of public accountability at all times.

The history of the Press in our country since independence has not been very endearing for many reasons which need not be mentioned in exhaustive detail now. Suffice it to mention the obvious, namely, that Pressmen and women have found it difficult in the past to perform as real watch-dogs of the freedom of expression which also protects the interests of the people and of the country. Some of our past and even current woes can be attributed to this absence of a robust and truly uninhibited Press to provide critical and informed commend on Government policy and public behaviour. The Press has also often tended to provide more coverage for relatively minor and transitory issues than for nationally very important problems. This has tended to divert serious attention and prompt action from very important and urgent national issues.

Right now, untold harm is being done at our ports, to an already sick economy which is being painfully nursed back to life and yet the press seems to highlight only the views of those who are causing all this harm instead of delving into their demands, performances and practices and the reasonableness or otherwise of the position of a minority holding us all to ransom. Even the early publication of some information of common knowledge on the crisis would have been more helpful to the public than what the press has so far done on the problem.

Sixteen days after the undertaking by officers of the Black Star Line to the Vice-President that they will return to work immediately, none of the ships has yet sailed although eight of them have been fully supplied for their voyages. I wonder when the press will conduct an impartial investigation and expose the real causes behind this act of holding the nation to ransom.

Mr Chairman, my Government's accommodation of Press criticisms, sometimes uninformed and unhelpful to the public during the last nine months demonstrates our desire to encourage freedom of expression. However, I wish to state also that just as the Press needs to be insulated against official encroachments, so must there be the firm recognition, acceptance and practical application of the fact that individuals, private and publicly owned institutions, the Government and national interests must all be protected against the excesses and unrestrained misuse of the Press.

It has been all too easy for the Press to paint itself as the underdog while being silent over its negative influences on the thinking and activities of thousands of people at home and abroad.

Already, some media manipulators have, under the guise of Press freedom, arrogated to themselves the right to use public property not only to gag Government, as someone once protested, but also to ride their private and personal hobby horses. For instance, one of the longest editorials ever written in our dailies in recent times was devoted to a personal matter, but at public expense. This does not conform with the principles of fair play, honesty and public accountability.

Many innocent citizens have often been attacked by the media; some of them have even suffered irreparable damage and injury without having equal opportunities to put their own cases across through the media so that the public can the better judge. The Commission should therefore pursue the principle of fair play and ensure that we all avoid moving only between extremes as we have tended to do in the past. In some countries, journalists have themselves set up disciplinary committees to monitor their own performance, and when necessary to enable aggrieved persons to seek redress. It is rather unfortunate that the Ghana Journalists' Association has so far not been able to develop such a self-monitoring system. I hope that they will now give serious thought to the issue and set up a unit which can ensure that its members keep within the ethics of their profession.

Mr Chairman, I now wish briefly to turn to Local Government Administration which is one of the more pervasive and important problems before us at the moment. Various local government systems have been introduced or tried before in our country. For want of either financial support, administrative sanity and competence or due to the inherently weak and non-viable nature of the units, all past systems have failed to ensure an enduring framework within which essential services for which levies are collected could be provided for the people they were supposed to serve. The net result of the handicaps and problems facing past systems has been the vicious circle of ineffectiveness in which Local Government Councils have tried to discharge their statutory obligations.

It is often argued that Local Councils did not have the means to discharge their functions or that they could not utilize available resources and therefore were not given the necessary financial support. The situation was that they did not demonstrate the capability to discharge the roles expected of them. The establishment of the Local Government Grants Commission by an Act of Parliament is therefore intended to remedy some of these defects.

Central Governments are henceforth required to provide grants-in-aid to regional Councils which should allocate them to the Local Government Councils established by or under the Constitution.

The Commission is expected to:

(a) determine the proportion of grants to be allocated to Regional Councils and the Local Government Councils;

(b) make grants to District and other Local Government Councils;

   (i)   for specific projects approved by Government;

   (ii) fund projects considered to be of priority in the national development programme;

   (iii) augment the income of District or other Local Government Councils whose revenues and resources are inadequate;

(iv) such other purposes as Government may direct and also to review, at intervals of not more than three years, grants made under the first function.

The Commission's work is not going to be easy in our present state of economic disrepair and the paucity of our financial resources. Undoubtedly, yours is an onerous task, a task which you will have to approach with ingenuity and determination, with all your mind and might, a task which calls for sacrifice, devotion and a sense of mission. The yardstick of your success will be your honesty, integrity and devotion to duty in the discharge of your functions.

Mr Chairman, many visitors, coming to Ghana to ascertain its economic potential, have without exception, expressed their surprise at our present poor economic position in spite of the rich natural resources with which the country is endowed. The conclusive impression is that the utilization of our natural resources has not been carefully and effectively regulated and managed to enable the country derive maximum benefit from them. Indeed, this view is also shared by the majority of Ghanaians as is evidenced by the provisions of Article 191 of the Constitution, under which the Forestry Commission is set up. Total earnings from cocoa, for years the mainstay of our economy, are being totally swallowed up by oil import bills alone. It has therefore become absolutely essential for us as a nation to look elsewhere for additional income which is increasingly needed for development. This long felt need for diversification can no longer brook delay if we are to survive economically. economically.

Fortunately, Ghana is richly endowed with forest resources comprising a wide range of timber which, when carefully and effectively regulated and managed, can substantially add to our foreign exchange earnings and also support our local construction and other industries.

Another natural resource which has not yet been seriously considered is game and wildlife, an area which when properly developed can also yield immense revenue. Countries such as Kenya have long developed theirs and are now using it effectively to promote tourism and foreign exchange earning. Besides encouraging tourism, this can also promote the development of local crafts, cottage industries and the export trade. It is for the foregoing and many other reasons that the Ghana Forestry Commission has been established and charged with responsibility to regulate, manage and utilize our forest and wild life resources efficiently for the present and future benefit of the country. To this end also, the Timber Marketing Board, Forestry Department, Department of Game and Wildlife and the Forest Products Research have been established.

Some radical innovations have thus been introduced in this set-up. If we want to improve upon what we have, we must be prepared to innovate boldly. Those among you who have been entrusted with the onerous responsibility of ensuring the successful operation of the Forestry Commission should take up these challenges before you and assiduously work to achieve the objectives of your Commission. If you succeed, as I am sure that you will, you shall contribute in no small measure to the stability of our dear country and to your own pride and performance satisfaction.

Distinguished guests, ladies and gentlemen, this occasion is an important turning point for our country. As usual, we have met full of hope and with great expectation for a better future. While it is right and proper for us to feel this way, we should also realize that whatever objectives and ambitions we may put down on paper these can be transformed into reality only by the determination and conscious effort of Ghanaians, that is, by all of us.

A lot of thought has gone into the elaborate establishment of these Commissions; efforts have also been made to provide the best talents available to man them. Their establishment subsumes heavy costs but not much attention has as yet been paid to the problems of funding them. I therefore charge members of the three Commissions to direct their priority attention to this fact in their determination to discharge their duties and responsibilities faithfully, diligently and conscientiously. To be truly free, the media must have independent means of financing itself so that the papers now existing at the expense of the taxpayer may become less burdensome to the public. This will also dispel any fears that they may misuse public property for their own ends, while paying scant attention to national objectives and the permanent interest of the country.

The Local Government Grants Commission bears an even greater responsibility to devise viable and lasting ways and means of funding the new system adequately and also ensure that waste, embezzlement of funds and very poor performance of all which have bedevilled the past systems do not return to destroy this new structure.

Mr Chairman, distinguished guests, ladies and gentlemen, it is now my special pleasure to declare the Local Government Grants, the Press and Forestry Commissions inaugurated.

27

The President addresses the Nation 28 July 1980

Speaking to his people on radio and television, the President expressed the feelings of the public, exasperated by the indiscipline and callous indifference of public officers in responsible positions.

A case in point was the current industrial action of the officers of the Black Star Line.

It is now ten months since I assumed office as President in our third attempt at democratic rule. Throughout the election campaign and especially since my assumption of office, I have repeatedly spoken candidly, often very bluntly, about the pressures on our resources, the precarious nature of our finances and about the urgent need for all of us to work assiduously for our national recovery and regeneration.

During the last ten months I have toured parts of all the regions to meet our chiefs and people closely and to outline some of our policies to them. I have also visited some projects, installations, water works, mines, farms, hospitals, schools and numerous other establishments so as to attain a deeper insight into the problems facing the economy and our country. These tours have given me and my colleagues a deeper insight into the extent of destruction that has been done to the economy over the past decade and the problems facing all of us. Since then I have repeatedly made appeals that we should all as Ghanaians take our collective destiny into our own hands and to work relentlessly to resuscitate our economy and save our nation from disgrace and shame.

Countrymen, the main reason for my taking some of your time this evening is once again to appeal to you to take seriously the point we have made over and over already, that only we ourselves can rescue our country from any further decline. We cannot expect others to help us solve our problems if we are not prepared to be serious and start tackling them ourselves.

My greatest concern has been the inability of some of our people, particularly those in vital sectors, to shake themselves out of apathy or show concern towards the worries and near despair of the majority of their fellow Ghanaians. In diverse ways we have all contributed towards bringing Ghana to its present sorrowful state. We all therefore have a duty to help repair the damage and destruction the present Government has inherited.

Unfortunately our attitudes towards work have not yet changed. Some officials have continued to demonstrate lukewarm attitudes, and nay, indifference towards work and towards the feelings of the majority of our people. They shy away from taking action on decisions taken that can benefit the public. People sit idly by and watch food go rotten while others need it even for sheer survival. They hesitate to act because they are afraid, perhaps, of hurting some personalities or harming some interests.

Eight Black Star Line ships have finished taking on cargo, including cocoa, to be delivered to buyers abroad for foreign currency, which will enable us to import some of the goods and raw materials needed to keep our industries going. Two ships have been ready to sail since 10 June 1980 and another four for the past fortnight. In fact all the thirteen ships should have sailed long ago but because of the industrial action not a single one of them has moved. Countrymen, this is the present situation eighteen days after officers of the Black Star Line had given an undertaking to the Vice-President to resume work and when Government had believed that an amicable settlement had been made to enable negotiations to be resumed.

The officers in charge of these ships have refused to move until certain demands they have made for salary increases and other increased benefits have been granted. The first of their demands is that all their salaries should be paid in a currency of their own choice to be named at will and at any time. At present the officers receive 60 per cent in foreign exchange and 40 per cent in Cedis. They are not satisfied with this and want all their salaries to be paid in any currency they themselves select. The second demand is for increases in their salaries ranging from 45 per cent to 100 per cent. Their other numerous demands will be revealed publicly and in detail later by the Minister responsible for Transport and Communications.

Fellow Ghanaians, enough is enough. We have had enough from these officers, each of whom was trained as a seaman and an officer entirely at the expense of the state. The public has spent money on their training so that they would serve us. You will be able to judge for yourselves how they have repaid us when the details are fully explained to you later. This situation has to come to an end.

If we sit back and do nothing to save the Black Star Line, its officers will totally destroy it.

I have therefore decided to assume the powers conferred on me by law, to take over personally the running of the Black Star Line. In exercise of these powers I have ordered the following measures to be taken in the interest of the nation:

(1) Officers of the Black Star Line who have refused either to resume normal work or to sail are to be dismissed forthwith.

(2) The Ghana Navy shall immediately take possession of all Black Star Line ships lying idle at Tema and Takoradi.

(3) The Auditor-General and the Police shall put together a team of investigators to thoroughly investigate the sea-going operations of the Black Star Line in recent years with special emphasis on the private trading activities of all officers and some members of the crew.

(4) Upon the completion of that investigation the Attorney-General will take appropriate action on any criminal offences and civil liabilities which may be disclosed by the investigation.

(5) Foreign crews should be recruited, as and when necessary, to make up for any short-fall in the complement of Ghanaian officers.

(6) Payment of overtime in foreign exchange to sea-going staff of the Black Star Line should cease forthwith.

(7) The payment of emoluments to the sea-going staff of the Black Star Line should henceforth be in the ratio of 40 per cent in foreign exchange and 60 per cent in Cedis.

I must stress at this juncture, that these unrealistic demands have in recent times not been limited to the Black Star Line alone. Similar unpatriotic demands, coupled with a total lack of any sense of duty have also been made by other sectors of our economy, especially, the Public Boards and Corporations.

Countrymen, these unpatriotic acts tend to sap our energies and divert our attention from our primary objective of restructuring our economy. As a government we will not shirk this responsibility and allow a few individuals to hold the whole nation to ransom and deprive us of our birthright.

Countrymen, I would like to point out to people placed in management positions that this government has allowed them sufficient time to adjust to the realities of the times in their respective areas of operation. From now on managers will be strictly held responsible for the maladministration and poor performances of their organizations.

We are about to complete reconstituting all the Boards of the Public Corporations and I would like to emphasize that I expect Board Members to take an active part in the welfare of the Corporations they are to oversee. It is completely unacceptable for Board Members to stand still always expecting Government to solve all their industrial problems. I expect all placed in positions of authority to rise to the challenges facing them and make meaningful contributions towards the resuscitation of the nation.

For a long time now we have hypnotized ourselves into the belief that

142

everything in Ghana is bad. This has led to the mass exodus of trained, skilled and unskilled labour from Ghana to neighbouring and other countries, seeking for jobs in even more difficult conditions than at home. The result is that our nationals keep getting into trouble in other countries bringing shame to their countrymen and sorrow to their relatives. Let us break out of this apathy and hold our heads high because Ghana has really not yet sunk beyond repair. We are not the poorest nation in Africa and certainly we do not live under the worst conditions in Africa. Let us rise to the challenge of rebuilding our nation for ourselves and for our children.

Countrymen, my statement over the weekend on the proposed exercise by the Electoral Commission seems to have aroused a lot of passion within certain sectors of our community.

I would like to make it clear that I have nothing against the Electoral Commissioner personally nor do I wish to interfere in the activities of the office of the Electoral Commissioner. However, as President it is my responsibility to ensure that all activities in the country are co-ordinated and synchronized to the fullest benefit of all Ghanaians.

In my address to the nation during the independence celebration, I made a similar call. On that occasion I had this to say:

Several other institutions have also been created in the Constitution to assist each of these wings to carry out its duties effectively.

It is very important for all of them to realize that at these crucial stages of our third attempt at democratic practices, entrenched and inflexible attitudes and confrontational stances can cause needless delays and even much eventual damage.

The various arms and establishments should therefore work together in a co-operative and harmonious spirit for the supreme national interest. We may not all hold similar opinions on all matters but even such differences can be reconciled through timely discussions and consultations. If we are to succeed, we must necessarily work in unity towards politically defined national objectives. The various parts of the one and same country cannot pursue the policies and attitudes usually associated with independent sovereign states. Co-operation, consultations and mutual understanding are among some of the ways in which our civilian experiment of checks and balances can succeed under the clearly expressed political mandate of the People's National Party Government.

Countrymen, when I made this call I was emphasizing the need for absolute co-ordination between all wings of Government to ensure that we set our priorities right within the boundaries of our limited resources. It is therefore my wish that an important exercise such as the replacement of the voter's register should not be rushed but should be carried out after adequate preparations have been undertaken and sufficient consideration given to the entire exercise. I have always made this point of view known to everyone and especially to the Electoral Commissioner himself.

As of now, steps have been taken in conjunction with the Council of State for me to meet with the Electoral Commissioner once again to resolve the issue of the timing of the exercise. I therefore hope that no one will play to the gallery and fan a non-existing confrontation between myself and the Electoral Commissioner.

Countrymen, our belief in freedom and justice and in the fundamental principles of human rights means absolutely nothing if we do not translate it into concrete terms. As a Government we are in duty bound to ensure that no one starves but can go about his or her normal life in peace and dignity.

We cannot achieve this in an atmosphere of confrontation, antagonism and lack of trust and confidence. It behoves us all to see our roles clearly in this enormous task of rebuilding our economy, restructuring our nation and saving Ghana from shame. I have no doubt that we have the ability and the capability as a nation to rise above our present gloomy state.

I hope that I can count on all of you to make meaningful contributions in the noble task of saving our dear country.

28

Thirty-second Annual New Year School

The Institute of Adult Education derived from the pioneer Department of Extramural Studies of the University of Ghana. Beginning as an institution which was to provide continuing education to adults in liberal studies, it operated as an educational movement with the People's Educational Association at the vanguard of organization in town, city and village in the years immediately preceding the independence of Ghana and during the early post-independence years. The date was 30 September 1980. The President was happy to report his early identification with the movement.

I feel greatly honoured to have been invited to open and briefly participate in this Thirty-second Annual New Year School. Indeed, I am doing so this morning with infinite pleasure, many happy memories and reflections after having been an involuntary truant for over two decades now—more precisely since 1956.

As the Vice-Chancellor has already said in his welcome address, I am very much at home not only in a gathering such as this but also with its venue where I have long had many personal friends whom I visited often in the recent past. It is also a fact that I used to be an active participant of the educational programmes which the former Institute of Extra-Mural Studies organized in my locality and, indeed, throughout the country in the fifties.

The New Year and Easter Schools, Seminars and Conferences I attended at the Wesley College, Kumasi in 1952, St Augustine's College, Cape Coast in 1953 and here in Legon in April 1954 have been of particular and great importance to me. Such activities were the first to open my eyes beyond the District and Regional levels to that of the nation and far beyond. They made it possible for me not only to meet and observe wider and wider cross sections of people and academics but also to visit many important sites and monuments, including Lake Bosomtwi, Elmina Castle and the Tsito Model PEA residential College.

Above all, such activities aroused in me the awareness of the need and the thirst for knowledge. I even realized from such contacts that I could sit the GCE 'O' Level Examinations and so, prodded by close friends, I took the plunge with them in June 1955 and to my surprise, passed in enough subjects to qualify me for the award of the certificate. In short the PEA has been at the root of all the studies I have, like many others, done at home and privately in higher institutions abroad later.

The sterling qualities and good example I observed in others during those New Year and Easter Schools aroused and sustained my interest in learning and a great yearning for more and more knowledge. Being one of the bridges which some of us have used to cross over or gain access to university studies, I think that the PEA has not done too badly at all. Indeed, on my own behalf and on behalf of many others, I must avail myself of this opportunity to commend it very highly and also to thank all those who have sustained it even against odds.

Mr Vice-Chancellor, the renewed national efforts we are all deploying to re-establish civilian democratic rule or the democratic way of life in Ghana, assumes that the general citizenry should have free access to information and therefore opportunities for that continued or life-long liking for the acquisition of knowledge which helps increasingly to improve upon the quality of life itself and leads to responsible citizenship. ship.

The Third Republican Constitution requires that, as far as our national resources permit, Government should make every effort to provide free basic education for all Ghanaian children and also free adult mass literacy and opportunities for life-long education. Aware of these provisions my Administration will do everything within its power and resource-availability to implement them as the economy improves. The extent of fulfilment however depends very much on the resources which we can muster as a nation and also on the efficient, honest and disciplined use of whatever resources are available to us at any given period of time. We must now therefore start to think seriously of spending more and more funds not on food alone as in the past decade but rather on rehabilitating and re-equipping our educational establishments, including re-stocking our institutional libraries, bookshops and teaching apparatus which have all either run down to hopeless levels or even totally disappeared.

Consultations and other preparations are currently in progress to draw up effective and less wasteful plans for providing free basic education to all Ghanaian children as well as opportunities for mass literacy and continuing education for our adult population. I therefore wish to take this opportunity to appeal very strongly to all concerned to redouble their efforts and expedite action on the said plans.

Mr Chairman, or is it Chairperson, it is hardly necessary for me to justify the need for life-long education before this type of audience over which you are presiding, since the very presence of all of us here today is the most telling indication and testimony that having tasted it ourselves, we have found it to be good for our well-being and the quality of our lives, even amidst our present economic problems, deprivations and hardships.

Through learning and honest intellectual discipline, we are more aware than others that the whole world is at present experiencing economic difficulties, tensions, conflicts, and irrational attitudes and that therefore our economic recovery and national salvation lie in our own hands through hard work and self-discipline rather than on our pursuing the beggar-my-neighbour policies of the recent past. Indeed, education and learning have even enabled us to philosophize about what has gone wrong in Ghana since the 1960s and also over our increasingly worsening economic situation since then.

The question we must now raise and answer for ourselves is whether or not we have been living and acting according to the searching analysis and the lucid conclusions we frequently draw on our national plight. My view is that we have not all been doing so. We have not been intel-lectually honest with ourselves and with the Ghanaian public. Thus, it has been alleged that even now some people do not want Ghana to recover under the PNP Administration because our success will make them lose face or keep them out of office.

Strange as this may sound, we are all aware that there has never been any smoke without fire in Ghana or anywhere else and my Ad-ministration has therefore not been surprised at some signs or evidence during the past thirteen months which seem to confirm these rumours. In this connection I wish to re-emphasize that such attitudes and tactics constitute a punishment not to my Administration but to the general Ghanaian public and are therefore rather dangerous. Since a word to a wise man is enough, I hope that those indulging in such dangerous games and antics would advise themselves before it is too late, since the public is watching all of us.

Mr Chairman, I am very well aware that some participants at this School have travelled here from far-flung places at personal financial sacrifices and hazards on our very bad roads, just as some of us had to do before independence when the roads were, in fact, not much better than now except that the traffic was less dense and without monster articulated trucks. In fact, going to Tsito recently I could not identify the spot where six of us, including one Sudanese and two Nigerians, were involved in a very dangerous accident—mainly because that road, has, at least, since then been tarred and had luckily, not yet been destroyed.

Being determined, solid and permanent converts to the philosophy, or is it ideology, of life-long practical learning or education *à la* PEA, it will be futile for me to waste words in trying to convince this audience that now, more than ever before, the need for learning, discipline and peace in all our institutions has become very urgent. Suffice it to add that education and life-long learning are of no societal use and benefit or can even be very dangerous if they are not harnessed to producing good,

147

honest and responsible citizens with sensitive feelings and concern for their uneducated fellow nationals who still constitute the main life blood of our economy and the sounder fabric of our national community.

Similarly, I need hardly belabour the obvious point to this audience that every citizen should be prepared to learn something new every day, particularly at this time of our collective efforts to resuscitate our economy, promote development and recover our self-respect, dignity and national prestige. At this stage, kindly permit me, Mr Chairman, to recall, however imperfectly, and also to renew and re-emphasize the appeal made in the opening remarks at the April 1954 International Conference of the PEA by the then Leader of Government Business, the late Osagyefo, Dr Kwame Nkrumah of blessed memory, and the comment of the Principal of the then University College of the Gold Coast, Mr Balme.

Among other things and appealing to the then young University, the Osagyefo pleaded that the University should make its studies and life-style relevant to the needs and aspirations of the society in which it existed. In his reply the Principal also said, among other things, that the University would have fulfilled its role if in a thousand years it is able to produce one genius.

A very young participant then, I still remember these two positions because they were seemingly diametrically opposed and, in fact, became so later until the University started to be accused, wrongly or rightly, of living in Ivory Towers. I have said 'seemingly' even today because the two positions are really not opposed, the one to the other, since there cannot be any genius outside organized society, and its needs and aspirations. I can therefore do no better than repeat the same appeal to you at this School, to all our lower and higher institutions and organs directly concerned with education and intellectual-cum-academic discipline, namely, that they should make their existence and learning relevant to the needs and aspirations of the total Ghanaian society, particularly, those of the uneducated taxpayer who helps to support these institutions and other educational facilities.

To underline this very urgent appeal I wish also to recall Matthew Arnold's famous phrase from his book entitled *Culture and Anarchy* that 'Culture is reading, but reading with a purpose to guide it, he does a good job who does anything to help this.' What should guide us all in our education, reading and learning, must be the need to produce good, honest, responsible and useful citizens.

One of the solutions to the many problems of our present educational system such as indiscipline in our institutions is making education and, particularly, academic life relevant to the needs and aspirations of our predominantly very youthful population. This calls for new approaches to the way we organize ourselves for living at peace in order to resume serious learning at our University campuses where good examples are far better than bad precepts which can, moreover, only tend to complicate the very serious problem of the generation gap.

Mr Chairman, as adults we cannot be credible to the younger generation if we preach one thing in lecture halls but practice the opposite in our private lives. Similarly, the younger generation can also not convincingly preach the virtues of accountability or condemn their elders as 'corrupt and decadent' if they, as adolescents, are not prepared to accept discipline, accountability, honesty and hard work while preparing themselves to take over the baton of leadership at the appropriate time which may not be as far away as they suppose.

Ghanaians have often questioned as to why our living conditions have deteriorated to such low levels in recent times despite our enormous natural resources endowment like our rich variety of fertile soils, arable lands and fairly adequate rainfall which frees us from the need for irrigation to produce most of our basic staple foodstuffs such as plantain, cassava, cocoyams and their edible leaves, yams, beans and so on. At least, my Administration knows and firmly believes that we can produce such foodstuffs so abundantly that their prices can be brought down substantially hence our strong emphasis on agriculture and our appeals for hard work in whatever role each citizen plays in the collective effort to rebuild our country.

Similarly, our environment leaves very much to be desired in cleanliness yet our schools and colleges still teach health science daily. Here again, if we all tidy up and burn the rubbish in our back yards during weekends or drop a little kerosene in the gutters, we can keep the environment clean and also eliminate the ear deafening, malaria-carrying mosquito.

We waste our staple foodstuffs during harvests only to hunger for them during the lean or off-seasons of the year. We tend to ruin things ourselves and then turn round to complain or rail at others for our plight. We must all therefore now start to re-think and re-organize our private lives and run our public affairs more rationally, seriously and honestly than we have done during the past decade.

As a people, we are acclaimed for our intelligence and ability to work hard everywhere, except at home. Here again, we must stop letting down ourselves and our country any more. Indeed, on an occasion such as this, we must admit that, as a people, we seem to apply our intelligence and knowledge actively not to improve upon our living conditions but to cheat our country, our fellow citizens and often even ourselves in the end.

Mr Chairman, one of the main objectives of adult education and life-long learning is that through it individuals or groups of them should improve upon their living conditions by applying knowledge directly to the serious business of living. Yet some of us have often tended to think that learning is useful only for passing examinations and that therefore once we leap over and successfully put these hurdles behind us we should stop showing any further interest in education for others or for ourselves. I sincerely hope, indeed, I believe that nobody at this School accepts or follows this line of thinking and behaviour. We in this gathering should at least therefore demonstrate in more purposeful and practical ways that we are concerned that it can and must be a task for life.

Our Universities and Research Institutions are allegedly storing away files full of research results which are not being put to any practical use in the public interest. If so, then perhaps, these results are not in the form and language which can be understood and applied by those of us not initiated in this sort of esoteric research and findings. The time has long been overdue to bring this sort of situation to an end and thus make academic research action oriented and its findings practical and implementable.

In other words, our research institutions should take the initiative in producing results in forms which can be used in the interest of the general public. In this regard I wish to go further and suggest that the Institute of Adult Education, in co-operation with other relevant institutions, should devise ways and means of promoting a science of culture in and for our society.

We need also to develop scientific, discipline and efficient attitudes and procedures for the solution of problems if we want to progress and move forward with our neighbours and the rest of the world. Being allegedly among the most intelligent of the black race, we cannot afford failure in this field. Indeed, we should be among the first to realize by now that traditional and anachronistic approaches of the past must give way to positive and scientific procedures and solutions to the rapidly changing and fast accumulating problems of our times.

Mr Chairman, I must confess my happiness at observing that the theme of the Thirty-second New Year School—'Citiens' Participation in Government'—falls perfectly in line with my Administration's policy of 'open Government and participatory democracy', a policy which also demands the practical application of knowledge to improving upon the methods of civic involvement in our socio-economic affairs. Is it enough to cast a vote, help elect a Government and then withdraw into one's shell and yet expect public affairs to be properly run? My Administration does not think so since democracy implies the active and unceasing involvement of all citizens in public affairs, particularly at the local level, in order to make it a reality.

Moreover, the challenges of our times require that individual citizens should be better equipped with information and the relevant knowledge which will enable them to give of their best to the total national development effort, enjoy his rightful share of national resources and, at the appropriate times, exercise his suffrage or vote more responsibly than at the time of the ancient Greek city-states. To reiterate the point, one of the cardinal objectives of education should be to produce good, honest, useful, responsible and patriotic citizens.

In conclusion, Mr Chairman, I hope that participants will make the fullest use of the opportunity being offered by this school to understand their rights as citizens and even more importantly, their duties and social obligations to their fellow, less fortunate citizens and to the nation at large. I also hope that as individuals and as members of organized groups and other voluntary organizations, you will all carry the messages from this School to your friends and relatives at home.

The message which I wish you to carry with you to others is simply this: Ghana is on the march towards economic recovery, progress and national prosperity and therefore expects every citizen, now more than ever before, to play his or her part in this noble task or assignment. We must all therefore move forward together as one united and determined people towards the recovery of our economy, our self-respect as a people, our national dignity and prestige.

And, now, Mr Chairman and colleagues, it is my great pleasure to declare the Thirty-second Annual New Year School open and to wish you all very successful deliberations and a Happy New Year of hope for prosperity.

29

The President commissions the Ghana Naval Flagships, 27 March 1981

The ships were Achimota *and* Yogaga. *The need for more effective control of Ghana's territorial waters grew greater and more insistent requiring the strengthening of coastal patrol. The speech treats these matters.*

This is the second time in just over three months that I have accepted an invitation to visit the Ghana Naval Base at Sekondi. On the first occasion last December, I presented my colours to the Western Naval Command to mark the occasion of the twenty-first birthday of the Navy. Today, I have come to commission two of the newest Ghana Navy ships, namely, *Achimota* and *Yogaga*. Of the two I have been pleased to confer on *Achimota* the honour of being my flagship. This occasion is also undoubtedly memorable and unique for all the officers and ratings of the Ghana Navy, for those of the Western Naval Command and, more especially for those who will man *Achimota*, my Flagship.

Distinguished guests, ladies and gentlemen, this 'out dooring' ceremony marking the twenty-second milestone of the Ghana Navy is yet another modest testimony of the determination of my Administration to rehabilitate and re-equip all our Armed Forces to enable them to contribute their quota in the efforts being made towards national recovery, reconstruction and upliftment.

The contract for these two ships being commissioned today and the two smaller ones commissioned last year, was signed in 1976. When I assumed office as President and thereby also became the Commander-in-Chief of the Ghana Armed Forces, I was faced with a huge bill which had already been committed for the ships. I was faced with only two options in this connection.

The first option was to renegotiate the contract and reduce the number of ships but this would have involved the payment of heavy penalties for default and at a time when the economy could not bear such wasteful expenses in foreign exchange. The second alternative was to negotiate for certain amendments which would reduce the overall cost of the entire acquisition programme of the Ghana Navy. In view of the near total collapse of the economy, I chose this latter course of action.

There could not have been any better demonstration of the fulfilment of my Administration's plans and determination to modernize the Ghana Armed Forces to the level which will restore their self-confidence and our national respect and pride in them. We are thus determined to recreate things befitting our national pride and prestige from the nothingness which the previous administrations of the last decade of the history and evolution of our country had left us as a people.

In this connection, I should like to remind you also, officers and ratings of the Ghana Navy, that you bear the heavy obligation of justifying the huge expenditure made in the acquisition of these ships. In operating them and their equipment you must constantly be mindful of the financial sacrifices involved in procuring them. Naval professional etiquette and practice which will ensure the long life of these ships, should be scrupulously observed at all times. Difficult as these practices may be, they are some of the challenges of the profession you have voluntarily and freely chosen to follow. As I once told some of you at your Ward Room in Accra, I personally admire your high spirit of adventure, the uniqueness of your profession and your etiquette.

As underlined in the commissioning warrants, the primary role of these ships, as the role of the entire Ghana Navy itself, is the defence of the Republic of Ghana against aggression by outside forces. This role also includes anti-smuggling operations, the protection of our marine resources, search and rescue operations, and such other duties, as may from time to time, be determined by the Government of Ghana.

You are all very well aware that our real enemies in peacetime and during this particular period of our national reconstruction are not only outside our borders but within our society itself. I refer to the big-time smugglers thwarting our efforts at economic recovery by their massive smuggling of cocoa, gold, timber, petroleum products and even food-stuffs across our territorial boundaries by land, sea and air. I therefore hope that the Ghana Navy will use these new ships to patrol vigorously our sea frontiers so as to check and eventually eliminate smuggling, and other subversive economic activites and illicit deals in our territorial waters and harbours. It is particularly imperative for the Ghana Navy, together with other security agencies, completely to eradicate pilfering and other acts of piracy in our ports and thus ensure that such much needed goods as spare parts, drugs, industrial raw materials and other commodities imported into Ghana (to improve upon the lot of our people and for the rehabilitation of our factories) do not leave the country or end up in the hands of only a few selfish and unpatriotic individuals.

The oil exploration activities off Saltpond, and the recent discovery of some gas and oil deposits in the Axim area have transformed our territorial waters into vital economic and security zones. Extra vigilance must be mounted to ensure the safety of oil rigs at all times. Our fisherfolk are also strongly advised to keep off such areas not only in the national interest but also in the interest of their own safety since both elements are very highly inflammable.

I wish to repeat what I said here three months ago about the roles which navies all over the world play in national defence and development and also to repeat that the Ghana Navy has not been found wanting in playing these vital roles. My Administration will therefore continue to make every effort, within the constraints of the economy, to ensure that these ships and others in the fleet, are maintained in the highest operational state at all times to enable the Ghana Navy effectively to fulfil the tasks assigned to it.

Distinguished ladies and gentlemen, I cannot conclude this address without referring to the builders of these ships, namely, Fr. Lurssen Werft of the Federal Republic of Germany. But for their trust, understanding and co-operation, this impressive ceremony would not have been possible today. Due to the precarious economic conditions of the country since the late 1970s, previous Ghana governments were often not able to fulfil payment obligations on due dates. Indeed, payments had to be rescheduled several times.

However, due to their tact, co-operation and understanding, Messrs Fr. Lurssen Werft continued patiently with the contract even in the face of such poor past performances. This trust and understanding reflects the high degree of good business relations established not only with Lurssen Werft but also with many other West German firms. We appreciate their gesture and are most grateful to them. We sincerely hope that the successful execution of this contract at long last has paved the way for much greater co-operation between Ghana and the Federal Republic of Germany at both public and private sector levels.

I should also like to record my personal gratitude to His Excellency the Ambassador at the Federal Republic of Germany who has greatly contributed towards the successful execution of the contract for these ships and also for the various substantial West German loans granted to Ghana over the past eighteen months, thus concretely demonstrating his trust in, goodwill and support for civilian rule in Ghana.

To the sub-contractors also, namely, Thomson CSF of France, Bofors of Sweden, Oto Melera of Italy, we say a big 'thank you'.

And now, Honourable Ministers, Nananom, distinguished guests, ladies and gentlemen, I have the greatest pleasure and honour to declare *Achimota* and *Yogaga* officially commissioned for service in the Ghana Navy.

30

Dinner in Honour of the President, given by the Governor of the Bank of England, London, 14 May 1981

The President visibly cherished the kind hospitality of Sir Gordon Richardson Governor of the Bank of England. He addresses his hosts and guests.

It gives me great pleasure to be invited to this Dinner and to have the opportunity of speaking to this august group of eminent bankers and businessmen. I wish to record my sincere thanks to you, Mr Governor, for the honour done me.

This occasion recalls memories of the long-standing traditional relations between our two countries and provides us with the opportunity to expand and strengthen those bonds for our mutual benefit. Links between the United Kingdom and Ghana have always been cordial and special. For instance, Ghana's financial institutions have a unique attachment to the Bank of England and the City. From the very early days, through the era of the West African Currency Board to the emergence of our own financial institutions in the immediate post-independence period, we have enjoyed the closest collaboration and support of the Old Lady of Threadneedle Street and the City's other financial institutions. The mutual benefits which have flowed from this special relationship for our two countries over the years have been so obvious to both sides that we need not recount them now.

It is however only natural, Mr Governor, distinguished ladies and gentlemen, that I should seize this opportunity to refer briefly to my country, its problems, its potentialities and the long pent-up expectations and aspirations of the Ghanaian public. Those who know Ghana well readily admit that it is a country with considerable economic potential and promise. But our economy has developed very serious structural problems demanding careful analysis, realistic evaluation and imaginative policy options for solving them now and in the immediate future.

155

Our economic revival hinges on substantial and rapid improvements being made in our financial resources. One of our preoccupations has therefore been to lay sound foundations which we consider to be vital for resuscitating the economy. Acute foreign exchange limitations in the economy have caused shortages of raw materials and spare parts, idle capacity in industry, under-employment and rising unemployment. These problems have been worsened by the ever increasing cost of energy and steeply falling prices for our exports. Our adverse balance of payments has therefore become very critical.

Despite these difficulties, we have, through improved discipline in the management of our external resources, managed to reduce our payments arrears by substantial amounts in our foreign exchange allocations for imports. We have set some policy measures in motion meant to improve upon our exports, intensify exploration for and exploitation of such minerals as gold, diamonds, bauxite and hydro-carbons. The measures also aim at achieving revival and growth in the cocoa and timber sectors.

You will therefore readily agree with me, Honourable Governor and distinguished ladies and gentlemen, that in view of the difficulties we inherited, these efforts have clearly demonstrated our determination to take and apply austerity measures, meant to revive our economy even at the risk of very serious socio-political reactions and repercussions and that therefore we ought not to take the patience and restraint of our public for granted any more, especially, in the face of the audacity of irrational elements who are always ready to incite others for destructive purposes simply for the love of destroying the norms and methods of the 'cake of civil society'.

After careful consultations and discussions we have now placed a bill before Parliament which will re-define the relations which ought to exist between foreign capital and entrepreneurship on the one hand and the exploitation of our natural resources and social objectives on the other. My Administration recognizes the need for fair rewards to risk capital and entrepreneurial and managerial skills, within the context of fair play and social justice. It is therefore in the interest of all of us that our efforts to achieve economic recovery and growth and progress should be carried through smoothly and efficiently. The stringent economic policies I have briefly summarized are being taken in such a democratic environment that free comments and criticisms easily create wrong or unintended impressions. Since it is impossible to envisage any successful operations within a relatively short period of time without contributions from our long-standing friends, we hope that you will appreciate our efforts and quickly respond to them concretely and massively. Indeed, that is why I am addressing you in these terms right now.

In this regard, we are happy to acknowledge the contribution which the United Kingdom Government has made, with the support of the

156

Bank of England and some of the City banks, to our efforts through various lines of credit guarantees by the Export Credit Guarantee Department.

I hope that as a practical demonstration of our long-standing friendship the Bank of England and other city financial institutions will, as they have done in the past, continue not only to be favourably disposed towards Ghana in her attempts at economic recovery but also greatly step up their concrete support and assistance. Hesitant support given in dribblets and too late often fail to provide effective solutions to serious problems. I also hope that British financial institutions will use their considerable influence abroad to get other multilateral financial agencies to show more understanding for our problems since too much pushing, too fast and too far tends to create abrupt reversals, psychological obstacles and resistance to changes even when they are clearly seen to be necessary. A proper appreciation of our local conditions and of the long pent-up expectations of our public as well as of the serious efforts we have so far made has therefore now become necessary and urgent.

And now distinguished ladies and gentlemen, may I ask you to rise with me in drinking a toast to the good health and personal well-being of the Governor and to continue co-operation between the business and financial communities of the United Kingdom and Ghana.

31
The President in Belgrade, Yugoslavia 18 May 1981

As a successor in the line of presidents of Ghana, Dr Hilla Limann, brough to mind the founding fathers of the Union of Non-Aligned Nations.

I deem it an honour and privilege for me and my entourage that you have been among the first, outside the continent of Africa, to invite us to visit your great country. This visit coming shortly after that of Mr Fadilj Hodza, a Member of the Yugoslav Presidency to our country, should strengthen age-old bonds of friendship between our two countries, governments and peoples.

Mr President, I wish at this juncture to warmly congratulate you personally on your election as President. I wish you great success during your tenure of office. I also congratulate your colleagues of the Presidency, worthy successors of the late Marshal Tito of blessed memory, for your magnificent works and achievements before and since death laid its icy hands on your immortal leader. Indeed, Marshal Tito will always be remembered as a great son of Yugoslavia who provided stability, unity and progress for his own country and also as one of the architects of the Non-Aligned Movement and an outstanding internationalist who devoted his life to the needs of peace, security and social justice throughout the world.

In this regard, Mr President, we are determined that the Non-Aligned Movement should remain faithful to the tenets laid down by such founding fathers as the late Presidents Tito, Nehru, Nkrumah, Nasser and their collaborators so that they would not have lived and died in vain. The Movement should grow from strength to strength as a major moral force in the maintenance of world peace and security and the fulfilment of the legitimate aspirations of the vast majority of depressed peoples of the Third World.

These great and dedicated men are no more with us, but the noble ideals which brought them together to fight a common cause in the interest of mankind, remain an ever-renewing source from which we can draw inspiration and maintain the original principles alive.

Mr President, the Non-Aligned Movement composed of small, large, strong and weak nations, has naturally not been spared its share of tensions and pressures. Efforts have been made from time to time to divide its members and sway the movement from the straight and narrow path of neutrality. We should therefore constantly be on our guard to resist all such efforts, since, like your great country, our strength lies in our unity. Being so large and diverse, the Movement is bound to have differences. But diversity should be a great source of strength with the different shades of opinion reflecting its democratic character. Our ability to reconcile differences and harmonize views has already stood the test of many stresses and of time. This should give us ever-renewing strength as our Movement grows into greater maturity.

Mr President, it was our Movement which first drew attention to the dangers inherent in the ever-widening economic gap between North and South and thus spearheaded the call for the establishment of a new international economic order as the basis for re-structuring the world economy to ensure equity, fairness and justice. We have all however, painfully become aware that the high hopes initially engendered are being thwarted by the vested, short-sighted interests of the North thus resulting in very serious economic depression at a time when the world is so richly endowed with wealth and idle funds. This sad experience however challenges us to pull more fully together the opportunities for co-operation which abound within the Non-Aligned Movement for our collective self-reliance. We span all the continents and produce a wide variety of complementary raw materials and skills. Despite our present disadvantages and weaknesses, we are potentially the most prosperous group of countries in the world. We should therefore be true partners through trade, exchange of skills and joint promotion of projects, to forge and reinforce the global grid of co-operation for our individual and collective fulfilment.

Mr President, the process of decolonization has reached Southern Africa where an oppressive and racist regime is making its last ditch but futile stand against the irresistible tide of freedom. The intransigence of the South African apartheid regime in ignoring the clearly expressed majority wishes of the United Nations constitutes a serious challenge to enlightened international opinon and should therefore be resisted until Namibia and eventually Azania are free from racist discrimination, oppression and exploitation.

Mr President, our world is still plagued by injustices, pressures and tensions, with the strong always trying to dominate the weak. Some nations still resort to the use of force or the threat of the use of force in their efforts to dictate to others by the use of superior and more deadly weapons of destruction. Our Movement should therefore strengthen its moral and economic force as a group to resist these attempts. We have to intensify our campaign not only for a limitation of weapons of mass

DG-1.

destruction but also for complete eventual disarmament so that the world can enjoy peace and security and the resources which are being wasted on armaments spent on peaceful economic development for the benefit of all mankind.

Mr President, it is a matter of great satisfaction that our bilateral relations have been based on the clear awareness and acceptance of the vital need for us to co-operate in all fields. Through our Joint Commission for Co-operation we have identified and undertaken several projects in Ghana for which your country has provided financial and technical assistance. For this, the Government and people of Ghana are most grateful and I hope that we shall continue to work even closer together in the years ahead to the mutual benefit of our two countries and peoples.

Your Excellency, I thank you most sincerely for the great honour you have done me and my country this evening in conferring upon me one of your country's highest national awards. This honour, which I share with all Ghanaians, once again reaffirms the very strong bonds of friendship that exist and should continue to prevail between our two sister countries. I shall cherish, as a lasting remembrance, this momentous visit to your great country.

Finally, Mr President, let me express on my own behalf and on behalf of my entourage our deepest gratitude for the warm reception which was accorded us on our arrival and the generous hospitality which we have received in your friendly country.

And now, Excellencies, distinguished ladies and gentlemen, may I kindly ask you to join me in drinking a toast to the health of His Excellency the President of the Presidency of the Socialist Federal Republic of Yugoslavia, to closer co-operation between Ghana and Yugoslavia and to world peace.

Long live the Socialist Federal Republic of Yugoslavia.

Long live Ghana–Yugoslav friendship and co-operation.

32

The President in Bonn

At a luncheon in his honour on 26 May 1981, the President said:

It is for me and my entourage a very great pleasure to have the occasion of meeting you and through you the great people of the Federal Republic of Germany. Even though my visit is very brief, I shall go back with the satisfaction that the Federal Republic of Germany was included in my first visit outside the African continent.

The relationships between our two countries have been characterized by understanding, genuine friendship, sympathy and mutual respect and it is my determination that these relationships will be maintained and even enhanced.

Mr President, Excellencies, about twenty months ago, the people of Ghana freely chose a form of government in which freedom and justice would prevail and in which human dignity would be respected. This option imposes a heavy responsibility on us, but we are confident that with the support of dependable and long-standing friends like you, we shall be able to overcome all our difficulties.

We attach particular importance to the special relationship between our two peoples. This dates from the nineteenth century when Bremen missionaries set foot on our soil, and the good work they started is being continued in several other spheres by your compatriots. This special relationship was recently further demonstrated when we had the pleasure of playing host to His Excellency Herr Richard Stucklen, President of the German Bundestag. To us, his visit reflected the confidence which your government has in our new democratic institutions, and we trust that you will give us the necessary co-operation to safeguard these institutions.

Mr President, we are extremely grateful for the substantial assistance that your Government provides to my country. We greatly value the assistance as well as the economic co-operation existing between our two countries and we hope that our visit will go a long way in strengthening that co-operation.

Mr President, on the international scene, my Administration views with grave concern the increase in violence and conflicts throughout the world. In the present times of economic interdependence, conflicts in other parts of the world have inevitable repercussions on all of us. It is partly for this reason that we expect influential nations like yours to continue to play leading roles in finding peaceful solutions to such conflicts. On the African continent, we are confident that the Federal Republic of Germany will continue to play a leading role among the five Western Contact Group of Nations in rapidly finding a peaceful and negotiated settlement in Namibia.

Mr President, Your Excellencies, distinguished guests, I would like to conclude these brief remarks by expressing to you personally and to the Government and people of the Federal Republic of Germany my deepest gratitude and appreciation for the kindness that they have shown to me and my delegation during our brief visit. When I leave your shores, I shall return home with very happy memories and also with the hope that the discussions we have held here will yield concrete results for the mutual benefit of our two peoples.

Now ladies and gentlemen, it is my very great pleasure and privilege to ask you all to rise and drink a toast to the health and prosperity of His Excellency Dr Karl Carsterns, President of the Federal Republic of Germany, to the Government and people of this great country and to the friendship between our country and yours.

33

Address to the German Association of Chambers of Industry and Commerce 26 May 1981

Evidently an important occasion, the President felt privileged to speak to his audience.

It is a great privilege for me to have the opportunity to address this august gathering of distinguished Members of the German Association of Chambers of Industry and Commerce. Even though my visit to your great country is a rather brief one, I am nonetheless grateful for this meeting with representatives of industry, trade and finance to exchange views on our long-standing relations and on investment opportunities in Ghana.

Mr President, given the crippling debts and the shattered economic infrastructure my Administration inherited, we urgently need large infusions of institutional and private investment since our own efforts are woefully inadequate for resuscitating our economy as quickly as our public expect. Rapid recovery will provide us with the resources needed to further stabilize our freely chosen socio-political system and also to enhance our mutually beneficial partnership for greater progress.

We fully appreciate the concern of prospective investors about guarantees for the commitment of funds. Indeed, we want trade and mutually beneficial economic ventures and in turn, we offer you investment opportunities. During the past twenty months, we have seriously tackled the problem of political stability. We are however also convinced that economic stability is the best guarantee for political stability. We seek to protect risk capital and to ensure the repatriation of earned profits. That is why we have tried, since assuming office, to create the expected investment climate. These endeavours deserve your positive, unreserved and massive encouragement.

Mr President, after nearly a decade of political setbacks, Ghana has freely and consciously opted for the democratic system of government in the firm conviction that it best meets the legitimate aspirations of her people. However, the ultimate success of this system also depends heavily on how quickly we shall be able to solve the enormous problems which have long hampered the aspirations and hopes of our people.

Aware of these socio-economic and political realities, we have taken steps to lay sound foundations for rapid recovery, steady growth and eventual take-off by reordering our priorities very carefully. We have embarked on the rehabilitation of our long-neglected infrastructures, industries and institutions directly connected with sound economic activities.

We have instituted measures of discipline in the administration of our public finances and streamlined our import licence programme. Besides effectively controlling public expenditure, we have also launched a policy of phased liberalization by removing institutional controls which hamper smooth economic activities and distort commodity and factor prices.

Our new import programme and careful husbanding of resources have enabled us to settle our short-term bills on due dates and also to make modest repayments of some minor old debts. I note with some satisfaction that these efforts seem to have improved our image and regenerated some international confidence in us as credit-worthy and dependable trading partners.

Distinguished ladies and gentlemen, our own foreign exchange resources have, however, greatly dwindled over the past decade. At the same time our import needs have greatly been encumbered by crippling crude oil import bills and thus severely limited our ability to import vital industrial inputs and spare parts to revive the economy. The result has been a traumatic, all-round reduction in the productive capacity of all sectors of our economy, hence our urgent need for substantial injections of foreign investment to enable us to bridge the foreign exchange gap. We will also welcome entrepreneurial and managerial skills for the efficient utilization and absorption of investment funds.

Our investment laws have been reappraised in our new investment Code now before Parliament. The Investment Code re-defines the areas of our economy in which foreign investment is most needed and also provides new guidelines on equity participation. In short, the Code seeks to protect and guarantee investment and offers investors a wide range of exemptions and incentives in the priority sectors of the economy. Limitless and attractive investment opportunities therefore await you in Ghana and I hope that you will avail yourselves of them.

My Administration has placed agriculture at the top of our priorities. We rate gold mining, prospecting for and exploitation of fossil minerals very highly. We have already organized an international seminar on Ghana's Gold Endowment and highlighted our gold ore potentialities and also drawn attention to numerous other minerals as well as off-shore natural gas. The timber and tourist industries also offer great investment opportunities.

In order to make investment meaningful, my Administration has embarked on the rehabilitation of our road infrastructure, railways and telecommunication facilities. We are also bending all our efforts to develop our enormous renewable energy resources. In addition to the existing Akosombo and the now almost completed Kpong Dam, plans are well advanced for the construction of the Bui Dam.

Mr President, distinguished ladies and gentlemen, we have drawn up and submitted to Parliament a five-year Economic Development Programme costed at about twenty-five billion cedis in local and foreign currency. For its implementation, we have initiated very ambitious domestic and external policies to restructure our economy and enable it to generate domestic and foreign savings. The Plan period, however, also reveals a yawning foreign exchange gap to be filled. I am therefore drawing your kind attention to this and invite your favourable consideration.

Mr President, the efforts my Administration has made since 24 September 1979 amply show our determination to give a powerful stimulus to business activities to lift Ghana out of the abyss and propel it to economic recovery, growth and prosperity. We therefore count on you quickly to translate your goodwill into meaningful economic activities. Furthermore, on the threshold of a new era of economic recovery, of democratic rule in an atmosphere of peace, stability, freedom and justice, you should assume your role in our collective endeavours to uphold, promote and defend this option. I am confident that the people of Ghana can count on your understanding, support and friendship.

34

Back in Accra from his European Tour

He speaks to the Press and dignitaries who have come to the airport to welcome him.

My entourage and I are very happy to be back home, safe and sound, after packing and unpacking our travelling bags almost every other day since 12 May on a tour which took us to the United Kingdom, Yugoslavia, Romania, the Federal Republic of Germany and Sierra Leone. We have simply been overwhelmed by the spontaneity and the warmth of the receptions accorded us everywhere abroad and now by you back at home right now. We are indeed very happy to be back amongst you.

We wish to take this opportunity to express our very sincere thanks to you all for this warm welcome and also for the many goodwill messages sent us during the tour. Those messages were a great source of encouragement to us. They demonstrated that although we were out of your sight we were always present in your minds. They convinced us that the nation was solidly behind us in our quest for ways and means of solving our economic problems.

The visits were primarily goodwill missions meant to consolidate, expand and strengthen our bilateral relations with the host countries. We therefore took advantage of them to explore ways of intensifying our respective economic co-operation ventures and activities. Apart from official Government to Government discussions we also made contacts with industrialists, bankers, Chambers of Commerce, individuals and journalists. In all our contacts and discussions we highlighted Ghana, West Africa, Africa, the Non-Aligned Movement, the Third World and global problems. Views expressed were frank and sincere on both sides and we can report that the visits were very successful, judging by the enormous fund of goodwill shown towards Ghana wherever we went. The perspective held out to us promises a bright future if we can make good and successful use of them. Since others wish us well so much, we can hardly wish ourselves ill. I therefore hope that we will all co-operate sincerely, honestly and actively with our friends and well-wishers abroad and help them to help us.

I am sure that you all join me in expressing my deepest appreciation and gratitude to the friendly people of all the countries visited for the very warm, cordial and friendly receptions accorded me and my entourage at every stage of our visit and also for their hospitality during our brief stay with each of them. We were received everywhere with great enthusiasm and open arms by people who appeared to be highly pleased to see Ghana back again on the international scene at the highest representational and governmental level.

The efforts we are making to resuscitate our economy and the determination of all Ghanaians to rebuild our country were sincerely and greatly appreciated. This goodwill necessarily made our job a lot easier. I can also assure you that no effort was spared in explaining the peculiarities of our situation and the reasons behind certain policy decisions we have taken, which sometimes were misconstrued by international agencies or even by our own public.

In all our discussions, our hosts appreciated the fact that the success of the democratic system of government we had freely chosen is a vital prerequisite for steady economic growth. We also assured them that Ghanaians firmly believe that the system best meets our aspirations, and guarantees for us all freedom, human dignity, justice and equality. We therefore appealed to our audience to fully appreciate and help us sustain our efforts at making democracy work in Ghana. Naturally, since political stability thrives only in an atmosphere of peace, economic stability and steady growth, the recovery of our economy became the focal point of all our discussions.

Our efforts at reordering of our priorities, the austerity measures we have taken, the streamlining of the administration of our national finances, gradual decontrolling of the economy and the concomitant new stresses being created were all understood and highly appreciated. Many private investors have shown great enthusiasm and interest in the economy of Ghana. In particular, the discipline we have imposed in the import-export trade and in the allocation of import licences, the repayment of short-term debts on due dates, and the many other economic policies initiated in the field of agriculture, transport and communications, mining and the draft Investment Code Bill have all evoked much attention and appreciation in all the centres we have visited.

The host governments and private sectors now understand our situation better and have pledged to assist us not only bilaterally but also in international circles. For instance, the United Kingdom, one of our traditional trading partners, agreed to increase its credit guarantee cover for exports to Ghana and therefore signed a new agreement for £40 million under the ECGD. Four major British Banks have also agreed to give us 180 days credit cover for exports to Ghana. The German government is also actively reconsidering the restoration of their guarantee scheme, the HERMIS, which had been withdrawn following repeated defaulting under previous Ghana Governments in honouring our debt obligations. In brief, greater understanding of our problems and of the efforts and sacrifices we are making to solve them have been generated in the United Kingdom and the Federal Republic of Germany.

Our visit to Yugoslavia where we took the opportunity to reaffirm our conviction in the principles of the Non-Aligned Movement co-founded by late Presidents Nkrumah and Tito of blessed memory, was extremely useful. It was mutually agreed that greater bilateral economic co-operation must be encouraged. Also, increased co-operation and contacts between all member states of the Non-Aligned Movement was urged in order to enhance its moral, political and economic strength in maintaining international peace and security.

On the bilateral level, major decisions on greater co-operation centred especially in the agricultural field, namely, the establishment of new farms for producing maize and also sunflowers for edible oil. To this end, experts are expected to arrive here within the next few weeks to start activities on chosen sites. One giant Belgrade agricultural company called PKB has also agreed to collaborate with GIHOC in creating new farms and revitalizing such GIHOC Divisions which utilize agro-based raw materials. Energoinvest already active in Ghana, is seriously considering participating in the Bui Dam project and rural electrification schemes.

As a long term plan, Yugoslav authorities have also expressed interest in extending the present Takoradi–Awaso railway line to Sunyani to open up access to bauxite deposits at Nyinahin in which they have expressed considerable interest. This also opens up perspectives for the construction of an integrated aluminium complex.

In Romania we reaffirmed our determination to be friends to all, enemies to none. We reviewed our bilateral relations and agreed on greater economic co-operation, especially in agriculture where, again, a number of maize farms are to be established within an agreed timetable. Romania has also agreed to resume joint exploration for oil here.

We took the opportunity to express the heartfelt gratitude of the Government and people of Ghana to the Government and people of Romania for the kind and loving care they took of the late Osagyefo Dr Kwame Nkrumah during his last days in that country. We visited the hospital where he spent his last days and paid homage to the memory of our first President. In brief, our economic revival was our major concern throughout the goodwill missions. At all stages we emphasized that the world had talked about co-operation for far too long and that the time had now come for concrete action. We have re-established confidence in Ghana and should therefore take all necessary steps to ensure concrete realization of the projects and joint ventures agreed upon during our tour.

As is our usual policy and practice, we met cross-sections of Ghanaians resident in the countries visited. To all of them we conveyed your fraternal greetings and held extensive discussions with them on the situation at home. We appealed to them to observe the municipal laws of their host countries and also to comport themselves so as to enhance the good name of Ghana. We encouraged students who had completed their courses of studies to return home and help rebuild the country. These meetings, held in an atmosphere of reunion, frankness and cordiality, were very fruitful. Your friends, relatives and fellow citizens send you their greetings and best wishes.

On our way back home, we stopped in Freetown, Sierra Leone to attend the ECOWAS summit where the need to implement decisions on greater economic co-operation in our sub-region was re-emphasized as a major step towards the realization of the objectives of the Organization and of North-South economic relations. The ECOWAS Summit also re-examined and completed deliberations on the need for a joint ECOWAS defence pact.

Once again, we are very happy indeed to be back home and thank all of you most sincerely for the very warm reception you have accorded us.

35

In the Federal Republic of Nigeria

Ghana shares with the Federal Republic of Nigeria a common background of colonial and post-colonial experience, history and, not least, political and economic institutions and aspirations.

Social interaction and accommodation of each other's nationals have characterized the long-standing accord and practice between the two states.

The President, Dr Hilla Limann, in his speech at a durbar followed by a luncheon, recalled these happy relations and looked forward to more mutual co-operation.

On behalf of the Government and people of Ghana and on my own behalf, I should like to thank you, the Government and the people of Nigeria for the warm friendship and generous hospitality accorded us since our arrival in this historic city. I should also like to express to you personally, Excellency, our profound gratitude for the many fraternal and kind gestures you have been making towards us since last July.

You have eloquently demonstrated your solidarity with us at a time when we are passing through a most critical period of our history. We attach great importance to this spirit of solidarity. Indeed, this prompted me to plan my first official visit outside Ghana to you personally, to express our appreciation and gratitude, but the calls on both of us on assuming our new offices have been so numerous and urgent that it has not been possible for us to meet earlier than now. I am therefore exceedingly happy to be here today at long last.

Ghana and Nigeria have shared close ties of cordial friendship and co-operation even long before our accession to independence. During our common, long colonial past, our two countries had to go through similar development and experiences. We have acquired similar attitudes of mind and even tastes. Our socio-cultural, economic and political evolution has followed the same path and it is not surprising that both of us have recently emerged from military regimes to popularly elected governments. Our constitutional preference for republicanism, based on the concept of separation of powers and checks and balances *à la* Montesquieu has also turned out to be largely the same. Indeed our

171

actions, reactions and interactions tend to be intimately linked and our destinies inseparable; events in each of our two countries, for good or bad, set our peoples thinking.

Excellency, the potentialities for our bilateral co-operation are limitless and we in Ghana are prepared, as I hope that you are also, to exploit these potentialities to the full through the Ghana-Nigeria Joint Commission of Co-operation which can be used as a veritable instrument of partnership for advancing the economic and social horizons of our peoples.

Your Excellency, the focal point of Ghana's foreign policy, like that of Nigeria, is Africa. I am happy to recall the central role played by our two countries in the liberation struggle, the unity of Africa and the solidarity of the Third World. Indeed the dramatic transformation of the map of Africa has resulted from the firm foundations our two countries laid in the 1950s and 1960s.

We therefore welcome with profound satisfaction and joy the happy outcome of the recent elections in Zimbabwe and the resounding victory of the Patriotic Forces of Dr Mugabe and Mr Nkomo. That victory is a fiting vindication of the common front taken by Africa and also the Commonwealth initiatives taken at the meetings held here in Lagos in 1965, in Lusaka and London during which Nigeria played a consistent and highly appreciated role. Given the right orientation, the Commonwealth association of which we are both members, can, like the OAU, play a vital role in Africa and in international affairs.

We should continue to assist young liberated Zimbabwe in the greater challenges of reconciliation, reconstruction and nation-building now confronting it. The new turn of events in Zimbabwe should also sharpen the conscience of all concerned countries to come forward and help complete the unfinished task of liquidating the remnants of colonialism and racism in Namibia and Azania. Until every inch of African soil is completely free from colonialism and racism, we have to consider our continent threatened. Our freedom is indivisible.

Your Excellency, the circumstances of our time compel us to direct our efforts and focus our attention on our mutual economic co-operation and development. The deterioration in the international economic order, the unprecedented levels of inflation and economic stagnation and the massive imbalances of trade payments constitute immense pressures on us all, thus threatening the stability of all African governments. We must therefore urgently evolve measures to redress these imbalances.

As developing countries, our progress can be guaranteed only when we pool our resources together and make a supreme effort to tackle the complex difficulties facing us since they do not easily lend themselves to segmentary solutions. We highly appreciate our membership of the Economic Community of West African States (ECOWAS) through which we can strive to foster the widest possible co-operation within our sub-region in which similar economic and developmental problems plague us. We commend the tireless efforts of Nigeria which was one of the initiators and moving spirits behind the establishment of this collective wisdom and vision designed to remove the constraints of limited domestic markets, skills, technology and investment funds. In the challenging task of promoting our collective will, I assure Your Excellency that you can count on the active co-operation of my Government. The recent ratification by our Parliament of the Protocol relating to the free movement of persons and goods clearly manifests our faith in the ECOWAS.

Naturally, we have also necessarily to look beyond co-operation within our sub-region to co-operation on a continental and universal basis. Indeed ECOWAS can realize its fullest potential only within the wider context of inter-African and world-wide co-operation. We, therefore, appreciate and heartily welcome your initiative in readily agreeing to host the Extraordinary Summit Meeting of the OAU to consider economic co-operation on a continental scale. Such an opportunity should enable us to chart a new course for the economic emancipation of our continent and thus make our political independence more real and meaningful.

Excellency, I should like to express our appreciation to you personally, to your Government and to all the people of Nigeria for the very warm hospitality you have accorded us and also our nationals in your great country. I hope that the latter will live in peace and harmony with their hosts and brothers so as to avoid any more unfortunate incidents as have repeatedly happened in the recent past. We trust that their stay here will help foster the spirit of African co-operation and unity. They should scrupulously abide by the laws of their host country.

May I now request Your Excellencies, ladies and gentlemen to join me in drinking a toast to the continued good health, success and prosperity of His Excellency Alhaji Shehu Shagari, President of the Republic of Nigeria, to the abiding friendship of Ghana and Nigeria and to African solidarity and unity.

Long live Ghana and Nigeria! Long live the ECOWAS! Long live the OAU and world peace!

36

In the Republic of Mali

In the speech of the President, on the occasion of his friendly visit to the Republic of Mali on 24 March 1981, his audience heard echoes of the past imperial co-existence of ancient Ghana, Mali and Songhai in reference to the latter-day understanding behind the Ghana-Guinea-Mali Union.

My delegation and I have been in your great country for barely twenty-four hours now but have already been impressed and even overwhelmed at times by the sincere and brotherly affection and solidarity shown towards us. These warm sentiments have been reinforced by the impressive reception and the expression of friendship so eloquently conveyed by your short welcome address.

Excellency, although overwhelmed, we are not surprised; friendship between our two peoples springs from the strong historical and cultural origins and interactions which have not been weakened even by time and distance or by our different colonial experiences. From time immemorial human and material traffic have regularly and unceasingly moved between our two counties. This has resulted in the establishment of large colonies of our nationals in each other's country. The contributions which these entrepreneurs have made to our respective economies have been vital and commendable.

Your Excellency, my visit to Mali would not have been complete without a visit to this great city. In the historic and productive interaction between our peoples, the City of Mopti occupies pride of place. It was from this great centre that the long cattle routes and trade started and went right down to Kumasi and far beyond to the Atlantic coast. It was also at the confluence of the Rivers Niger and Bani here that the famous fishing centre exported its products not only to Ghana but to other neighbouring countries of our sub-region. Indeed, our own Volta Lake is stocked with fish supplied from this fish depot. The legendary resourcefulness and enterprising spirit of merchants of Mopti are worthy of emulation in our efforts to develop our natural resources on a co-operative basis.

Perhaps the Governor of Mopti may wish to examine with his counterpart of Kumasi the possibility of twinning their two cities with a view to putting their long-standing historical ties on a firm and formal footing, the better to broaden the special relations existing between them. The Mopti–Kumasi axis provides a ready-made foundation for this. . . .

Your Excellency, on behalf of my delegation, on behalf of the Government and people of Ghana and on my own behalf, I must express our deepest sense of appreciation and gratitude to you for this refreshingly genuine brotherly and African welcome accorded us since our arrival yesterday. Kindly therefore permit me also to transmit through you the fraternal salutations and sentiments of friendship from the Government and people of Ghana to your good self and the Government and people of the sister Republic of Mali.

Excellency and distinguished guests, I consider this visit a veritable pilgrimage and a re-affirmation of our common roots and history. As I have already hinted, this was part of the area of the great African Empires of Ghana, Mali and Songhai whose intellectual and cultural excellences were renowned throughout the world and have become our collective inheritance, the source of our instinctive sense of human sensitivity and dignity, our pride in ourselves and our unflinching determination to live nobly even in 'dignified poverty'.

Your Excellency Mr President, this visit recaptures the visions and ideals which inspired the bold and unique adventure in political union of the Ghana-Guinea-Mali Union. Though brief in its existence, it was the first concrete expression of Africa's desire for freedom in unity and diversity. It set the stage for what has long become our Continental Organization, the recent Lagos Plan of Action and the Economic Community of West African States (ECOWAS).

Distinguished guests, recent revolutionary technological developments have accelerated time and annihilated space. The world has therefore shrunk into a much smaller community now than ever before. The new challenges facing mankind call for frequent consultations and collaboration in our search for sanity, peace, stability and an equitable world economic order.

The major unresolved problem facing the international community has long been the deteriorating global economic order with its resultant stresses, tensions, irrationalism, conflicts, fatalism and the growing helplessness of mankind in the face of unemployment, inflation, energy crises, dwindling resources and chronic imbalances of payments which frustrate the legitimate aspirations of our peoples. We must all therefore do some hard rethinking to evolve solutions and sensitivities which can respond quickly and adequately to the plight of mankind.

In this regard, Excellencies, the Third World faces the formidable challenges of pulling its peoples out of the depressing conditions of poverty, hunger, illiteracy and diseases to levels that befit human dignity. Our collective salvation can be secured through our regional and continental organizations which have been designed for our political liberation and economic emancipation. It is to this end that we strongly support the ECOWAS and the Lagos Plan of Action.

On the bilateral level, we must increase and strengthen our co-operation in all fields without which our sub-regional and continental co-operation will be meaningless. That is why we attach great importance to the Ghana-Mali Joint Commission for Co-operation which has just completed its sixth Session in this beautiful city.

Mr President, our efforts to maintain peace, stability and harmony in our sub-region and throughout the world are being systematically assailed by ill-conceived and misguided policies of others, even within our continent. This weakens us economically much to the benefit of our external detractors, including apartheid South Africa. If we cannot deplore the tragic cruelties of our own societies, how can we continue to condemn those who oppress our brothers and sisters elsewhere?

South Africa which still keeps Namibia in colonial bondage and oppresses the black population of Azania under its inhuman system, can only continue to laugh at us, defy enlightened world opinion and United Nations resolutions if we are heartless towards ourselves. We therefore condemn human cruelties and unusual forms of punishment in every part of our globe. We condemn South Africa's aggressions against the Frontline States. Only a determined, united and sensitive Africa can ensure the success of our objectives of social justice and the liberation of Namibia and Azania.

Mr President, the problems of Chad and the Western Sahara pose serious challenges to our organization's ability to solve its problems in peace, freedom and justice we must, in all fairness, judge ourselves by the same yardstick we use to judge others. Just as the people of Namibia have a right to self-determination, so do the people of Chad and the Western Sahara.

Mr President, under your leadership, Mali has maintained a high profile and effective presence in the OAU and the ECOWAS. In our bilateral relations your wise counsel has been invaluable in our joint efforts to strengthen our common bonds and co-operation. These qualities have enabled you to manage your domestic affairs successfully against all odds. I wish you continued and increasing successes in the years ahead. You can count on the support and solidarity of the Government and people of Ghana as we struggle together to fulfil the aspirations of our two peoples for a better tomorrow in peace, stability and unity.

Long live Ghana-Mali friendship, co-operation and solidarity!

Long live the ECOWAS!

Long live the OAU!

37

Official Visit to Senegal: Arrival statement at Yofi-Dakar International Airport 19 February 1981

I feel very highly honoured to be the first Head of State to have been invited by His Excellency President Abdou Diouf and his Administration to pay an official state visit to the Republic of Senegal. Mr President, I and my entourage have come to share with you the happy event of your smooth assumption of office.

We bring you the very best wishes of the Government and people of Ghana for your howling success now and for the future.

The smooth process of the recent changes here in the 'Gateway to West Africa' from Europe and the maturity and serenity accompanying them have attracted the admiration not only of Ghanaians but, indeed, of all other peoples and governments throughout Africa and the entire world. I therefore wish personally to renew my very warm congratulations to you, your Government and the people of Senegal.

Your Excellency, my entourage and I are deeply moved by the very warm welcome just accorded us. We very highly appreciate the kind sentiments you have expressed about us and our country which forms part of the real geo-political and physical heartland of our sub-region and continent as evidenced by the fact that whenever Ghana catches a cold, the whole of Africa sneezes, so much so that the infection tends to spread far beyond our continent. Dakar was the last point of retreat of Free Fighting France in 1940–1. Takoradi, in the then Gold Coast, now Ghana, was the real launching pad from where the Allies regained their balance and re-launched their offensive which eventually determined the course and end of World War II.

We wish to assure you that Ghana cannot, dares not, must not and shall therefore not remain in the backwaters of history and that my Administration is determined to bring about our economic recovery and growth for the upliftment of the living conditions of our people, within the general framework of the forward movement and progress of our people, within the general framework of the forward movement and progress of all mankind.

No power in the world should therefore write our two countries off now or in the foreseeable future. Being kind-hearted and generous, we have never demanded the payment of the inestimable debt and compensation that both the West and the East owe us despite their present affluence and arrogance. Curiously enough, the countries of the Axis of that time have been more genuinely helpful to us and our sub-region since then. 'Caveat Emptor' or 'Let the buyer beware'. 'Magnas est veritas et prevalabit'.

In coming here today we have realized a long-felt wish. The land of Leopold Sedar Senghor has always commanded our interest and respect and we are therefore very happy to be here among a people with whom we share very many ideals and aspirations. Indeed, our goodwill visits to the countries of our sub-region would not be complete without our coming here. We are grateful that you have promptly made this possible so soon after our brief meeting in Lomé.

The visit brings my Government in contact with yours in a personal and most desirable way and affords us the chance to meet your people, to learn of your future plans for them and of your past achievements. It also affords us the opportunity to exchange views on the current problems confronting our two countries and Africa; on the continuing search for a more just, equitable, humane and socio-economic world order, on the ways and means of protecting and defending the independence of our continent, and above all, on how to enhance the freedom of our peoples while improving upon their social, economic and political well-being.

In short, Mr President, this visit will sharpen our awareness of what we have in common, what we can achieve and how we can work in close co-operation towards the advancement of our peoples. I look forward to fruitful discussions with you.

38

In The Gambia

At a State durbar held in his honour by Sir Dawda Jawara, President of the Gambia, on 18 February 1981, the atmosphere was good neighbourliness and the theme was 'Each His Neighbour's Keeper'. Cooperation between African States in fighting for freedom, decency and economic well-being was the theme of the following address.

I have risen with the greatest respect and humility to reply to the toast of my brother and colleague, President Jawara.

First, I wish to re-emphasize the profound gratitude of my entourage for the warm, spontaneous and tumultuous reception accorded us since our arrival in Banjul. This gesture, Mr President, has underscored the brotherly feelings that have always characterized Ghana-Gambian relations. We are most grateful for the great honour done me and Ghana by extending your special invitation to us to attend your sixteenth independence anniversary celebrations. This has also enabled us to realize our plan to complete our goodwill visits to the member countries of our West African sub-region before we travel further afield. We are most grateful to you for your understanding, patience and kind gesture. Above all, we are particularly grateful for conferring on me and members of the Ghana delegation these gracious Awards.

Mr President, sixteen years is a short time in the history of the majority of the nations of our present world. However, in our continent we attach great importance to such occasions. The evolution of our countries requires us to pause, from time to time, to take stock of our work and draw up the balance sheet of our successes and failures. This, like similar celebrations, therefore calls for sober reflections on the lives of the members of our respective societies and the health of our nations hence my wish to take the liberty this evening briefly to refer to the evolution of the Gambia.

Long before I ever dreamt of engaging in open, active politics, I had watched your political scene with keen personal interest, particularly, ever since I stopped over here on 17 January 1965, in my search abroad for knowledge. I have, more precisely and intensively, admired as a student of political science, the peaceful and stable atmosphere that has reigned in the Gambia since 1965.

Your Excellency's ability, throughout these years, to maintain your economic and social momentum in the Shylock-like realities of our global economic difficulties, worsened by ever-escalating fuel crises and the uncontrollable natural phenomenon of the Sahelian drought and crop failures has been remarkable and has thus attracted much favourable attention in Africa and further afield. The secrets which have made such singular achievements possible therefore greatly interest me and many other African political leaders.

The vast majority of the people of modern Ghana as recreated by the late Osagyefo of blessed memory are only too happy to be associated with their brothers and sisters of the Gambia for their identical values outlooks and ideals. We sincerely hope that these cordial and excellent relations will continue to grow from strength to strength in the coming years.

It is to this end that the People's National Party Administration has directed the urgent conclusion of a formal Co-operative Agreement between our two countries and we have happily noted that our respective experts have recently met here in Banjul and successfully concluded negotiations on a wide range of subjects that would enhance benefits for our peoples by bringing us even closer together as envisioned by Osagyefo Dr Kwame Nkrumah of blessed memory and others like your good self, in the concept of the unity of independent and sovereign states of Africa. The objective of the People's National Party Administration of Ghana, Mr President, is to intensify inter-African co-operation in which none of us would merely be at the receiving end, but relations which should be based on or inspire mutual respect and trust.

Mr President, the type of vertical co-operation between the developed and developing countries in which aid is almost exclusively geared towards the production of commodities required by developed countries neither promotes the rapid solution of our common problems nor benefits the vast majority of our respective populations.

The consolidation of bilateral and inter-African relations is therefore absolutely necessary to enable us to concert our efforts, skills, means and potentialities and thus move ahead into a position of strength so that we can help our other less fortunate brothers and sisters elsewhere, particularly in southern Africa, who still labour under alien domination and also in the less richly endowed parts of our continent. To this end, Mr President, the ECOWAS provided opportunities for the intensification of our co-operation in partnership with others. Ghana is fully committed to its goals and aspirations since it holds great promises for the economic development of our sub-region for a sound start.

Admittedly, the kind of regional integration ECOWAS envisages will take a long time to materialize. But even now we are all delighted that its institutions are gradually taking shape. The entry into force of the Protocol on the Free Movement of Persons brings the idea of an

ECOWAS common citizenship a step closer to realization. With the passage of time we may all come to feel and act as citizens of one great federated country.

The beginnings of unity inherent in the idea of common citizenship evokes heart throbbings since it represents one form of the dream of African Unity which the Founding Fathers of modern Ghana, led by the late Dr Kwame Nkrumah together with Your Excellency and other great sons of Africa, living and dead, have greatly cherished.

Mr President, as Africans we cannot turn a Nelson's eye on recent events in southern Africa. The joy of Zimbabwe's achievement of independence was shared by us all. Namibia's freedom can no longer be delayed. But the racist Pretoria regime seems to be determined to subvert the time-table endorsed by the United Nations for Namibia's orderly attainment of true national independence. The breakdown in the recent Geneva pre-implementation talks was a deliberate act of sabotage.

We should condemn this unfortunate turn of events and remain committed to the recognition of SWAPO as the sole authentic voice of the people of Namibia. We shall support any sanctions and other measures which the United Nations may impose to compel South Africa to enable Namibia to progress unimpeded to genuine independence.

Mr President, Banjul has recently been the site of the formulation of the African Charter on Human and People's Rights. This was not surprising, for in this beautiful and peaceful country, you have established a climate of tolerance and understanding which has ensured respect for the dignity of man, the sanctity of his person and the realization of fundamental human rights. It was therefore fitting for the Ministers assembled here to have recommended and that this Convention should be known as the Banjul African Charter on Human and People's Rights. For my part, I endorse this proposal. I am told that the Charter was adopted on the Birthday of the Holy Prophet Mohammed, Peace be unto Him. It was a propitious gift to the people of the Gambia on the eve of their sixteenth birthday as an independent sovereign nation.

I congratulate you, Mr President, and through you, the worthy people of the Gambia. I wish you all eternal enjoyment of peace, security, stability, progress and prosperity which together with political independence, are indivisible.

Ladies and gentlemen, I now wish to invite you to join me in a toast to the people of the Gambia and to their most outstanding son, the Father of the Nation and President of the Republic, His Excellency Alhaji Sir Dawda Jawara.

Long live the independence of the Gambia. Long live Ghana–Gambia co-operation and solidarity. Long live the ECOWAS. Floreat United Africa.

39

In Benin

The President of Ghana addressed the leader and the people of the People's Republic of Benin, 16 May 1980, during his goodwill visit to that country.

My delegation feels deeply touched by your warm words of welcome and by the generous hospitality showered on us since our arrival in your beautiful capital of Cotonou. On behalf of the Government and people of Ghana, we wish to thank you for this demonstration of cordial friendship and solidarity which reflects the traditional ties between our two countries.

We have come personally to renew the old, tested friendship between our two countries and peoples, to get acquainted with each other, to compare experiences and to derive mutual benefit from such a direct contact. At all levels of discussion, we have been impressed by the genuine hospitality, goodwill and understanding which the brotherly people and leaders of the People's Republic of Benin have always shown towards Ghanaians and unfolding events in Ghana.

Your Excellency, permit me to congratulate you on your recent election to the high office of President of the People's Republic of Benin under the new constitution which is the fundamental law. By your resounding election the people of Benin have demonstrated their un-shaken and massive confidence in your outstanding qualities of leadership.

One of Ghana's cardinal principles is a strict adherence to a policy of non-interference in the domestic affairs of other countries. We also fervently believe that every sovereign country has the exclusive right to choose its own social, economic and political system which is best in fostering the welfare and progress of its people. We therefore admire and applaud the magnificent achievements of the people of Benin in this regard. You have amply demonstrated that with hard work, dedication and inspired leadership a country like yours with limited natural resources can accomplish a great deal, to the discomfiture of cynics and prophets of doom. This remarkable achievement is a tribute to Your Excellency's great vision, to the combination of ideological clarity and African pragmatism which have generated the economic gains so far made by your talented people under your able leadership. Naturally, this has provoked envy, hatred and enmity among mere slogan-mongers, traitors and quislings who shamelessly collaborated with reactionary international forces to invade your country in order to reverse the positive gains of the October Revolution. However, thanks to their eternal vigilance and steadfastness, the people of Benin heroically and courageously repelled that aggression and thus stoutly defended and consolidated their gains. We are confident that the measures adopted by the OAU to check the incidence of mercenary adventurism in Africa in the wake of your experience, will forestall the recurrence of such activities elsewhere.

Excellency, we are proud of our joint collaboration in the political field, and particularly in the area of decolonization and the elimination of oppression and apartheid in Africa. As a result of our concerted efforts the reactionary forces of colonialism and racism have been routed and are everywhere on the retreat. The emergence of Zimbabwe to independence is the culmination of many years of joint struggle. This should strengthen our hands and encourage us to continue to struggle till Africa is truly free and united. For this final onslaught on the bastions of colonialism and racism, Africa needs to mobilize its energies and forces rather than waste them in wanton fratricidal wars. We thus fervently appeal to our brothers now engaged in destructive civil wars to lay down their arms and find peaceful solutions to their differences in the supreme interest of their people and of mother Africa.

Your Excellency, I am happy to observe that our co-operation also encompasses the economic and social sectors as well and has been expanding in scope. Thanks to the success of your agricultural revolution, your country has been filling a significant gap in making up Ghana's shortfalls in the supply of maize and other food items. The Ghana–Benin Permanent Joint Co-operation offers a sound basis for greater co-operation and mutual self-help for the benefit of our peoples. The potential for fruitful bilateral co-operation is, indeed, great and we are determined to exploit it to the full. This will be supportive of our wider co-operation in ECOWAS which seeks to promote the economic growth of our sub-region as a whole.

I take this opportunity to thank the Government and people of Benin through you for the kind hospitality which you continue to extend to Ghana nationals in your country. I do hope that they prove themselves worthy by their contributions in advancing the overall progress of your country.

On this note, I now invite you, Excellencies, ladies and gentlemen, to join me in drinking a toast to the continued good health of President Kerekou, to abiding friendship between Ghana and the People's Republic of Benin and to the happiness and prosperity of the brotherly people of Benin.

Long live Ghana–Benin friendship and co-operation! Long live ECOWAS. Long live OAU and Africa Unity. Thank you.

40

In Upper Volta

Ghana and the land-locked neighbour north of Ghana, the Upper Volta, have enjoyed good neighbourliness since the early days of Ghana's independence. As a result, while other nations go to war over border disputes, the two countries approach their border problems through mutual negotiation and friendly demarcation of boundaries. In his speech on 9 April 1980, the President expressed satisfaction at the continuing solidarity between the two states.

It is with the greatest pleasure and a profound sense of satisfaction that I rise, first of all, to say how happy I am to be here today and to convey to you personally, Mr President, and to the people of the Upper Volta, the warmest fraternal greetings and regards of the Government and people of the Republic of Ghana.

Kindly allow me also, Mr President, to say how deeply touched I have been by the warm and spontaneous brotherly reception accorded me and my delegation and therefore to express, on my own behalf and on behalf of my delegation, our sincere gratitude for this gesture of friendship and brotherliness. Such warm demonstrations, further enhanced by this sumptuous dinner, undoubtedly transcend my individual and humble person. They reflect the historic, natural and unbreakable bonds of affinity which have always united our two peoples geographically, ethnically, and linguistically. Indeed, opportunities such as this only serve to remind us more vividly of the roots of the special links and bonds that join our two peoples so very deeply that they are merged into the immemorial past.

The 380 kilometres of artificial border that separates us has remained just that 'artificial' since it has not and never will succeed in severing or even weakening the strong and natural ties of blood and ethnicity between us. Our links with you in Upper Volta are not mere extensions of our physical proximity, but something more. They are the links and bonds of one big family with the same problems, joys and sorrows, in scope as well as in content. Given this background and understanding, it should be easy and beneficial for us to evolve common or joint solutions to our problem at all times.

Barely six months after assuming the reins of government, and despite the many problems facing our country and people, I have deemed it necessary to undertake this goodwill visit primarily to reaffirm my personal and official endorsement of our special ties and also to demonstrate our commitment to the unavoidable policy of good neighbourliness that inevitably proceeds therefrom. I have come to explore also with my colleague and dear brother ways and means of deepening as well as diversifying the existing areas of co-operation between our two countries and peoples.

This visit has already afforded me the opportunity to share and exchange views on issues of bilateral interest, on issues affecting our subregion, Africa and the international community at large.

As no country can live in isolation, neighbours such as ourselves must consult each other frequently and at all levels with a view to assessing the importance and implications of the changing drama of human interactions and how we can best face up to them. May the Bui Dam Project be a major breakthrough in our joint endeavours to improve upon our common lot.

Mr President, recent events in Africa give us joy and distress at the same time. I refer both to the happy outcome of the recent elections in Zimbabwe and the painful fratricidal civil war in the Republic of Chad. We welcome and applaud the resounding victory of the Patriotic Front Alliance, a victory which has also eloquently vindicated the common stand of Africa and of all lovers of freedom and justice. We stand ready, and indeed call upon all countries of goodwill, to assist in safeguarding the sovereignty and integrity of independent Zimbabwe in the difficult taks of rebuilding her war-torn economy to enable the long suffering and valiant people of that country to enjoy in peace the fruits of their struggle and immeasurable sacrifices. On the other hand, we thoroughly deplore the destructive conflict in Chad and hope that sanity and good sense will prevail in that sister country.

The situation in the rest of southern Africa is disturbing since our brothers and sisters in Namibia and Azania are still victims of the inhuman apartheid regime.

Racialist policies constitute a veritable threat to world peace and security and should therefore continue to be strongly resisted. Africa should collectively pledge to the valiant freedom fighters of Namibia and Azania continued and unflinching moral and material support until victory is won. South Africa should realize before it is too late that the inexorable march of history cannot be stemmed for ever and must therefore start to co-operate fully with the United Nations in the on-going negotiations for a peaceful transfer of power to the black majority of Namibia led by SWAPO.

Mr President, it is most disheartening to see Africa continue to weaken herself by dissipating her energies on internecine wars and/or territorial claims instead of pooling her resources together and closing her ranks for the final onslaught on racism, under-development, poverty, disease and hunger. We should therefore fervently appeal to our brother Africans to stop making such claims or wanton fratricidal wars, lay down their arms in the supreme interest of the lives of their peoples and work together in the common interest of mother Africa.

Your Excellency, our joint commitment to the success of our bilateral and regional organization makes it imperative for us to set the example of working effectively together to promote co-operation between our peoples in all fields and at all levels. The progress of our Border Demarcation Commission and Permanent Joint Commission for co-operation have both facilitated and promoted peace and unity between our peoples and should therefore be commended and encouraged in their good work. After this visit we should both spare no effort to make them effective instruments for mutually beneficial co-operation between our two peoples and governments.

Mr President, every close observer of the Upper Volta political and economic scene has been impressed by your personal contribution to the deep-seated needs of peace, stability and also with your beneficial involvement in the constitutional and developmental processes of your country. Indeed, thanks to your political astuteness and maturity, your unflinching commitment to the requirements of national survival, unity and progress and thanks also to the support of your people, great strides have been made in the economic and institutional developmental efforts of the Upper Volta.

These examples are worthy of emulation in our sub-region and farther afield.

An erroneously cheap campaign stunt had it last year in Ghana that I was Voltaic and should therefore be rejected by the electorate. This did not harm my prospects and I was elected. It however underscores the need for perfect peace and harmony between our two countries and peoples henceforth. Indeed, I fervently hope that nothing shall be done on either side of our common border to embarrass our two Governments and responsible citizens. Such unfortunate incidents as the one which recently involved the burning of some Upper Volta registered cars should therefore not be seen out of context or exaggerated to excite and inflame passions—the insurance companies involved should settle the matter amicably according to their regulations.

Your Excellency, kindly allow me to conclude, by once more expressing our commitment to the strengthening of the bonds of brotherhood existing between our two countries based on meaningful co-operative efforts both bilaterally and multilaterally. Our faith in the continuing solidarity and progress of our two countries and peoples are abiding and must forever remain unshakable.

With this faith and conviction I invite your excellencies, distinguished

187

guests, ladies and gentlemen, to join me in drinking a toast to this great son of Africa, His Excellency the President and our dear brother, General Sangoule Lamizana to whom we wish long life, good health, prosperity and happiness.

Long live His Excellency, President Lamizana. Long live Ghana–Upper Volta Friendship, Co-operation, Solidarity and Perfect Understanding. Long live the ECOWAS, the OAU and Africa.

41

In Guinea

At a rally organized by the Guinea Democratic Party in Conakry on 8 March 1980, the visiting President of Ghana recalled the fraternal relations between President Sékou Touré and the late Osagyefo Dr Kwame Nkrumah.

It is a great honour for me to be with you today and to have this golden opportunity to address you and the valiant people of Guinea.

Since my assumption of office as President of the Republic of Ghana, this is my first visit abroad. I can assure you that this is no mere coincidence. I could not think of going anywhere else before coming here. Even though it is my first visit to your country, I already feel very much at home.

Your excellency, I bring fraternal greetings and felicitations from the people of Ghana to you personally and to the friendly and brotherly people of the Republic of Guinea. I also bring you special greetings from the People's National Party which has been given a clear political mandate by the majority of Ghanaians to reshape the destiny of their country. The National Chairman of the Party is here to testify to those special greetings.

The friendly relations that exist between our two sister countries date back to the very early days of our independence, the twenty-third anniversary of which was celebrated only two days ago. The strong bonds between our two countries created during the early days of our independence were the results of the great foresight of President Ahmed Sékou Touré and the late Osagyefo Dr Kwame Nkrumah of blessed memory. Their foresight was not understood by their contemporaries; their aspirations, were only partially shared by their counterparts; their belief in the absolute need for the total emancipation of the African was however never shaken. The struggles they went through and the sacrifices they made were immeasurable. Today, we enjoy the fruits of their selfless and devoted services.

Your Excellency, the People's National Party which now forms the Government in Ghana believes in and draws inspiration from the pioneering work started by the late Osagyefo and yourself. We further firmly believe that it is only when the task of true political freedom and economic emancipation has been accomplished that Africans can co-exist with other nations in peace and harmony. The struggle for the total liberation of Africa, initiated some twenty years ago by these gallant leaders, should be given the fullest support as long as any inch of African territory remains occupied by colonialists.

The time has therefore come to launch a final assault on all the vestiges of colonialism, imperialism and neo-colonialism in Africa. It is in this spirit that my Government and, indeed, the people of Ghana, warmly congratulate the ZANU-PF, led by Mr Robert Mugabe, on their magnificent achievement in securing true independence for the people of Zimbabwe. We consider this as a major step towards liberating the whole of southern Africa from colonial rule. We salute the Zimbabweans and assure them of our inflinching support in their efforts to take the destiny of their country into their own hands and reshape it for their collective benefit.

Your Excellency, comrades, the People's National Party Government has assumed office in Ghana after the country had gone through a period of economic crises, gross mismanagement and total disregard for the principles of accountability. Consequently, we have launched an intensive campaign to eradicate corruption from our society. We are also actively demanding accountability at all levels. It is my Government's determination to harness all our human and material resources and use them judiciously, to the benefit of all Ghanaians. We are determined to reactivate the good works and programmes started by the late Osagyefo who in his great foresight built such an infrastructure as was once the envy of Africa but which has sadly been allowed to deteriorate beyond all recognition.

Your Excellency, my Government is ready to play once again an active role in African affairs and indeed to participate fully in the politics of the international community. We shall therefore give our fullest support to efforts being made to unify the West African sub-region through the establishment of the Economic Community of West African States (ECOWAS). Economic co-operation among ourselves in the sub-region should be one of the first steps towards a total economic and political unification, the foundations of which were laid by Your Excellency, the late Osagyefo Dr Kwame Nkrumah and Dr Modibo Keita of Mali. As the late Osagyefo declared, the independence of Ghana is meaningless unless it is linked with the total liberation of Africa. This is still our belief and we will continue to struggle not only for liberation but also for the unification of our continent.

Comrades, we in Ghana take great pride in the magnificent achievements of the people of Guinea under the Parti-Etat Democratique and dynamic and able leadership of His Excellency President Sékou Touré. We have watched and are still watching with keen and great interest your considerable achievements in the industrial sector, especially in your mining industry and also in the field of agriculture.

We salute you for your steadfastness and discipline. Above all, we salute your patriotism which characterizes all your activities. My presence here today will enable me to gain inspiration from you, your Party and your dynamic people. I have also come to assure you of the desire of Ghanaians to live in closer harmony with their Guinean brothers and sisters. The People's National Party is ever ready to forge closer links with the Parti Démocratique of Guinea so that we can assist each other in improving the socio-economic standards of our people and bring lasting peace to our two nations, to Africa and the rest of the world.

In conclusion, let me express the sincere gratitude of the People's National Party Government and of all Ghanaians for the support the Government and people of Guinea have given us over the last decade. We value that support and wish that the friendship and brotherly relations between our two countries will grow from strength to strength.

We salute you, Your Excellency, we salute the Parti Démocratique of Guinea and we salute the heroic people of Guinea.

Long live the Guinea-Ghana accord. Long live the revolution to free Africa.

DG–N

42

In Togo

Luncheon/dinner speech by President Limann in reply to the one delivered by President Eyadema of Togo.

My delegation is deeply touched by your warm words of welcome and by the generous hospitality to which we have been so lavishly treated since our arrival in your lovely and historic city of Lomé. Mr President, I am particularly happy to be here for as Your Excellency, no doubt recalls, I lived here in Lomé from 1968 to 1971 and was so much at home that I rarely visited Accra, even though it is so near. Though I make my current visit in a different capacity, it is to me a true homecoming, and this gives me profound joy and satisfaction.

Our two countries are immediate neighbours bound inseparably together by ties of geography, history, culture and economics. We are destined to live together because of imperative necessity, common interests and aspirations. We are here to renew our cordial traditional friendship and co-operation and to get to know each other. We believe that personal contacts at all levels are invaluable for forging friendship and promoting better understanding between nations. I consider it my sacred duty therefore during my tenure of office, to work to deepen further the already happy relations existing between our two countries through such personal contacts.

Mr President, we are deeply impressed with the vast improvements which have occurred in your country in all fields. The remarkable progress in the area of infrastructure, the spirited economic developments and steady growth and the general improvement in the quality of life of our Togolese brethren attest to your foresight as well as your wise and able leadership. All this has been accomplished in circumstances of political stability which has created the right atmosphere for the pursuit of your economic and social objectives. It is not therefore surprising that at the recent Presidential elections the brotherly people of Togo elected you to your high office.

The massive endorsement of your candidature and of the constitutional proposals, are an unambiguous manifestation of the people's confidence in your tested leadership. May I take this opportunity once more to congratulate you warmly on your election.

Mr President, the thrust of Ghana's foreign policy is Africa and it is only natural therefore that political developments in our continent should be of particular interest to us. As African countries, the OAU has been a unique forum for the harmonization of our policies and for the articulation of a coherent voice on the evils of colonialism and the obnoxious policy of apartheid. As a result of our concerted action significant victories are still being scored in the area of African decolonization. . . .

As the remnants of colonialism and the discredited doctrine of racism sing their swan-song, we have a moral responsibility to intensify the struggle at a time when the reactionary forces are making their last ditch effort in the face of the growing forces of freedom. In view of the justness of our cause total victory will surely be ours.

In the light of the resounding gains made in Zimbabwe, Pretoria is now appealing to the races to close their ranks. The people of Azania are not deceived by this clamour for unity. The sole criterion for unity and a truly multiracial society is the dismantling of apartheid and the unqualified acceptance by all races of the concept of the principle of one man, one vote. Anything less will be meaningless and unacceptable.

Mr President, the present disarray in the international economic system which has deteriorated and dislocated the economies of developing countries makes it imperative for smaller neighbouring countries like ours to promote close co-operation. We are in this regard pleased with the progress made so far to strengthen our bilateral relations. Trade between our two countries should be increasingly accelerated within the framework of the Ghana-Togo Permanent Joint Commission for Co-operation which unfortunately has been inactive since 1977. In the interest of meaningful co-operation, it is essential that our Joint Commission resumes work immediately.

The CIMAO project involving our sister countries of Togo, Ivory Coast and Ghana and which I am happy to learn has started production, is a shining example of sub-regional partnership for mutual gain. The supply of clinker from an additional source so close should assist Ghana's cement factories, now producing under capacity, to keep pace with the growing demands of the building and engineering industries. We are satisfied with the progress so far made in implementing the various provisions of the Economic Community of West African States (ECOWAS) an institution in whose establishment your country played a central role. Ghana's Parliament has recently ratified the Protocol on the free movement of goods and persons. This is a clear manifestation of confidence in the future of ECOWAS as an instrument of closer co-operation and collective self-reliance in our sub-region.

In the wider international sphere—in the United Nations Conference on Trade and Development, (UNCTAD) in General Agreement on Tariffs and Trade (GATT) and particularly in the African, Caribbean and Pacific Group, we have been collaborating closely together because of our mutuality of interests. In the difficult negotiations for a better economic and trading relationship between the European Economic Community (EEC) and the African, Caribbean and Pacific Group (ACP) which led to the signing of the Convention based on equality and justice, the valuable contribution made by the Togo delegation did not go unnoticed. The signing of Lomé I and Lomé II Conventions was a tribute to your praiseworthy efforts.

Mr President, our visit has been rather unavoidably short but fruitful. We do look forward to a longer visit which will enable us to visit the regions and thus acquaint ourselves with developments in your country. In conclusion, I wish to thank Your Excellency, the Government and brotherly people of Togo for your generous hospitality and for the excellent arrangements which have ensured the success of our visit.

May I now request Your Excellencies, ladies and gentlemen to join me in drinking a toast to the continued good health of President Eyadema and the happiness and progress of the fraternal people of Togo.

Long live Ghana-Togo friendship. Long live ECOWAS. And long live OAU and African unity. Thank you.

43

Lagos: First OAU Economic Summit 28–9 April 1980

Many observers see the First OAU Economic Summit which was held in Lagos on 28 and 29 April 1980 as a propitious omen. The President, who attended the Summit, reminded the assembled Heads of State that nations do not live by politics alone. He was understood to be welcoming the first ever get-together of African Leaders to talk economics. His mood was shared by the other delegates. He called for definite action in proposing a treaty, establishing African economic community.

Kindly permit me to congratulate you on your election as Chairman of this historic Economic Summit. I should also like to take this opportunity to convey through you to HE President Shagari, the Government and brotherly people of the Federal Republic of Nigeria, fraternal greetings from the Government and people of the Republic of Ghana. Furthermore, I wish to express my delegation's warm gratitude and appreciation for the traditional and fraternal hospitality we have enjoyed since our arrival.

Mr Chairman, one of the cardinal objectives of our organization since its inception has been to accelerate the decolonization process of our Continent. We have pursued this objective with determination indeed and have won great victories. With the independence of Zimbabwe, this process is now almost complete.

I wish to take this opportunity to express our profound joy and satisfaction at seeing Zimbabwe take its rightful place amongst us as the fiftieth member State and to wish the Zimbabwe delegation a very warm welcome. Our organization is strengthened and enriched by this new addition and we must wish the people of Zimbabwe success in their efforts at national reconciliation, unity and reconstruction. A strong and united Zimbabwe will surely advance the cause of the unfinished task of the total liberation of Africa. Any other approach will be illusory. With our continued unflinching support, Namibia and Azania will also be rid of colonialism and racism, and fit to join our ranks. This adds a new dimension and greater depth to the present Summit.

Indeed, Mr Chairman, winning the struggle for political emancipation now makes it very urgent for us to wage the even more difficult battle for the economy, emancipation and development for our Continent, especially now that we are all only too well aware of the devastating effects of neo-colonialism on our peoples and governments. The legacy of the colonial system ensured that our economic activities were dominated by and served the needs of metropolitan economies. This legacy is still with us since our economies have not yet been restructured and made responsive to our own needs.

That system deliberately discouraged us from trading among ourselves. It foisted artificial tastes on us which have stimulated demand for foreign goods and services, to the neglect and detriment of our own agriculture and industry. Our peoples are even now reluctant to bestir and save themselves from hunger, disease and poverty. This seems to be so partly because we have tended to do too much politics in the past. Our Charter enjoins Member States 'to co-ordinate and intensify their co-operation and efforts to achieve a better life for the peoples of Africa'. On this, there are no conservatives, moderates or radicals in Africa today.

It is therefore timely that we have now met at this first, all important, Economic Summit to adopt strategies that will enable us enter the year 2000, not in our traditional role as suppliers of raw materials and importers of finished products, but as partners in international trade, production, marketing and distribution of goods and services. We must all now recognize that the fight for our economic and social progress like the struggle for political freedom, will largely depend on the effective mobilization of our own domestic or internal resources, side by side with the need for complementary external factors. Our economic activities should therefore now be both horizontal, that is among us, as well as vertical, that is, between us as a group and the developed economies as a group. Indeed, it is now time for us to direct our efforts to the promotion of greater trade and other economic relations among ourselves.

It is the conviction of my delegation that our economic dependency on the industrialized countries has largely been responsible for our continued poverty, under-development and the erosion of our political independence. Excellencies, we must now come out with a united determination to break down the barriers of economic exploitation and thus mobilize the economic and social forces of this abundantly endowed continent for her positive development and progress. We must strive relentlessly to consolidate our collective self-reliance to enable us to face efficiently the development challenges of the decades ahead.

In the light of this, Ghana fully endorses the proposals that have been laid before us in the Plan of Action. In particular, we accept that the removal of tariff and non-tariff barriers is an essential step towards ensuring the free movement of goods and services within the sub-regions. We support the establishment of an African Monetary Fund as a means of providing impetus to intra-African trade and accelerating our economic development. Such a Fund, Mr Chairman, should reduce our dependence on foreign Financial Institutions for balance of payments support, and shield our financial and economic policies from undue external influences. The terms normally imposed by some of these financial institutions as pre-conditions for lending are not always in the best interest of our countries.

Excellencies, while we are not oblivious of the many difficulties inherent in the very process of promoting regional economic integration, we are nonetheless confident that given the political will and determination, practical and realistic solutions can be found to these difficulties. We therefore sincerely appeal to those of our sister States which have pioneered the building of sub-regional economic institutions not to abandon or dismantle them despite any temporary problems that may be encountered.

We in Ghana have always believed in the efficacy of economic collaboration as the vehicle of accelerated growth. We are happy that considerable progress is being made, in collaboration with our neighbours, in the development of our water resources for power and irrigation.

Mr Chairman, it is our conviction that the time has now come for us to initiate bold and positive moves towards an African Economic Community. Whereas localized difficulties might place impediments in the way of sub-regional economic grouping, we might find it easier to co-operate and foster relations within the framework of an economic community on the continental scale.

Mr Chairman, I wish to invite your attention to the objectives to which, as proposed in the Protocol on the African Economic Community, we pledge ourselves to attain in the next decade. It is my firm belief that in order horizontally to integrate our economies and harmonize our financial and trade policies, we need a clearly defined political will and direction. To move further towards this desirable goal, and in the spirit of our Monrovia Declaration, I would propose for your consideration:

(i) that we set up, without any further delay, a Ministerial Drafting Committee to draw up, within a given deadline, the Treaty establishing the African Economic Community, and,

(ii) that the Draft Treaty be submitted for our study and consideration at our Summit Meeting in 1981.

Mr Chairman, the problems inhibiting Africa's development are well known, having been very well documented. What is required of us now

197

is, above all, the political will to take those decisions and create those institutions which can translate our desires and ideals into concrete realizable action. This Summit offers us the unique opportunity and we should make full use of it. It is in this spirit that I have proposed for our serious consideration the establishment of a Ministerial Committee to prepare a Draft Treaty establishing the African Economic Community.

44

The 18th Assembly of African Heads of State in Nairobi, Kenya, 24 to 27 June 1981

At that first appearance of the President of the Republic of Ghana at an OAU Summit, the President felt at home with his colleagues and made some useful contributions to the debate. His intervention during the debate on the Western Sahara issue narrowed the debate and focussed the attention of the Assembly on the need for less rhetoric and more action.

It is with the greatest pleasure that I express, on behalf of my Delegation and in my own name, profound gratitude to His Excellency the President of Kenya, the Honourable Daniel Arap Moi, the Government and people of Kenya for the very warm and fraternal hospitality accorded us ever since our arrival.

My Delegation also joins me in expressing to you, Mr President, warmest congratulations on your election, by unanimous acclamation, to the Chairmanship of the 18th Session of the Assembly of Heads of State and Government and of our organization. We salute you as a pillar of this organization and also as a statesman who has greatly contributed to the stability and progress of the republic of Kenya, of this sub-region and of Africa as a whole.

I seize this opportunity to wish you every success in the discharge of the very heavy responsibilities entrusted to you and pledge to you the whole-hearted support and co-operation of my Delegation and Government. I wish also to express our deepest appreciation for the able, tireless and dedicated manner in which the esteemed predecessor of your exalted office, His Excellency Dr Siaka Stevens, President of the Republic of Sierra Leone, discharged his duties throughout last year. We render him our grateful thanks.

Mr Chairman, your capital city, Nairobi, has justifiably gained recognition for its beauty, just as your country, Kenya, has deserved the everlasting memory of that fiery, indomitable and great leader and statesman, the first President of Kenya, Mze Jomo Kenyatta of blessed memory, who was instrumental in wrenching independence, against all odds, for the brotherly people of Kenya. It would have gladdened the heart of the Grand Old Man to see today the full blossoming and fruits of the relentless campaigns he waged for Kenyan and African emancipation. This well attended summit is a great tribute to his achievements and memory. Mr Chairman, we are happy that you are his worthy successor and that under your wise and able leadership, this Assembly will make further progress towards achieving the lofty objectives our organization is setting itself for the coming year. May Kenya also benefit to the fullest measure from this leadership.

At its inception, the main objective of this Organization, Mr Chairman, was to assist our brothers and sisters who were still dependent to free themselves from colonial rule and oppression. Since then, its achievements have been so impressive that they have confounded its earlier and over-rash detractors who can all now also feel proud with us of these achievements.

However, our mission has not yet been totally accomplished. The 18th Summit is meeting at a critical moment in the history of our continent, due to the continuing explosive situation in Namibia and Azania. We followed with concern the pre-implementation talks held on Namibia in Geneva from 7 to 14 January this year. Those talks were stalled not by SWAPO but by the subterfuges and the intransigence of racist South Africa. The softening or shifting of the position of the members of the Contact Group towards South Africa, when they should unambiguously have reaffirmed their previous stand ensured the temporary failure of the United Nations Plan for Namibia's independence on schedule.

This unfortunate trend must shake us out of our complacency and spur us to renewed determination and greater efforts. We must draw the necessary lesson from the curious triple veto exercised by three members of the Contact Group which had initially done so much to convene the UN Security Council to debate the issue on the basis of Resolution 435 (1978) which calls for a negotiated settlement for Namibian independence. Why are these powers now turning their backs on a resolution they had so much helped to shape? We may have drawn hasty conclusions or misinterpreted their motives, but we are still entitled to deplore these delaying tactics, remain even more resolutely committed to our recognition of SWAPO as the sole, authentic and legitimate representative of the people of Namibia and reaffirm that Security Council Resolution 435 (1978), which endorsed the United Nations Plan on Namibia, is the only basis for a negotiated and peaceful settlement on the independence of Namibia. We must oppose any attempt to change, qualify or modify that plan.

In the face of South Africa's intransigence, the OAU should close its ranks and assist SWAPO to overcome the impediments in its way towards eventual liberation. We must step up our moral, material and diplomatic assistance to SWAPO to enable her to foil South Africa's attempts to promote and instal a puppet regime as a step towards any actual UDI in Namibia.

For the moment, we condemn the intensified repressive measures being adopted by the racist South African regime against African workers, students and even children in Azania and also the futility of the whole Bantustan system. Similarly, we condemn the frequent acts of aggression perpetuated by South Africa against the Frontline States, particularly, Mozambique, Angola, Zimbabwe and Swaziland and the threats of aggression continually issued against these countries and Lesotho as well as Botswana.

Mr Chairman, moves to revive the South Atlantic Treaty Organization which includes the racist South African regime should also be deplored and carefully watched. Indeed, the United Nations Organization should ensure that such an Organization is not established.

In line with Ghana's Foreign Policy on African Affairs, my Delegation is prepared to endorse any corrective action, including the imposition of sanctions, that this Summit will recommend against the apartheid South African regime, either directly or through the United Nations system.

Mr Chairman, please permit me to refer briefly to our relations with one another as independent African states, as members of the Non-Aligned Movement, the Group of Seventy-Seven and the Third World. It is regrettable that the OAU continues to be distracted from devoting its full attention to the imperatives of our economic development and the welfare of our peoples and the final onslaught against apartheid, racism and internecine tensions and conflicts among its members. These distractions seriously undermine our ability to mobilize our resources, concert our actions and project a united front in international affairs. Inter-African conflicts also give grounds for powers outside our continent to exploit our minor differences for their own ends through power block confrontations at our expense. We must therefore devise a mechanism for the prevention of such conflicts as well as for their ready and effective solution as they arise. Whether we achieve this end by reinforcing the existing institution of the Commission of Mediation, Conciliation and Arbitration or by evolving the newly proposed organ of an OAU Political and Security Council, is for us to determine, but its need has become very urgent. Whatever system we choose should be able to solve disputes and maintain peace and stability in such areas as the Western Sahara, Chad and the Horn of Africa without interference by outside powers.

Mr Chairman, our Organization should focus increasing attention and devote more of our time, energies and resources to the economic development problems of our continent. In particular, we must step up economic activities among ourselves within the context of the Lagos Plan of Action and horizontal or South-South co-operation. In this regard, we should promote greater constructive co-operation, especially economic and technical co-operation, between member countries of the OAU, the Non-Aligned Movement and the group of Seventy-Seven, in such areas as energy which we have so far not explored to advantage. We should seriously re-examine within these organizations the crippling effects of rising crude oil prices on the economies and the living conditions of the peoples of the vast majority of the members of our Organization and of the Third World which are always at the receiving end of all adverse economic developments. We should also explore new initiatives in revitalizing a more meaningful and imaginative Afro-Arab co-operation which will ensure the means of solving our mutual problems by expanding and strengthening our multilateral and bilateral economic co-operation and arrangements for our mutual benefit, while respecting the principles of non-interference in our respective internal affairs, and strictly observing our equal rights to choose our friends and practise political and economic systems which best suit the cultural backgrounds of our peoples. The economic salvation of our individual countries and the entire continent lies in our own hands and can only be achieved by our own endeavours and industry. We, however, welcome genuine and mutually beneficial foreign assistance from government and private sources. While foreign governments may pursue economic aid policies which show understanding of our problems, foreign private companies sometimes impose agreements or conduct their business in a manner which may evoke public displeasure and embarrass their own governments. In all our economic relations, the welfare of our people should be our supreme concern.

Finally, the issue of refugees has been gaining increasing concern in recent years among African countries. With the African refugee population currently standing at the staggering figure of five million displaced persons out of a world total of ten million, new problems and burdens have been created for some of our member countries and for our Organization. The eventual adoption of the African Charter on Human and Peoples' Rights will ultimately enable us to achieve peace, security and harmony on our continent. In the meantime, the refugee problem has to be tackled now. My Delegation stands ready to play its full part in support of any measures and assistance programmes to secure the welfare and happiness of our hapless brothers and sisters.

Mr Chairman, we have as our Agenda Item No 10 the date and venue of our next Summit. We should like to take this opportunity to thank, most heartily, the President, Government and brotherly people of Kenya for offering to host the 18th Ordinary Session of the Assembly of Heads of State and Government and for the excellent arrangements that have been made, at considerable national sacrifice, for the success of our meeting. In deciding the question of our next Summit, we should take cognisance of certain criteria and conditions which we have so far applied more or less unconsciously.

It is gratifying to note that more than a simple majority of Heads of State of Member countries are present at this Summit and it is not the case with Kenya that any Head of State who is not present here with us has deliberately been excluded by the host Government. Any Member State which seeks to host a Summit of our organization must allow the participation of all and the exclusion of none. Our organization is characterized by our commitment to a set of cardinal principles among which are:

(a) non-interference in the internal affairs of States;
(b) peaceful settlement of disputes by negotiation, mediation, conciliation or arbitration;
(c) unreserved condemnation, in all its forms, of political assassinations as well as of subversive activities on the part of member states.

In order to enhance the credibility of our organization, we should select for our venue a member country which has over the years shown respect for and loyalty to the principles to which our Organization is committed.

Mr Chairman, my second condition relates to normal procedure. Those who want to be Chairman of this organization normally attend meetings. He who seeks the honour of hosting a Summit should also sufficiently respect this organization to want to attend its meetings and actively participate in our deliberations.

In his address to the Opening Session yesterday, the Secretary-General of the UN accurately and succinctly described the present state of international relations. To refresh your memories, I quote: 'I cannot recall a more critical period in international relations than the present. Confidence between nations is at a low ebb; violence is endemic at both the local and international levels; a new armed conflict has broken out in Asia, and dangerous situations continue to exist in various parts of the world; East-West relations have suffered a serious setback; the arms race, which is both a consequence and a cause of the prevailing distrust between nations, is accelerating relentlessly; and the North-South dialogue, to which so much hope had been attached, has become stagnant.' The OAU has an important and unique role to play in urgently and resolutely meeting these challenges of our time. And the OAU can discharge this historic responsibility if it has for its spokesman, in the capacity of the current Chairman, a person who enjoys international credibility, acceptability and respectability.

Mr Chairman, with these few remarks, I wish to conclude and I thank you.

May our liberation struggle be crowned with success. Long live the OAU. Long live African unity.

Intervention during the debate on the Western Sahara Issue, Friday, 26 June 1981

Mr Chairman, when I asked for the floor during our morning session it was to have raised a point of order. That point of order was however not to try to ask you to rule any speaker out of order. It was in order to make some suggestions which would enable us to dispose of the matter placed before us, namely, the issue of the Western Sahara. I am therefore grateful to you, Mr Chairman, that you have rather put me down to contribute to the debate.

First and foremost, in line with my original request, I wish to appeal very strongly to my brothers and colleagues not to reopen a general debate on this issue which was exhaustively discussed at the last Summit in Freetown. It would be mean or ungenerous, Mr Chairman, even fastidious on our part, if we do not acknowledge that the council of wise men and all the parties involved in the Saharan issue had worked hard, shown a spirit of conciliation and generosity to meet the main demands of the resolution which His Excellency, President Shehu Shagari of Nigeria moved during the last Summit and which was adopted, not by a division, but by our unanimous acclamation. I am very sure that in your capacity as our Chairman, you will render them homage and grateful thanks on our collective behalf.

Mr Chairman, after the eloquent and lucid speech, the vibrant and passionate appeal made by His Excellency President Ahmed Sékou Touré; after the generous, magnanimous, constructive and conciliatory speech made by His Majesty King Hassan of Morocco, and after the very useful interventions and contributions made by the President of Mauritania, the leader of the delegation of Mali, the President of Madagascar and the leader of the Cape Verde delegation, it should be possible for us to bring to an end discussions on this most useful and constructive report presented to us this morning by the Secretary-General. I therefore wish to propose that without any further discussions we accept and adopt the report. I also wish to suggest that we commit this report, together with the relevant addresses delivered during the morning session, particularly, those by President Sékou Touré and His Majesty the King of Morocco, to a Select Implementation Committee and mandate it to implement, on behalf of the Summit, the recommendations of the report.

I leave the composition of the Implementation Committee to a meeting of the committee of wise men, with the participation of interested parties such as Morocco, Mauritania and Algeria, and which meeting should take place during this Session and draw up the modalities of implementation.

These suggestions are meant, Mr Chairman, to expedite our

deliberations so that we can exhaust our Agenda on schedule and thus avoid ending this well attended Summit in an anti-climax of rushed, last minute proceedings and the deferring of items we can easily dispose of at this very successful 18th Summit Meeting. The parties concerned having risen above themselves, and even excelled themselves, the Summit cannot do less than this.

45

Annual Festival of the People of Manya Krobo, 2 November 1979

A month after the changeover from military rule to civil authority, the President answered the invitation of the Manya Krobo people to join them at their annual festival, a most authentic cultural display, which, being close to Accra, the seat of diplomatic personnel and tourists, never fails to attract visitors to it.

I wish, first of all, on behalf of my Administration and on my own behalf to express my profound gratitude for the honour done me by inviting me to address this august gathering of the Chiefs and people of the Manya Krobo Traditional Area, and for the warm reception accorded me and my entourage.

I share with you, on this auspicious occasion, the joy of participating in the celebrations of the Ngmayem Festival.

No doubt the Konor is one of the longest-reigning chiefs in the whole country today and the fact that various governments, including even colonial ones, had sought his advice on matters of national interest is a pointer to his inherent wisdom.

It is for me needless to recall here the important role he has played and continues to play in the history of this nation and the development of this area in particular. He has given selfless and devoted service to the nation and my Administration hopes to draw from his rich experience in the crucial times through which our country is passing.

Our nation is indeed endowed with rich traditions and customs and I am highly privileged to be here today to join you at the peak of your annual festival. I congratulate all of you and wish you, individually as well as collectively, success in all your endeavours. The aspirations of the people of Manya Krobo reflect the new hope that has now been kindled in all Ghanaians.

Permit me to avail myself of this opportunity to express my very sincere gratitude to the chiefs and people of this area for the overwhelming support they gave the People's National Party during the

DU–O

Parliamentary and Presidential elections. Now that the battle is over I hope that you will continue to give me and my Government the necessary support so that, with co-operation from all sides, we can lift this once promising nation from the depths to which it has now sunk.

Nenemei, distinguished guests, ladies and gentlemen, it is always sad to compare the glorious past with our present circumstances. We must however not despair of our present predicament. The past is gone. Great mistakes have been made. But we do not have to cry over spilt milk. What we have to do now as a people, is to learn from and be guided by the mistakes of the past and start rebuilding Mother Ghana to recapture the glory that once made her the envy of Africa.

The civilian administration was ushered in a month ago amidst great tensions within our society. Yet the changeover brought new hope and new aspirations to all of us. It is therefore, our sacred duty to ensure that we do not fail in our collective objectives. My administration will work unceasingly to this end.

A month ago the nation was gripped with fear and distress. Mobility ground to a halt in the most cruel fuel crisis we had ever experienced in our lifetime. During the months of June, July, August and September we had to pay $21 million a month for fuel which had previously been consumed six months earlier. In addition, the nation had to find spot cash of more than $50 million to pay for the emergency stocks that had to be rushed in. This has only worsened an already sad foreign exchange reserves situation, not to say anything about our national indebtedness. But within the past month, even without the full complement of Ministers, my administration has successfully tackled the fuel crisis and brought some relief to all motorists. We have been able to restore the sixty-day credit facility from Nigeria. This shows the zeal and determination with which we want to tackle all our national problems. I must, however, caution that it is impossible for us to work miracles overnight. After many years of neglect and destruction we need some time to rebuild.

Fellow countrymen, the future is not as bleak as it seems. We have the human and material resources to transform our nation to a great country. I implore you therefore to look forward to the future with hope and confidence instead of looking backwards to our gloomy past which only sickens all of us. We must recreate faith and confidence in ourselves. We must not yield to despair.

We can build a prosperous nation but we must eschew laziness, cheating, industrial strife and social conflicts. Yet, in the last few weeks the peace of our country has been seriously threatened by strife and even tragic incidents involving bloodshed and loss of life and property. There has also been a resurgence of strikes which have led to huge losses not only in man-hours of work but in precious foreign exchange. I must

208

emphasize that if we are to succeed, and I know that we will, then we must instil confidence in ourselves, in our institutions and in our ability to tackle and solve our problems peacefully.

The current unrest in the country has continued to create an atmosphere of instability. This distracts Government's attention from evolving and pursuing the policies which can cure our ills. It also creates lack of confidence in us by the outside world. I, therefore, appeal to you and all Ghanaians to give the Government the kind of stable atmosphere needed for the solution of our numerous problems.

Nenemei, distinguished guests, ladies and gentlemen, as an agricultural country, it is important for us to turn our attention in the years ahead to developing our great potential in this field. Food production has gone down thus bringing in its wake high prices even of local foodstuffs. My government is working out plans to help farmers by making available the necessary inputs and incentives which will enable them greatly to raise food production again. To this end, I call on farmers throughout the country and particularly in the Manya Krobo area to intensify their efforts to produce more food for local consumption.

As a short-term measure, we are taking steps to ensure that such vital implements as cutlasses, hoes and hand-saws are quickly made available in the country for our small-scale farmers who are mostly engaged in food production. We will follow this up by ensuring that local manufacturers who produce these implements are given adequate support to increase their production so that we do not continue to import them from abroad anymore.

Our factories are at the moment producing below capacity; many of them have even ground to a halt. As a result, many of our able-bodied men and women are under-employed or completely unemployed. We are determined to restructure our industries; with sound planning and a judicious use of our resources we can revive all our factories and get them back into high level production.

But, again, we must all be realistic and accept that these things cannot be done overnight. What has been destroyed over a period of seven or more years cannot be rebuilt in one month even if we had the funds which we so woefully lack now.

We are planning to redirect labour. This will involve the retraining of our people for more productive areas of work. An uncompleted survey of the Civil Service alone has already revealed the staggering figure of more than 3,200 messengers who can be trained and redirected into areas of economic activity which will be more useful to them and to the nation. Hence our determination to encourage some of these young men to retrain and acquire skills which will enable them to enter into more productive sectors of our economy. To this end we are taking steps to make the necessary facilities available, but again, this cannot be done overnight.

Nenemei, ladies and gentlemen, this country is endowed with vast resources. All we need is to redirect our energies and attention in developing them. In your own Region alone we have the great potential of the Kibi Bauxite which successive Governments have failed to exploit, but which we plan to tackle. Endowed with other potentials such as uranium, diamonds and timber your Region is also one of the major cocoa-growing areas in the country. Much potential also exists in the rivers that cross your Region. Your own part of the Region is endowed with rich farming land. My Government is working out positive investment plans to enable these resources to be exploited to your benefit and the benefit of all Ghanaians.

Nenemei, distinguished guests, ladies and gentlemen, I must, in conclusion, thank once more the Chiefs and people of the Manya Krobo Traditional Area for inviting me to participate in this historic festival.

I pray that you will always display the same degree of togetherness and industry in your attitude to matters of national interest. I invite all of you to envision Ghana as a country in which hunger and degradation will disappear, yielding place to our sense of pride, confidence and dignity.

I congratulate you and wish you well.

46
Hogbetsotso at Anloga

Throughout Ghana, the various ethnic communities celebrate their distinctive annual festivals centring around a harvest observance or a historical occasion representing the community's migration to the present location, a war experience or deliverance from a natural disaster such as a famine, plague or flood.

The Ewes of the Anlo Traditional Area have their annual 'Hogbetsotso'. It was to the 1979 celebration, held on 3 November to which the President had been invited at which the following speech was delivered. Such occasions call back the sons and daughters from far and near to homecoming and reunion.

It is my special pleasure and honour to participate in the celebration of the Hogbetsotso festival of the people of Anlo which commemorates the revolt of your great ancestors against irredeemable tyranny and their march to freedom and progress.

On this memorable occasion, I wish to thank the Awoamefia, the Fiaga and the citizens of Anlo for the honour done me by inviting me to share in the joy of these festivities which, in the true Ghanaian tradition, can be described as a family gathering.

I must say that I am overwhelmed by the warmth of the reception accorded me and my entourage and I have no doubt that this show of goodwill is the outward manifestation of faith and confidence in my Administration.

At this juncture, I wish to avail myself of this opportunity to introduce to you formally, Mr Daniel Yawo Agumeh, the Deputy Regional Minister for your Region. Government has full confidence and trust in Mr Agumeh and I hope that you will give him your unqualified support and co-operation in the discharge of his duties as Acting Regional Minister.

Togbuiwo, distinguished guests, ladies and gentlemen, our country stands at the crossroads of history today. After passing through many abuses and hardships, we now have the opportunity to chart a new way of life that shall lead to peace, progress and prosperity. Failure to do so will shatter our confidence in ourselves as a people capable of solving our problems. Indeed, it will open the flood gates to unmitigated disaster. My Government is therefore determined to prove our worth as a people and redeem us all from poverty, want and deprivation.

The odds which face my government today seem to be as challenging as those that faced the people of Anlo when they rose up against oppression and bondage and embarked on a struggle, full of tribulations and privations, in their determined march to freedom and justice. We can draw inspiration from the shining example of your ancestors who through perseverance, selflessness, hard work and sacrifice faced and overcame monumental problems centuries ago and founded the great Anlo State of today. Guided by this example, we can as a nation also overcome our present problems and build an equitable and just society in which the interest and welfare of all our people shall be met.

However, a dispassionate assessment of the present chaotic state of our economy and the many pressures still being exerted on it ought to engender some realism, sympathy and understanding from all men of goodwill. At this crucial time when our country is faced with awesome challenges, I cannot over-emphasize the need for absolute peace in the country so that the Government can vigorously address itself to our pressing national problems.

The recent disturbances among sections of the community, particularly the tragic clashes between the people of Peki and Tsito in which precious lives were needlessly lost, endanger the well-being of our society and distract Government's attention from many demanding national issues. If we are to forge ahead as a people, united in our determination to open fresh chapters of progress for ourselves and our children, then we must insist that all feuding tendencies and conflicts which can undermine our united resolve must cease so that, united, we can redirect our energies towards our collective revival and regeneration.

Togbuiwo, distinguished guests, ladies and gentlemen, like other parts of Ghana, the Anlo area has many needs which its people rightly expect the Government to provide. Some of these have just been enumerated in the Awomefia's address. They will be closely studied so that nationally integrated solutions to them would be worked out.

I have listened with keen interest, particularly, to the passionate appeal of the Awoamefia for the implementation of the Wakuti Dam and Irrigation Project. This multi-purpose project now involves the development of a 40–45,000 ton Havi Sugar Project in the Abor-Akatsi area designed to set up the third sugar factory in the country at a cost of ₵168 million.

The report of the Havi Sugar Project is under serious study and negotiations are proceeding with four foreign companies on it. The Government's policy is to encourage the development of industries in the rural areas. We shall therefore pursue these negotiations vigorously to ensure that the project gets off the ground.

Under a bilateral agreement signed between Ghana and the Peoples'

212

Republic of China, land has also already been acquired for the Afife Rice Project and by 1981, the time the project is planned to reach maturity, ₵14 million would have gone into its implementation. It is our hope that this project will produce positive economic and social effects on the lives of the people in the area. The success of the Project is also expected greatly to augment food supplies in the country.

Togbuiwo, one of the pressing issues in the Anlo Area has been the perennial Keta sea erosion problem. Between 1953 and 1971, various measures were taken to find a permanent solution to this 'human survival' problem. A team of Dutch experts recently completed a hydrographic survey at Keta with a view to locating possible changes in the sea bed contours and possible movements of shore bars. The construction of an outfall at Kedzi to combat flooding of the township of Keta is also envisaged. As Togbuiwo are aware, substantial funds have been sunk into this important project which my Government intends to pursue vigorously so as to alleviate the suffering of the people of Keta and its surrounding towns. This is in line with the Government's avowed aim of offering Ghanaians a new lease of life.

Togbuiwo, the infrastructural development of the rural areas of Ghana is a programme to which the Government is fully committed and I can assure you that we will fulfil these obligations towards the long neglected rural people who actually produce the bulk of the wealth of our country. To this end, I am pleased to announce that concrete steps are being taken to provide electricity to the region from the Akosombo hydro-electric power grid and that the Federal Republic of Germany has already released 28 million Deutschmarks to the Government for the implementation of the first phase of the project.

Togbuiwo, the deterioration of health and medical services in the rural areas and the debilitating diseases which afflict our people is also a matter of great concern to my Government. One of our priorities is the rehabilitation of and the provision of drugs to our existing health centres, clinics and hospitals to make them functional again before new ones can be built where necessary. The Government is making efforts to give the necessary assistance to work currently going on, on the Regional Hospital at Ho. Important as curative medical care is to my Government, we shall also direct very serious attention to the field of preventive medicine.

Togbuiwo, distiguished guests, ladies and gentlemen, as you are well aware these are hard times for our country. In more recent times, the need to take emergency measures to procure fuel for the country has taken a heavy toll on our resources.

Since assuming office we have striven to ease the difficulties of mobility caused by a virtual fuel blockade. Our efforts in this field have not been trumpted about and so very few people seem to appreciate them which is, perhaps, why numerous demands are being made on us from all sides while it is impossible for us to do everything overnight after seven or more years of criminal neglect to and destruction of our economy.

In view of predictions of a worsening of the world energy crisis, long term solutions have to be sought for the fuel problem. To this end, onshore prospecting for oil in the Keta Basin, abandoned since 1967, shall be resumed. The Government is also negotiating for the acquisition of offshore blocks along the Keta coast between Dzita and Denu. We are determined to support these efforts. It is hoped that similar support and encouragement will also continue to be forthcoming from the people of the Volta Region and from all other Ghanaians.

Distinguished guests, ladies and gentlemen, I would like to take this opportunity to thank all the people of the Volta Region for voting so massively for us in the recent parliamentary and Presidential elections. By your votes you have reposed confidence in the Government of the People's National Party. I can assure you that we shall strive to retain this confidence and trust. I also thank you very sincerely for embracing my appeal to form voluntary vigilance or watch committees to check smuggling and other evils in our society.

However, I wish to point out that, at this crucial time in our history, there are neither winners nor losers in the quest to open new vistas of hope and progress for all our people. The crying need at the moment is a united resolve by all of us, irrespective of party affiliation, to overcome our problems. To this end, we intend to run a government in which equal opportunities will be open to all. Being a people's government, we believe in 'participatory democracy' and shall therefore encourage every citizen to participate fully in formulating and implementing policies. Our ultimate objective is to build a welfare state in which all Ghanaians will be better fed, better clothed, better housed, better and more usefully educated, better protected against unemployment, disease and the other vicissitudes of life. These goals can be achieved. We therefore implore you to give us your unreserved moral and material support to translate our plans into reality. Let us, together, take our collective destiny into our own hands and not sit back again unconcerned or indulge in hairsplitting arguments and carping criticism while our country is burning, and then only later point accusing fingers at one another again when things go wrong.

My guiding principles include the healing of wounds, reconciliation, national unity, national confidence, national pride and national dignity, in the service of all our peoples.

In supporting me and my Administration you will be contributing immensely towards the realization of these objectives. I have no doubt that you and all Ghanaians are rising up to this challenging occasion.

I thank you all very much for your understanding and co-operation.

47

Akyem Abuakwa People entertain the President at their Odwira Durbar 5 January 1981

Kyebi, the seat of the late Nana Ofori Atta I, who was a prominent national leader and paramount chief of Akyem Abuakwa, was inscribed in the annals of Ghana as an important citadel of tradition, culture and indigenous authority. There are stirrings at the offices of government planners, where the proposed bauxite project is at last coming off the drawing board. When it does, Akyem Abuakwa area seems destined to play a vital role in laying a firm economic foundation for Ghana.

Kindly permit me at the outset, to express in my own name and on behalf of my entourage, our sincere and profound gratitude for the very warm and cordial reception you have accorded us since our arrival in Akyem Abuakwa and at this colourful durbar of your reunion for moral stocktaking as a prelude to your future comportment and activities. We have been deeply touched and overwhelmed by your friendly and spontaneous welcome and also highly impressed by this most colourful display of the rich culture and tradition of the Okyeman. We thank you most sincerely indeed, for inviting us to this festive, very serious and culturally important function today.

I am particularly happy to attend your Festival because, as the Okyenhene has rightly said, this is my first official visit to Kyebi, the seat of Akyem Abuakwa, since my assumption of office as President and Head of State of Ghana over a year ago. Consequently, I wish to avail myself of this opportunity to express my sincere thanks to Osagyefo the Okyenhene, Nananom and people of Akyem Abuakwa for the support, goodwill and understanding shown towards the PNP and my Administration during the general elections and throughout the past fifteen months. We are most grateful to you all.

Okyenhen, Nananom, distinguished guests, ladies and gentlemen, large gatherings of Chiefs and peoples at such festivals bear eloquent testimony to the inherent unity which prevails among you and all Ghanaians. Such occasions form an important part of our way of life and the concrete manifestation of our rich cultural heritage. They offer

215

us, at the local level, unique opportunities for taking stock of the past and of the present. Even more importantly, they encourage us, as the Okyenhene has rightly emphasized, to look ahead to the future with renewed hope and determination.

Such festivals also provide the occasion for all citizens to settle their differences and disputes, to repair the strained relations between them and their neighbours, and help others to renew and strengthen old bonds of friendship. Even future lifelong mates meet for the first time or make final engagements on such important occasions. They are therefore of permanent moral value to both the individual citizens and the community at large. I take this opportunity to wish you all a very happy, prosperous New Year and a successful reunion. May the festival promote greater happiness, progress and true prosperity to all the Chiefs and people of Akyem Abuakwa in particular.

Nananom, we have watched your rich display of culture with admiration and while congratulating all the participants in this magnificent durbar, I wish to make the fervent appeal that you should endeavour to preserve, for posterity, if possible in written form, some of the rich and beautiful traditions of our cultural heritage.

Sufficient efforts do not seem to have been made in the past to preserve these cultural values and manifestations in any permanent form which runs the risk of falling into oblivion and lost beyond recognition. Already, such intrinsic moral values as obedience, honesty, loyalty, selflessness and respect to elders which are all inherent in our traditional culture are being eroded. Indeed, if this trend is allowed to persist, we may lose the best part of our history and our cultural identity. It is therefore my sincere hope that Nananom, elders, parents and all concerned citizens shall redouble their efforts at home, on the farms, in schools and other institutions to reinstil the old virtues of discipline, honesty, probity, selfless devotion to duty, good neighbourliness and public spiritedness in our people. Indeed, the need to reinstil such moral values into our people has become even more urgent now than before.

Discipline and honesty in our private and public lives are among the most important preconditions for success in our crusade for moral regeneration, economic recovery and national reconstruction. It will avail the majority nothing if we do not redevelop and sharpen our moral conscience and ensure that a few people do not loot what belongs to all.

Nananom, as a people and a nation, we have started a new phase, a new era of hope for a better tomorrow under civilian rule. It is very heartening that the Odwira Festival of the Okyeman is so much devoted to the noble objectives of regeneration and renaissance in the values of charity, honesty, good neighbourliness, brotherliness, harmony, cohesion, unity, progress and national greatness. Your example in this sphere, as in the sphere of self-help and self-reliance, are worthy of emulation by the whole nation.

I therefore wish to avail myself of the opportunity offered me by this occasion to appeal to the whole nation to take up the task of the moral regeneration of our society very seriously. The Osagyefo's address has dealt extensively with the mineral wealth of this traditional area. His survey has been extensive and I wish only to add that this is true of several other parts of our country thus indicating how richly endowed we are in human and natural resources.

The time has therefore now come for all of us to rededicate ourselves towards the fuller, disciplined and honest use of these rich potentials through hard work. Indeed, we cannot take full advantage of them if we persist in our old habits of greed, laziness and selfishness or continue to wallow in apathy and insensitivity towards our national duties.

My Administration has declared 1981 a Year of Action. This means that we shall redouble our efforts on the national scale and on all fronts as we have done throughout the past fifteen months. I should however like to repeat that it is the individual contributions of all citizens which make up the total national effort. You must all therefore take up the new challenges and improve upon your present best.

Nananom, personally aware of the praiseworthy contribution of the sons and daughters of the Akyem Abuakwa Traditional Area to the history of our country, I commend and salute all of you for your magnificent achievements in self-help projects and for your praiseworthy contributions to our total national effort. However, kindly permit me to emphasize that you should not rest on your laurels in the face of the even greater tasks ahead of us. We have a duty to restore the lost glory of our country. In this, Akyem Abuakwa has a leading role to play.

Distinguished ladies and gentlemen, I would like to reassure Nananom that my Administration is very well aware of the potentialities of the Akyem Abuakwa traditional area and that every step is being taken to exploit them to the fullest for the benefit of the people of this area and for the rest of the country.

Plans are well advanced for the exploitation and processing of the enormous Kibi Bauxite deposits into alumina. Indeed, I hope that it will not be too long before Nananom will see concrete action towards the implementation of this project.

As you are already aware, we have just launched a major campaign towards the exploitation of our varied mineral wealth. The gold and diamond prospects of this area shall be among the first to be exploited and developed. Government has also embarked on programmes aimed at improving upon various institutions and social amenities in this Traditional Area.

Thus over six million cedis has been allocated for improvements in facilities for your schools and colleges alone. In addition to a West German loan, two million cedis have also been provided for water supply projects at Asuom, Kyebi, Asamankese, and other surrounding areas. Similarly, plans are well advanced for the extension of electricity within this Traditional Area. These efforts shall complement the commendable contributions which the people of this area are already making through self-help projects. I, therefore, appeal to Nananom to redouble their efforts and greatly improve upon your excellent record of leading your people to help themselves.

Nananom, distinguished ladies and gentlemen, I cannot conclude this short address without commending Osagyefo Kuntunkununku II very highly for the shining example he set for all professionally trained traditional rulers to emulate, by his professional medical services to his people at the Kibi Hospital in time of great need. This singular act has demonstrated the Okyenhene's high sensitivity to the plight of his people. Excellencies, our people expect much from our traditional rulers who must therefore be as responsive to their needs as the Okyenhene has been. I commend him very highly indeed and hope that other traditional rulers will emulate his shining example in their various fields of endeavour.

Honourable Ministers, Members of Parliament, distinguished ladies and gentlemen, I wish, once again, very sincerely to thank Osagyefo the Okyenhene, the Chiefs and people of Akyem Abuakwa for this very warm and friendly reception.

May this festival bring greater understanding, peace, progress, prosperity and happiness to all of you, the chiefs, elders and people of this traditional area and to all Ghanaians.

48

The Fetu Afahye Festival at Cape Coast

I have the greatest pleasure and honour to address you on this festive occasion when the sons and daughters of the Oguaa Traditional Area are celebrating their annual Fetu Afahye. On behalf of my entourage and on my own behalf, I thank you most sincerely for the very warm and enthusiastic welcome you have accorded us at these durbar grounds. We are indeed grateful and beholden to you for this opportunity to attend and participate in this grand annual festival.

The pomp and pageantry, the grandeur and the general atmosphere of merrymaking of this function eloquently testify to the rich variety of our cultural heritage and its importance in the lives of the people of Oguaa as, indeed, in other parts of our country.

The coming together and intermingling of the old and the young from all walks of life who have travelled here from far and wide for this festive occasion underscores the unifying force of such festivals which serve as rallying points among all our people. Indeed, they are powerful and permanent sources of national unity. I therefore ardently hope that this deep sense of unity will pervade the totality of our national life.

Occasions such as this also provide unique opportunities for taking stock of our past collective and individual performances, that is, our failures and achievements in our efforts to serve the communities in which we live.

They sharpen our awareness of our civic and social responsibilities and renew our resolve to mend our ways and rededicate ourselves to greater service and achievements in the future. On this occasion, therefore, you may wish to resolve again to stand firmly together and provide selfless and devoted service not only to the Oguaa Traditional Area but to the Region and the Nation as a whole.

Nananom, Excellencies, in this season's spirit of introspection, self-assessment and stocktaking, I am happy to inform you that at the national level the People's National Party Administration is leaving no stone unturned in its efforts to introduce major and permanent changes in the unenviable economic situation we have inherited. The changes are designed to promote continued stability, social transformation, greater progress and prosperity for all Ghanaians, who have suffered for far too long from the effects of self-centred, ill-conceived and short-sighted decisions, fits and starts and makeshift policies which have proved only too detrimental to all aspects of our national life.

In our determination to arrest further humiliations and indignities, we have had to analyse carefully all aspects of our national problems in taking decisions affecting the vast majority of our people. This determination, this policy, is also meant to check those who had long plundered the nation but now make cheap political stunts, saying that we are slow, while carefully hiding the fact that when they had the opportunity, they were very quick only in destorying the economy through sell-outs and the reckless abandonment of viable and socially benefical projects throughout the country.

Countrymen, my Administration has boldly adopted the policy of open Government, participatory democracy, fair and constructive criticism. However, we are also prepared to react appropriately to malicious criticism and wilful distortions and reject dangerous solutions recklessly propagated for cheap political reasons. In the past such tactics only worsened the economy, stagnated progress at home and damaged our national image abroad.

That is why we have refrained from playing politics with our vital and permanent national interests. It is therefore a great pity that the confidence tricksters are still busy at their old tactics and are determined to retard or even sabotage the efforts we are making to clean up the mess they have created. We challenge them to tell the public the full implications of their defence of narrow privileges and reckless proposals for currency adjustments and price increases in the face of inadequate supplies and also the budget cuts they suggest against the numerous demands for development projects and increased amenities being made by the public.

One immediate consequence of ill-conceived proposals is that petrol will have to cost ₵18 per gallon within twelve months and ₵36 within eighteen months and all this at a time when it is being confirmed that there is a glut of crude oil on the world market. We therefore say no to throwing dust into the eyes of the public. We reject the policy of those who have inflicted wounds on the nation and now want to pour perfume on the ulcer and make it fester the more.

Fellow citizens, some of the major national issues which have preoccupied my Administration since we assumed office and led me to tour our country more than twice and also West Africa and four European countries include the following:

(i)   continual appraisal of our shattered economy and the careful reordering of our priorities,

(ii)   the survival of democracy and the restoration of law and order in the place of anarchy,

(iii)   the poor state of our gold, timber and cocoa industries, among others,

(iv)   good relations within our Sub-Region,

(v)   the inflow of foreign investment into vital sectors of the economy; and

(vi)   the restoration of Ghana's image abroad.

Thus, for nearly two years now the People's National Party administration has worked tirelessly to recreate peace, stability, personal safety, individual liberty, fair play for all and freedom from fear. Our determination is to ensure that these primary requirements of free, democratic societies prevail in Ghana. We emphatically reject Apollo 568s, disqualifications and Aliens Compliance Orders in our country which is the cradle of African liberation and respect for the dignity of the black and other disadvantaged races.

My repeated appeals for national unity and singleness of purpose are meant to buttress this determination and our relentless march towards salvaging our economy and restructuring our society. It is for the same reasons that we have been strictly observing the basic principles of mutual respect between all arms of Government, especially between the Executive, the Legislature and the Judiciary. Those who mistake approaches to be signs of weakness or slowness are therefore committing serious errors of judgement and underestimating the intelligence of Ghanaians, who know only too well the records and the past performance of the present so-called critics and new defenders of the common man. And by the way, which Ghanaian is really what such critics spitefully describe as common?

I wish to take this opportunity to reiterate my call to all placed in positions of authority to exercise caution in the use of their powers and privileges. The nation as well as the outside world, is watching all of us in our respective efforts to practice true democracy and lead our country out of the abyss, national disgrace and shame. At home the electorate is the final and sovereign judge. To it we are prepared to submit ourselves, decisions and actions all the time. Abroad, our friends will continue to distinguish between true Ghanaian patriots and nation-wreckers who are always ready to sell their country for a 'mess of potage'. In contrast, the People's National Party Administration will forever defend the cause of Ghana at home and abroad. Since we support and defend the good causes of others, we cannot do less for Ghana.

My Administration attaches the greatest importance to our cocoa industry which is still the backbone of our economy. Most of you are aware of the neglect and destruction which has taken place in that industry under previous regimes. These included the inadequate and erratic supply of inputs, the shortage of labour caused by obnoxious policies such as the Aliens Compliance Order, gross inefficiences and embezzlement in the administration of the industry, transportation difficulties and a general disrepair of existing infrastructures such as roads and bridges.

During the past two years we have been taking steps to reconstruct feeder roads for the speedy evacuation of cocoa; we have placed orders for sufficient and appropriate types of transportation—we are streamlining the administration of the industry through the promulgation of the new Cocoa Marketing Board Bill. The steady provision of basic inputs such as implements, spraying machines and improved varieties of seedlings has been considerably stepped up even at the present highly subsidized prices and despite our general policy of gradually removing subsidies. We have successfully renegotiated a new international Cocoa Agreement without which the industry would have been totally destroyed. The previous Agreement had lapsed before we assumed office and much time, hard work, patience and funds had to be devoted to its renegotiation. And yet others did their level best to wreck it even at the final stage of those negotiations and efforts.

As stated in the Manifesto of the People's National Party, we had long recognized the need for price incentives to cocoa farmers to enable them to meet their legitimate aspirations, to encourage and promote increased cocoa production and output and to reduce the incidence of smuggling of cocoa across our borders. That is why we have been working relentlessly on that industry, in conjunction with other major economic policies as I have already indicated.

Those who seem to want to destroy the whole industry itself should now publicize the real intentions of their cheap and reckless propaganda which only complicates our attempts to conclude delicate negotiations with international agencies in the interest not only of that industry but of the economy as a whole.

During our tour of Europe we successfully persuaded all the countries we visited to sign and ratify the International Cocoa Agreement which has now come into force pending ratification by our own Parliament. This is one of our major achievements for which all fair minded observers have given us much credit and praises despite what some of our local critics think and rail about.

Nana Omanhene, when the People's National Party assumed office in September 1979, our country faced a total economic blockade and indeed had been boycotted by investors and our trading partners for a long time. This had been caused by past reckless decisions, unstable and unattractive conditions as well as gross mismanagement of our economy.

It was therefore imperative for that blockade to be lifted, before we do anything else. You will recall that we were able quickly to remove the petrol queues. About this the economic pundits and our political critics are now silent. The regulations governing investment and strangulating the economy had also to be reviewed. This had not been meaningfully done since the time of the late Osagyefo who introduced the first ever

222

regulation in 1962–3 which enabled him to create the extensive infra-structures which were all neglected or abandoned after 1966.

Nananom, earlier this week I had the pleasure of inaugurating both the governing body and the new high powered Ghana Investment Centre. This has completed the long process we started nearly a year ago to review our laws on foreign investments in Ghana. The New Investment Code Act is therefore another major achievement of the People's Natonal Party Administration. It creates a new, attractive investment climate. It safeguards investments and should therefore promote ef-ficient and profitable operations of business ventures in Ghana since it also guarantees the repatriation of honestly earned profits.

The international goodwill we have painstakingly re-established in just two years, particularly within financial circles, as a result of the stream-lining of our financial administration at home and our policy of settling our short-term import bill has already paved the way for investors to take advantage of this new investment climate. In short, the campaign we have mounted for massive investment and the credit worthiness we have tried to recreate have now provided the climate investors need. A bright future is therefore ahead of us if we can continue to put our own house in order and maintain peace and stability. As I emphasized in my last Sessional Address to Parliament, 'a house divided within itself cannot stand', furthermore, it behoves us all to work even harder, provide self-less services to our nation and lift it out of the sorry state of the recent past.

Nananom, on your local scene I am happy to announce that we are determined to change the face of the Central Region for the better, as planned in the First Republic when the University was sited here in the teeth of much blind opposition as usual. To this end, sad cutting ceremonies have already been performed at Cape Coast here within the last two months for the commencement of work on two important in-dustries, namely, the Oguaa Unity Manufacturing Company Limited, and the Loyalty Garment Factory. These are beginnings of major programmes under the current Five-Year Development Plan during which period various industrial developments will be set up in the Cape Coast Industrial Area at a currently estimated cost of over ₵100 million.

Another project that I should like to mention is the expansion work proceeding apace at the Cape Coast Water Works for which I have directed the Regional Minister to ensure adequate supplies of inputs to enable its speedy conclusion.

Nananom, we are equally determined to improve upon facilities in all the educational institutions in the Oguaa Traditional Area which con-tinues to be the cradle of education in Ghana. For the daily convenience and comfort of the travelling public we have inaugurated the Tata Bus Service here in this city and former capital of the country. We hope to augment the present fleet of seven buses in due course.

DG–P

223

Nananom, chieftaincy disputes have however continued to sap our energies and divert our attention and resources from these primary objectives and socially beneficial programmes. I therefore appeal to all chiefs in this Traditional Area as indeed in other areas to bury their differences and unite in providing leadership to their people and also to rekindle the spirit of self-help among our rural folk. In particular, I appeal for peace in the Himan Traditional Area where there have recently been some clashes between Mfuom and Gomoa farmers over land disputes. Such clashes benefit no one. In contrast, everyone suffers from their immediate and remoter effects. You should therefore institute measures to ensure security of persons and property, peace, tranquility and progress within this old and renowned traditional area. Do not create the 'desolation' of Dagban and Wulensi 'and call it peace'.

Finally, Nana Omanhene, on my own behalf and on behalf of my entourage I wish, once more, to thank Nananom, elders and indeed the people of Oguaa Traditional Area for this warm and friendly reception today. We wish all of you a very happy festival, peaceful celebrations, prosperity and success in your collective and individual endeavours.

I thank you very much.

49

Twenty-fourth Independence Anniversary Celebrations

On the eve of the twenty-fourth anniversary of Ghana's independence, 5 March 1981, the President wished his people by radio and television many happy returns of the day!

With the historic words of 'Ghana, our beloved country, is free for ever', the late Osagyefo Dr Kwame Nkrumah of blessed memory, proclaimed our political independence twenty-four years ago. This lit the flame of pervasive euphoria and measureless hopes for a better future throughout independent Ghana and our continent which has continued to burn since then. As the poet would have put it,

> Bliss was it in that hour to be born,
> But to be young was very heaven.

Having boldly and proudly stepped out of 113 years of colonial rule to take our destiny into our own hands and reshape it to our heart's content, we were also determined to help the whole of our continent shake off colonial rules so that all Africans can be masters of their own fate.

On the eve of this twenty-fourth re-enactment of the drama of 6 March 1957, we must set the stage by first paying tribute to the gallant and self-less Founding Fathers, the sons and daughters of our Motherland who sacrificed their sweat, toil, blood and lives to win for us the Freedom we have all so greatly cherished since then. This happy, historic and unforgettable event however also requires us soberly to reflect on our successes and failures in the pursuit of Freedom and Justice in our lives so that we may the better understand our present problems and how to solve them now and in the years ahead.

During the last twenty-four years we have passed through many economic crises and socio-political upheavals. But we have also always managed to contain them and remained firmly united in diversity, convinced that we share one common national temper, outlook and fate. We have maintained our political independence through our resilience, tolerance and understanding, despite economic mismanagement, shortages, deprivations, hardships and even starvation.

225

We have often felt cheated and bitter that peace, stability and economic development have eluded us and thus made our political independence sound like a cruel joke or a hoax. Only our proverbial good humour even in adversity, which has baffled many observers and thus attracted their respect and admiration, rather than their unmitigated contempt, has sustained our will power to continue living together as a united national community.

Acutely aware of this discrepancy between the high expectations of our political independence and the harsh realities of our poor performance, the People's National Party Administration has not taken, and dares not take, the good qualities and the tolerance of our citizens for granted. Indeed, we came into being with the sole purpose and determination to harnessing and directing these qualities for the recovery of our economy, self-respect, sense of dignity and national prestige. We shall therefore do everything within our power to promote the orderly achievement of all-round improvements in the lives of all citizens.

While we can all congratulate ourselves that things have not fallen apart due to our innate determination and perseverance we must also concede that we have misapplied our political liberty and undisputed intelligence to destroy our economy and negate the great expectations of our fellow citizens.

This analysis and frank admission must be the starting point from which we can take heart and resolve to make amends through more responsible, honest and hard work for better successes and achievements in the years ahead. 'Pas de pitié pour les dupes' and posterity will never forgive us if we continue in the course which has destroyed all that Ghanaians hold dear. We must all now take seriously the appeal I have made several times already about the need for the moral reformation and regeneration of our society. The slow, imperceptible erosion of our moral fibre, rectitude and values has been one of the root causes of our present socio-economic malaise and should therefore be tackled now very vigorously by all concerned citizens, institutions and organizations which have this task as part of their *raison d'être* in society.

Since assuming office, my Administration has laboured relentlessly in tackling our problems realistically and fearlessly. In doing so, we have never minced our words in laying bare the truth and facts as we see them about our present national economic situation. The facts we have repeatedly exposed to the public are based on our careful examination of the long, accumulated problems of the past which we have not created but which we are determined to resolve with the collective mandate you have given us.

To this end, we have undertaken extensive on-the-spot investigations through Regional and District tours, supplemented daily by information and complaints readily and widely volunteered by concerned citizens.

Our mature and candid appreciation of the facts of our present situation reveals the depressing enormity of our national problems and the ever-increasing resources at our disposal to solve them.

The most telling example of this bleak picture of our present economy is that while our demands for local and foreign goods have continued to grow with the rapid growth of our population, our domestic production and foreign earnings have been dwindling sharply for more than a decade now. Thus, our main foreign exchange earner, cocoa, fetched over £2,205 sterling per tonne barely two years ago, but now fetches less than half that price, that is, only £890 per tonne. Cocoa production and exports have also dropped substantially from year to year since 1965. This has greatly depressed the lives of our farming community and also emptied our national coffers amid the heightened and long pent-up demands of our wage and salary earners.

Countrymen, these and many other reasons have convinced the People's National Party Administration of the absolute necessity of diversifying our economy, particularly for our local food production and the sources of our external earnings. To this end we are vigorously directing our efforts towards the diversified exploitation of our abundant natural and human resources.

The renewed emphasis on agriculture and food production, the Seminar on our gold endowment organized earlier this year and the encouragement we are giving to crude oil exploration are among the concrete steps that we have already taken towards the diversification of the economy and the fuller utilization of some of our rich natural and human resources endowment. However, in order to succeed, we need the understanding, co-operation and honest hard work of all concerned citizens who want to help save our nation from further decline through hard work and selfless devotion to duty, and then move on to achieve greater successes in the years ahead.

But we cannot succeed in this long march towards restructuring our economy and restoring our once enviable infrastructure to tolerable standards if we do not refrain from negative attitudes, indifference and despondency at home or recklessly running down our country abroad. We should not cut off our nose to spite our face. We should not hastily abandon our dropping jaw merely because others are slow in coming to help us bind it up.

As we start the twenty-fifth year of our existence as an independent and sovereign nation, each and everyone of us must resolve to translate our politicial independence into true freedom, justice and happiness for all our citizens within the shortest possible time. We must give such a fitting account of ourselves from now on that by this time next year the Silver Jubilee celebrations of our Independence will set yet another example for all Africa to emulate three or more years later.

In preparation for that great event, we as individuals, families and organizations must tidy up all our surroundings and renovate our disfigured buildings. My Administration will tackle the problems of the roads, transport and official accommodation facilities in the city of Accra for that historic occasion.

Countrymen, even though we have made much progress since 24 September 1979 in our determined efforts to reinstil democratic principles in our national life by upholding the freedom of speech and respect for the African personality and human dignity, we must nevertheless continue to be extra vigilant at all times in order to help safeguard our newly established institutions, values and the democratic way of life which we have freely chosen for ourselves after many experiments and false starts in the political and economic wilderness.

To this end, in all our utterances, attitudes and actions we should studiously avoid creating the sort of wrong impression and situations which can be exploited by adventurers and anarchists to erode the principles, way of life and systems of values we have so painstakingly and freely adopted for ourselves. Indeed, our ability to maintain peace and stability shall continue to depend on the degree of sanity, self-discipline and responsible conduct we can instil in ourselves and in our society. In short, the price of political liberty, economic progress and social justice is eternal vigilance, stability and orderly changes of governnent which ensure uninterrupted development.

During the past year we have worked painstakingly to regain the goodwill and respect of friendly countries within our continent and farther afield. Our nationals abroad have already begun to hold their heads high with this gradual restoration of our lost national image. Our voice within the comity of nations has started to command respect and serious consideration. We must therefore continue to work harder to discipline ourselves and to maintain law and order in our society so that our sense of dignity at home and respect for our country abroad can take deep and unshakeable roots.

Excellencies and fellow citizens, we shall intensify our resumed active role in African and wider international affairs. With the struggle for the political independence of our continent drawing to an end we must steel our will-power for the greater and more complex battles ahead. We should intensify our economic co-operation with other countries so that, together, we can the better take the next major steps to review the inequitable international economic order that now exists between the Third World and the developed nations. We must step up horizontal co-operation within the southern hemisphere of our planet since this, in fact, holds the key to the future survival of mankind. This is an incontrovertible fact which can neither be understood or accepted now by fundlords the world over, but it is inevitably irreversible.

Compatriots, with determination and hard work, success shall certainly crown our efforts. I therefore wish you all, on this festive occasion very happy twenty-fourth Anniversary celebrations, many happy returns of the day and for the months ahead. May you all enjoy the full meaning and values of true Freedom and Justice in our society.

Finally, fellow citizens, in view of the uniqueness of the declaration of our independence and its repercussions on the rest of the black race, my Administration has decided that while other national holidays will be maintained, only the 6 March shall be celebrated each year with full national honours, pomp and pageantry embracing all sections of our community since this is the one single event in our national evolution and history which unites us as a people.

Long live Ghana!

50

Armed Forces Parade: Twenty-fourth Independence Anniversary Celebrations

As Commander-in-Chief of the Armed Forces, the President took the salute and addressed the soldiers, the school children and the large turn-out of people on this colourful occasion.

It is an honour and a pleasant duty for me to address this distinguished cross-section of the old and the young of our national community on this historical occasion of Ghana's accession to political independence on 6 March 1957.

We have gathered again today in high spirits to commemorate the drama which was first staged twenty-four years ago when our national flag was hoisted and the late Osagyefo, Dr Kwame Nkrumah of blessed memory pronounced Ghana free forever from colonial bondage. The majority of our total population of today were born after 1957 and can therefore not easily relive the spontaneous, infectious and hilarious atmosphere of the new nation which was overwhelmed with joy and pride on that historic occasion.

Howbeit I take this opportunity warmly to congratulate all Ghanaians and to wish you a happy twenty-fourth birthday anniversary and many pleasant returns for the day and throughout the months ahead.

The importance of the 6 March to us as a nation has never been under-estimated by any citizen since 1957. We have all acknowledged it as the living symbol and reality of our independence, national unity and collective fate. Its significance however needs to be brought vividly home to the youth all the time, so that they can appreciate its historic importance and role of all those who help to sacrifice their all in order that their contemporaries and their children might live free from foreign rule, domination and discrimination. We cannot fully appreciate what we take for granted today because we have either forgotten, with the older generation, or are not aware, as with the younger generation, the certain things which are now our birthright were denied us before 1957.

We must therefore continue to treasure or hold dear our independent sovereign national status by recapturing and rekindling each day that spirit of selflessness, sacrifice, singleness and unity of purpose without which the gallant Founding Fathers could not have won us freedom from colonial oppression and recreated modern Ghana from its ancient and long-forgotten past and the bounds of its imperial sway.

This historic annual event also affords the opportunity for us to bury our differences, prejudices and the petty daily squabbles of human nature and rather constantly renew our resolve to emulate the shining examples of those who have made it possible for our beloved Motherland to be free for ever. By their sacrifices they have won political independence for us. Through self-discipline, hard work and devotion to duty we can also win our economic emancipation to give fuller meaning to our national motto of Freedom and Justice. Indeed one of the lasting tributes we can pay to our Founding Fathers will be to rescue our economy from destruction, our people from indignities, disgrace and shame and our country from its lost prestige and glory.

Fellow citizens, for these reasons, among many others, the PNP Administration has decided to underscore the importance of 6 March each year with full national honours, pomp and pageantry involving our citizens of all sections and walks of life. Consequently, for the first time in more than a decade small groups of all such sections of our community have been requested to participate, however, modestly, in today's celebrations as a minor rehearsal for the Silver Jubilee Celebrations of 1982 and the years ahead.

The rich variety of colour, skills and professionalism on display before us today vividly portrays the human resources endowment of independent Ghana, built up largely after 1957. We must therefore fully harness this endowment to our enormous natural resources for the benefit of all our people since our salvation lies in our own hands. From this platform, I wish to renew my strongest appeal through you to the whole nation to rise up as one solidly united people to the challenges of our times and redouble the efforts we are already making to rebuild Mother Ghana into a peaceful, stable and properous nation.

The independence of Ghana marked the real beginning of the struggle for the total liberation of the African continent. This struggle has scored many phenomenal political successes. There is, therefore no doubt that Namibia and Azania shall in due course, also join the fold of independent nations to complete the total political liberation of our continent.

Our economic recovery, development and strength, as our political independence, will also greatly speed up the economic emancipation of our continent. Let it therefore not be said that our generation was found wanting when Mother Ghana and Africa needed us most. Our immediate task is to rebuild Ghana from its present ruins and make it the prosperous and proud nation that it used to be, in the vanguard of African liberation. Our youth in particular, should therefore constantly be taught to realize, accept and be prepared at all times to fulfil, Ghana's historic role in Africa.

Officers and men of the Ghana Armed Forces, the Police and Prisons Services, I wish to avail myself of this opportunity very warmly to congratulate you all on your smart turn-out today and also on your high performance in Ghana's peace-keeping operations in the Middle East. I also extend my congratulations to schoolmasters and children, voluntary organizations and cultural groups taking part in the twenty-fourth independence celebrations today.

Finally, Excellencies, distinguished ladies and gentlemen, once again I warmly congratulate all participants and also thank all spectators and indeed the whole nation on this happy and memorable anniversary. I wish all of you greater successes in your personal and collective endeavours.

We shall overcome! Long live Freedom and Justice! Long live Ghana! Thank you all.

The next day, he witnessed a parade of voluntary organizations at the Black Star Square and addressed them.

It gives me great pleasure to address this magnificent parade of school children, workers, voluntary organizations and indeed the whole nation through them on this second anniversary of civilian rule.

All too soon another year has turned its full cycle and we have again gathered on a second occasion of our return to democratic rule in self-respect and human dignity. I therefore wish to extend to all of you gathered here and indeed to all Ghanaians at home and abroad very warm felicitations, a very happy birthday and many, many returns.

Watching this march-past has made all of us immensely pleased and very proud indeed. In particular, we have been deeply impressed by the youthful exuberance and commitment which strongly re-affirm our belief that Ghana's abundant youthful human resources are her greatest renewable asset and must be well organized and directed towards the social and economic transformation of our total national community. Failure to plan for our teeming, and still fast increasing youth will spell the doom of the future of our country.

As I have stated on numerous occasions, the role of youth is very crucial to the success of our endeavours to reconstruct our economy now and rebuild our nation for the present and future generations of Ghanaians. Indeed, after my election as the People's National Party's Presidential candidate in 1979, I declared that my nomination was both a tribute and a challenge to the youth of Ghana and that I had accepted that challenge on their behalf. Since April 1979 I have increasingly forged links and closer co-operation with youth groups from all walks of life and also with workers organizations at all levels. I see in this co-

232

operation the most viable approach in the crusade to lift our country from economic despondency and social gloom which were the legacies left to us in 1979 by previous Governments and the maladministration of the last decade.

Again, as I have repeatedly stated, the need for profound and radical changes in the moral fabric of our society should not be underestimated any longer. After many years of apathy, corruption, inefficiency and indiscipline in high places, respect for rules and regulations, the pride and confidence of our people have suffered serious erosions thus leaving the younger generation justifiably bewildered and uncertain of their future.

We must therefore reverse these unhealthy trends through the slow but steady process of rebuilding our moral base, re-instilling discipline in ourselves and re-establishing respect for our elders, institutions and also respect for law and order. We should always remember and apply the simple courtesies in our daily lives since these lubricate relations in all organized human societies. To say 'thank you', 'sorry' or 'please' does not lessen but rather enhances one's importance, self-respect and dignity as a human being. In fact, this is one of the main differences distinguishing *Homo sapiens* from wild beasts.

We must also discard the erroneous notion held by many people and particularly by public servants that Government is one big alien cornucopia to be cheated or plundered for personal gain or else to be held in contempt and abused. Government is all of us. It represents the aggregate aspirations of the people it serves. Its success or failure therefore affects, directly or indirectly, all of us, young or old, rich or poor.

As the greatest asset of this nation, it falls more on the youth to help protect and safeguard public property acquired from the taxes parents and other adults pay and which the youth will inherit as their birthright. You should therefore all regard yourselves as part of Government and be actively involved in the 'open and participatory democracy' being practised under my Administration.

For this reason and, indeed, for the sake of future generations, it is our collective duty to support policies of public interest and to redouble our efforts in providing selfless and dedicated services for increased productivity at all levels. To this end, I appeal to all the youth, workers, farmers and fishermen of Ghana once more to move into the forefront of the crusade for the social and economic resuscitation of our nation so as to ensure a brighter future for the present and future generations. It is the duty of all of us to leave Ghana, when we do, better than we met it when we were born.

Distinguished ladies and gentlemen, I should like to reassure you that my Administration is determined and indeed will do everything humanly possible to bring about sound economic recovery and improved stan-

233

dards of living for all our people. It is to this end that we have never shied away from taking bold decisions that may at first appear to be harsh but which will definitely revive our ailing economy.

We are grateful to all concerned citizens for their understanding, support and stoical acceptance of what we dare not shirk in order to salvage our sinking ship of state. We are not deterred by the few who delight in upsetting the apple cart. We submit ourselves to the public and to posterity for judgment.

In the last two years, my Administration has been working quietly but tirelessly to provide the basis for the effective and meaningful arrest of the decline facing our economy and to recreate avenues and the proper climate for sound economic recovery, growth and eventual take-off.

In the rural areas where the majority of our people still live and produce the real assets and wealth of our country we have been trying to provide such facilities as good drinking water, electricity, medical facilities and adequate inputs for farmers, without much fanfare. . . . We are glad that our rural people are determined to help us so that we can help them as we have often promised.

Even the selfishness and refusal of so-called regional distributors to send supplies meant for people in the countryside has not undermined their determination to help save the country. We are however aware that despite what we have tried to do over the last two years, much still remains to be done, particularly for our farmers, miners and workers in other vital sectors who are still the real pillars of our economy and source of wealth.

The irony of our present predicament is that our country can boast of some of the most abundant natural resources on our continent. If we therefore still wallow in poverty, it is the result of our own over-complacency, indiscipline and mismanagement. We must mobilize and harness these resources now and put them to good use for the benefit of the present and future generations of all our people.

As I have often emphasized, the problems facing us are also complicated by international economic factors over which we have hitherto had little control. We have worked steadily and courageously over the last two years to awaken awareness in the dangers inherent in this lopsided, blind and soulless approach to our peculiar problems. We are grateful to those who are developing some understanding for and appreciation of our point of view.

One glaring example of these external factors has been the price of petroleum products. Thus, after passing a law last year which linked the internal price of petroleum products to the world price of crude oil, many were those who mistook our intentions to be mere gimmicks to evade our responsibility to check inflation.

In contrast, when a couple of weeks ago, the price of crude oil was abated by the modest margin of $4 per barrel we quickly kept faith with our promise and reduced the internal prices of petroleum products according to our laws, without prompting from anyone. This demonstrates our determintion to pass on the benefits of improved external economic developments to our people. We hope that this reduction will be passed on to our people in the countryside.

Similarly, now that an International Cocoa Agreement has been accepted for application and cocoa prices are rising and stabilizing on the world market, we have the basis for determining an equitable cocoa-producer price for our farmers, as stated in our Manifesto. This is how to manage an economy and not the reckless policies which have created the present mess. Yet our ears were being deafened recently with such policies again out of cheap political gimmicks, intellectual dishonesty, or logic walking on stilts.

Improved world market prices for cocoa and other exports will not only enable us to increase that local producer price to cocoa farmers but also increase our ability to provide greater quantities of raw materials and inputs for increased productive activities here at home. Let us all therefore play more honest politics in the coming year to enhance peace and stability and thus promote increased all-round productivity in foodstuffs, fishing, textiles and other commodities for home consumption and export.

Distinguished guests, gallant youth and workers, in congratulating all of you on your smart turn-out and impressive displays, I wish to place on record my sincere gratitude especially to our workers and farmers for their immeasurable contributions to the urgent needs of our dear country. Despite our present problems no one can write off Ghana any more, thanks to our own unaided efforts over the last two years of civilian democratic rule.

Ghana is an external historical and geo-physical factor which exists and will forever continue to do so with or without the understanding, acceptance, co-operation of other artificial and ephemeral creations and organizations. I therefore salute our gallant farmers, fishermen, workers, our teeming youth and all those who understand these elementary facts and are prepared to continue contributing to our recovery and thus sustain the democratic way of life we have freely chosen for ourselves.

Some of us were born under colonial rule but thanks to the founding fathers of modern and independent Ghana led by the late Osagyefo, Dr Kwame Nkrumah of blessed memory, about seventy per cent of our present population were born in freedom and must therefore strive to continue being free, self-confident, disciplined and proud of the historic mission of independent and sovereign Ghana.

Once more, I wish all of you a very happy second anniversary of our civilian democratic rule.

51

Second Anniversary of the Third Republic

The second anniversary of the return to civilian rule and democratic government, 23 September 1981, was hailed by the citizens of Ghana as an auspicious occasion. The President spoke to his people on radio and television.

Fellow Ghanaians, on the eve of the second anniversary of civilian rule, I take this opportunity warmly to congratulate all of you for our collective achievement in successfully practising democracy over the last two years.

Despite the difficulties we have encountered over the period we are convinced and have amply demonstrated as a people that the democratic system of government best guarantees our liberties, safeguards our legitimate aspirations and enables us freely to discuss our problems and take practicable decisions. This record has been the result of our individual and collective efforts and sacrifices despite the yearnings of most of us for relief from the neglect and deprivations of the past.

I therefore thank all of you most sincerely for your patience and for making it possible for us this evening to reaffirm the statement I made exactly a year ago, 'that the third attempt at democratic rule was no longer an experiment but a permanent reality'. Let us all earnestly resolve yet once again that democracy is indeed here to stay forever.

As our customary and traditional annual festivals demand, we should also critically re-examine our past performances, review our shortcomings or failures on this occasion and rededicate ourselves for more devoted and selfless services to our motherland in the months and years ahead. This analysis and self-criticism is also relevant to the Silver Jubilee of our independence and sovereign nationhood which we shall observe next March during the year of civilian rule.

Compatriots, as Head of Government and Head of State I have often been addressed as the Father of the Nation. In all humility I speak in this role tonight in bringing forward a few home truths for all of us to reflect upon soberly and calmly.

Democracy is said to be one of the most expensive forms of Government, but in our present circumstances must we swallow this view uncritically? I am convinced that we can operate this system effectively, efficiently, beneficially and yet less expensively if we all do for ourselves what Government by its very nature has not been designed to do and cannot do.

We should constantly remember that our past so-called liberators and redeemers satisfied only their individual simplistic views which they rammed down our throats against the wishes of the overwhelming majority of our people. Indeed, such claims sprang only from selfish motives. Similar opportunists are now reliably reported to be planning and training in some foreign lands, supported with funds from those who are more interested in destabilizing other societies than in the lives and welfare of human beings. In fact, the very system we have freely chosen for ourselves in Ghana is hateful to such adventurers and their foreign sponsors.

It is therefore our individual and collective duty to be vigilant and guard against them. The price of freedom is eternal vigilance. Our public performances, utterances and behaviour should also discourage rather than give the slightest cause for such confidence tricksters, adventurers and fanatics to exploit for their diabolical ends.

I appeal to all of you, especially to the youth who have more to lose from further spoilations of our country, to be extremely vigilant against those now actively engaged in recruiting and training some of our nationals for the sole purpose of destroying our motherland and throwing us back into shame abroad and dictatorial rule at home. The rule by decrees and fiats has failed to lead us to the Elysian fields of peace and happiness we were promised on past occasions.

In contrast, we have enjoyed our liberties and self-respect for two years now and should therefore not carelessly allow these inherent birth rights to be taken away from us any more. We must be prepared to live in and defend our freedom even in dignified poverty. We can, we must and we shall rise again even through our own unaided efforts, just as we have done before by being the first to win our political independence against all odds.

During the past two years, my Administration has laboured relentlessly and painstakingly to ensure personal liberties, fair play and, above all, freedom of expression without fear of harassment. These are among the necessary ingredients in the successful practice of civilian democratic rule.

Fellow citizens, the representative parliamentary democratic system may not be as perfect as the direct democracy practised by the smaller societies of the ancient Greek city states but it enables our people to express their will through those they have freely elected to Parliament. However, this also demands that the institution of Parliament itself should always rise above private and personal interests and thus ensure the success of this system in Ghana.

Within two years and after a long lapse of time and discontinuity of parliamentary life, our Members of Parliament have already learnt the ropes and made considerable progress. While commending them for this achievement, I should also like to appeal to them once again to make judicious use of their immunities, powers and privileges by avoiding issues that easily provoke unnecessary confrontations between Parliament and the Executive, Parliament and the Judiciary, Parliament and the individual members of the public, or which damage our permanent national interests. Merely playing to the gallery on sensitive national issues also only tends to make others despise us as a people.

At these early stages of our democracy the public can easily become disillusioned with Parliament, from which concrete ideas and suggestions are expected in enacting laws for our national recovery and a better tomorrow. Public disillusionment of this nature has often been easily exploited by the enemies of the democratic way of life everywhere in the past. We should all therefore learn from hindsight and apply the natural and elementary instinct of self-preservation.

Countrymen, it is sad to note that the Judiciary has not yet fully awakened from its deep slumbers of the past. Despite my repeated appeals, that system has not yet been streamlined to speed up the trial of even petty cases which keep piling up throughout the country. Of late, we have rather been treated to frequent and heavy doses of personal squabbles and recriminations within the system at a time when our people expect better examples than this and quicker adjudication of their cases. Another particular concern to me has been the unfortunate results of legal technicalities which becloud common sense and smother plain truth.

This has become a great demoralizing factor to our peace officers, security agencies and the general public and should therefore be checked within the Judiciary itself and by our 'learned' citizens. On our part, Government has initiated policies and measures to deal with the problem of national indiscipline and therefore appeals for the co-operation of all concerned officials and citizens who should expose and have the courage of their convictions to substantiate, reports against wrongdoers.

Fellow Ghanaians, friends and well-wishers, the Executive machinery has long been plagued with numerous problems and bottle-necks. As you are all well aware, this machinery is made up not only of Ministers and Deputy Ministers but also the whole range of public services and Corporations.

It is a sad commentary that after two years of civilian rule, 'open government and participatory democracy', many people placed in positions of trust still lack confidence in taking and implementing simple decisions. Some officials even consider themselves to be so insulated in their positions that they watch foodstuffs and meat go rotten, squander substantial funds on fictitious articles or frills or on less urgent exercises, and then call that independence even of the general public and of taxpayers.

Many Heads of Departments command scant respect from their subordinates due to their poor backgrounds and incompetence and yet refuse to advise themselves, withdraw and redirect their other talents and energies elsewhere. Holding on to functional positions as if they were sinecure jobs can undermine our determination to take our destiny into our own hands under civilian rule. Incompetence, lack of feeling and sensitivity to public expectations while clinging only to privileges and fringe benefits at public expense can lead to ridicule and the slow death of civilian rule. As a people, we should not tolerate or condone such practices any more, if we want to protect our hard and painfully re-established democratic institutions.

The first year of civilian rule was spent as a honeymoon by everybody. During the second year people placed in positions of trust were given the benefit of the doubt to prove their worth. Henceforth we must all be judged by results. Those unable to acquit themselves creditably should therefore give way to others able and prepared to tackle the difficult tasks and move forward in the hard times confronting us.

Fellow citizens, customary usages, land and chieftaincy disputes, coupled with inter and intra-ethnic disturbances have tested our energies and meagre resources very severely in recent years and also diverted much attention from the primary objectives of restructuring our economy and rebuilding our country. The great losses of life and property caused by such disputes and disturbances have been most deplorable and greatly harmed our reputation as being among the most intelligent, tolerant and peace-loving people in our continent. Our traditional rulers, should therefore help to reverse these negative trends.

Indeed, the institution of chieftaincy being one of our most important cultural and traditional heritages should play a more positive role in our efforts in rebuilding our shattered economy.

Our customs, land ownership and tenure systems must undergo change, develop and move with the rapid developments of our times, before it is too late for us to innovate without being wholly new and foreign, or to conserve without being wholly old, decadent and unprofitable.

Compatriots, the examples I have briefly sketched this evening are meant to demonstrate to all sections of our community that we still have a long way to go in making a lasting success of civilian democratic rule in Ghana. My purpose is not to paint a picture of despair or doom. Indeed, civilian rule is very much alive now, but lawlessness and too much complacency, if allowed any further scope, can turn it into a sour and sterile system. We should not forget so soon the harrowing experiences and humiliations we have endured before regaining our present liberties.

My Administration has been particularly worried about too much complacency, indiscipline and graft which have long taken deep roots in our public life. For instance, an efficient, disciplined and, above all, honest Police Service is indispensable for maintaining law and order and ensuring fair play for all. In contrast, disciplined law enforcement agencies create the impression of aiding and abetting crime. Yet the hierarchy of the Police Service does not appear to appreciate this. The whole nation still earnestly looks up to the Police and security agencies to greatly improve upon their performances to earn public respect and confidence in them.

The top hierarchy of the Police Service should therefore be either bold in reinstilling discipline in the system, or give way to others who can and are prepared to do so. The Police have a duty to perform and must produce results; I am confident many of its members are prepared and capable of producing the results the nation expects and demands from the Service. Mere time-servers should therefore now advise themselves accordingly. The nation demands nothing short of this.

For the first time ever we have been able to live with and can boast of a free press. As such, no journalist, broadcaster or editor has been molested for expressing views contrary to those of government and often even very harmful to our national interests. Our method has been to appeal to the Press itself for responsible reporting and self-discipline in the national interest. We are happy and grateful that these appeals have often been heeded and accorded respect whenever they deserved it.

Conscious of the vital role of the Press in the success or failure of any open society, I wish tonight to repeat my appeal for this form of self-discipline and to emphasize that over-sensationalization of events in Ghana, wilful distortions and quite often sheer misrepresentations can do untold harm to our economy, democratic way of life and our national image. Press freedom should not be surrendered for the mere financial gain now being termed 'Solidarity' or 'Item 13' as an accepted item of vocabulary in journalistic circles.

In fact, press freedom will be meaningless if people have to pay for their side of the story to be heard. The Press should rather defend the weak, the disadvantaged and the have-nots more than the wealthy and privileged sectors of our society. A few of our journalists appear to take some delight in running down their own country to the outside world, but is this really fair to their motherland? I wish to make a special appeal to such journalists to realize that our democracy is too young to be subjected to the licentiousness, fabricated scandals and shocks which older democracies and mature economies can absorb.

Fellow citizens, the year ahead should mark a great watershed for all of us. Efforts we have so far made to revive our economy must now begin to yield results. In fact, the chances of recovery in all areas of economic activity have been greatly increased and enhanced. Agriculture shall continue to receive top priority attention and resources. Tractors, harvesters and other implements are expected shortly from Brazil, Great Britain and a number of other friendly countries to augment the supplies of our tools for greatly increased small-scale productive agricultural activities, buttressed with a package of incentives for farmers soon to be announced.

Several agreements have also been reached with friendly foreign governments and international agencies for large-scale farming to greatly increase our food production efforts and output. As of now adequate supplies of spare parts are available in the system for the use of serious farmers who should therefore help to ensure that these are not smuggled out of Ghana to their detriment.

Our attempts in the past two years towards rehabilitating broken-down machinery and equipment have now placed industry on a relatively sound footing for increased productivity in the coming year. We shall intensify our efforts in the supply of raw materials while continuing with the policy of reducing waste. Malpractices such as over-invoicing and under-invoicing, short-landing of goods and evasion of taxes shall all be more closely scrutinized and checked.

With the New Investment Code Act and the high powered Investment Centre, the scene has been set for greater investments in such vital areas as gold, diamond and bauxite mining and also in the timber and tourist sectors. The Board of the New Investment Centre shall streamline and expedite the processing of investment enquiries and procedures.

My recent tour of four European countries having helped to dispel the doubts that have existed in the minds of investors on our investment policies, I am confident that economic activities will gather increasing momentum in Ghana in the months and years ahead. I therefore appeal to you all to welcome punctually, honestly and with courtesy investors who will be visiting us in increasing numbers.

During the coming year we expect considerable changes in our raod and other infrastructures which had long been neglected and are now in a most deplorable state. Substantial funds have been allocated for the importation of road construction equipment and these are expected to arrive soon for greatly increased activities in the reconstruction of our roads and bridges.

Compatriots, we have devoted the last two years to laying solid foundations for arresting further decline of our national fortunes. The years ahead therefore hold out many chances of a brighter future for us. But to realize this, the need for discipline, hard work, honesty and selfless devotion to duty is also imperative on all of us. Indeed, unless we change our old habits we shall fail to realize our objectives and may even end up in national disaster again. Indeed, the dangers of the disintegration of our society may not come from economic difficulties alone but from the lack of adaptability, flexibility and from indiscipline within our national community. They may also come from the most unexpected quarters with trivial immediate causes, as was the case in the past year.

Most of our present problems spring from carelessness, inefficiency and indiscipline on the part of managements and our fellow workers. In fact, the waste, greed, corruption and mismanagement we see all around us result mainly from the lack of initiative and discipline.

Thus, indiscipline at our airports, harbours and other points of entry into Ghana has grown to such proportions that visitors and indeed even local travellers are often scared by the chaos, the confusion and the fear of losing their personal belongings. Entering or leaving our country should therefore be made safe henceforth by the competent authorities.

Officers should be held accountable for their actions in order to check the tempo of indiscipline in the public sector. Public property such as houses, vehicles and equipment deteriorate rapidly due to indiscriminate use, lack of maintenance and ineffective controls. Disregard for laws and regulations in all spheres of our national life should be checked and the risks of living in an anarchic society removed.

It is imperative for all of us to make Discipline our watchword and challenge wrongdoing and the insolence of office in the coming months and years and thus move ahead in progress and success with each passing day. With this appeal and confidence, I wish you all once more a very happy anniversary. May success crown our individual and collective efforts and each day bring us closer to the achievement of our national objectives and aspirations.

I thank you all. Good luck and goodnight.

52

Meeting of the Association of Professional Bodies, 6 May 1981

Taking advantage of the representative nature of the meeting of Professional Bodies, the President spoke on many matters of concern to professional associations and the general public. Among other things, he referred to the courageous role played by members of the professions against the proposed imposition of undemocratic civilian rule; the advent of press freedom in the country; the true nature of the legacy handed down from the preceding military regimes and other effects of economic mismanagement.

On the positive side, he welcomed the draft Investment Code Bill which was tabled in Parliament.

I am very happy and highly honoured that this occasion has offered me the opportunity to address all of you at this combined meeting of the Recognized Professional Bodies Association for the first time since I assumed office. I had before had occasion to meet only some individual associations and a number of professionals in their private capacities to discuss and deliberate on various socio-economic matters affecting the well-being of our country.

On this first occasion therefore, I wish warmly to congratulate you for the courageous stand you took, together with other bodies and students four years ago, against attempts to impose nebulous political systems on our country which were not acceptable to the vast majority of Ghanaians. Thanks to that bold and sustained struggle Ghana enjoys a democratically elected Government based on the multi-party system today. The country should, I hope, be eternally grateful to you and all those who took part in the fight for the return to constitutional and democratic civilian rule. I have no doubt that you will continue to protect and defend this happy outcome of your struggle and sacrifices.

The social, political and economic conditions against which you had to fight have greatly changed in many ways since my Administration

245

assumed office. Socially and politically, we can say today that we are free and practising an open Government in which no one needs to subscribe to any particular political party or movement before he or she can be heard or vindicate the right to live in peace or without undue harassment. Our press and institutions of mass communication are open to all to express their views on matters of national importance. Our Judiciary is independent and free to interpret our laws and the constitution without fear or favour. We can boast of having not detained anyone because of his or her political views or religious beliefs.

On the economic front, the picture has become increasingly clear that the mismanagement, incompetence, secretiveness and arbitrariness which provoked you to stand up against military rule four years ago are now making their fullest impact felt on all of us. Our internal situation had however been compounded by external forces over which we have had little or no control. As is well known to you all at this meeting, as a people we have been rather too dependent on imports for a long time now. This has led to the present great concern about our foreign exchange earnings. We have developed and greatly expanded many costly tastes and life-styles without the means to satisfy them. This is one of the problems facing our urban centres, fanned in particular by an articulate minority who are usually quick to whip up anger, though not over fufu, banku, akple, tuosafe or kenkey nut imported in tasteless and sometimes rotten condition.

In the face of lower prices for our exportable raw materials, massive smuggling and crippling oil import bills, which now stand at almost 40 per cent of our total hard currency earnings, our foreign exchange resources have dwindled increasingly while our demand for imported commodities, equipment and productive inputs has greatly expanded over the last decade. To worsen matters, our population has also grown at the fast rate of 2.7 per cent per annum, thus greatly raising the dependency ratio and placing acute strains and stresses on the costly goods and services that our present meagre resources can purchase abroad and ship home at additional high freight costs.

The consequences of the decade-long economic mismanagement are vividly portrayed in the poor state of our roads, steep decline in agricultural and industrial production, breakdown in the transport and communication systems, water supplies, hospital and health services and the run-down of educational institutions. Our lack of means to import adequate supplies of goods and services to match our greatly expanded demand has inevitably made prices shoot up considerably, thus eroding the purchasing power of all our citizens, including you as highly qualified professionals.

We have tried to mitigate this situation by granting some wage and salary awards which had been held up artificially for a long time and also by giving more fringe benefits. However, these awards have, unfortunately, not yet been matched by any substantial increases in productivity, hence inflation has persisted at a higher rate than we would have liked. This dilemma has spurred us on to take further steps to improve upon our foreign exchange earnings. These include the provision of urgently needed inputs for the export sector and the removal of the crippling controls under which it had long operated. We are also making efforts to attract investment into such areas as agriculture, gold mining and exploration for crude oil which stand the best chance of making an early impact on our present poor hard currency earnings performance.

However, we still need to do very much more than this before we can get the economy to turn round from depression towards recovery and this is precisely what we are trying to do in the draft Investment Code Bill now before Parliament. I therefore hope that you will all view the attempts we have made and are making dispassionately and objectively and give them your fullest support and backing.

If we want to recover then we must provide the conditions and political climate that can attract investment. If we continue to be the dog in the manger then we shall starve the horse drawing our economic cart and also die ourselves of starvation because we cannot eat and digest fodder. Similarly, as I have once stated, we cannot continue to be an island of low costs and cheap goods in a world of rising prices and high production costs even if we had the means which, of course, we lack woefully now.

Indeed, Mr Chairman, until the measures we have taken and will continue to take begin to bear fruit and thus enable us to provide adequate quantities of the goods and services we need, it would be less than frank and candid on my part to give your Association the impression that the tasks ahead are now easier than before the advent of civilian rule. The difference is that we can all now discuss and find commonly acceptable solutions to our problems since what touches all must be decided by all, and not by unworkable decrees and fiats. We must therefore apply our long coveted and reborn freedom responsibly.

The enormity of our problems, difficulties and hardships has made some of our citizens to lose faith in our country, even to the point of seeking their livelihood and fortunes abroad. Admittedly and as I have often said, the times are difficult and the forces with which we have to grapple to turn the tide are complex and formidable. The hard times at home are great, though illusive, expectations abroad have led our engineers, doctors, lecturers, teachers, architects, accountants, skilled, semi-skilled and even unskilled citizens, whom we can ill-afford to lose in these crucial times, to leave our shores in large numbers in recent years for presumed new Eldorados. Yet having worsened the manpower situation by their departure, the same nationals still expect us to overcome the problems they have left behind before they may return to enjoy better conditions later. This has been one of the paradoxes or ironies of our situation for a decade now. It has not started with the present regime.

Mr Chairman, much has been said about shortages, high prices, the inadequacy of remuneration, lack of job satisfaction and poor conditions of service among the causes of the exodus. Yet many of our nationals have been imprisoned in almost all foreign countries which are supposed to be better off than Ghana at present.

We must therefore begin to examine the present phase of our evolution as a people more critically, dispassionately, objectively and unemotionally than we have so far done in the recent past. We should not, as I have said many times already, bury our heads in the sand of our moral problems pretending that we have hidden ourselves from them. If we do not face our problems squarely and honestly, we will never be able to solve them.

For instance, higher salaries, job satisfaction and better conditions of service have to be related also to our present economic and social circumstances. We must work hard to produce more before we can enjoy the good things of life for which we are all craving. It would be unrealistic for us to offer or promise rewards which cannot be matched by increased productivity and the capacity of the economy to bear them.

Ladies and gentlemen, my Administration greatly appreciates the constraints under which most of you have worked for a long time. You lack adequate manpower, equipment and material which you would wish to have. However, these are the results of the many years of economic mismanagement, coupled with forces beyond our control. These crying shortcomings are the very problems against which you fought four years ago and which we of the present generation have been called upon to solve. In this regard it is incumbent on us to husband our limited resources with unrelenting care so as to maximize the results we can obtain from them. But can we really claim that we have started to obtain the maximum from the resources we have been making available even over the last twenty months for the operation and maintenance of our water supplies, our hospitals, roads, transport and communication systems, our educational institutions? How many times have scarce resources not been wasted for lack of the proper operation and maintenance of plant and equipment? How many times have we not locked up large sums of money in useless stores only to turn round to say that we have not money for simple, inexpensive but very vital inputs? How much are we losing by sub-standard professional work and unethical practices? As educated, enlightened and professional élites, are we living up to the expectations of the public whose sweat, taxes and

248

sacrifices have made us what we are today? Are we retaining the respect and high regard which the public had for us in the past?

In the light of recent, and glaringly unexpected, unprofessional and unethical developments and practices within some of your associations, you may wish to ponder very seriously over these nagging questions. We are all being critically observed and judged by the public which has educated or elected us for our various callings. I am confident that if we manage our resources more professionally and efficiently now than in past irresponsible periods, we can turn the economy round as quickly as we all want. These failings and weaknesses within our society, institutions and professions may have affected only a few members but their cost to the nation, in terms of wasted economic resources and even the loss of human life has been incalculable. We should therefore not tolerate, condone or practise wrongdoing in the public sector any more.

For instance, jobs should not be certified any more for payment when in fact they have been done shoddily or not done at all. Official time and facilities should not be diverted for private personal use and interest. The few have, perhaps, give a bad name to the many. However, the many within the various professions who are conscientious and are giving dedicated service, against many odds to the nation, should not lose heart now, having come this far and endured so much.

We are grateful to all such professionals. Their determination and abnegation is an example of the spirit which the present times demand. Only such sacrifices can help turn the tide and generate the wealth which will benefit all in future. Nothing great has ever been achieved without sacrifice, commitment and singleness of purpose. The economic salvation of our country is the challenge which we must all now face in this spirit if we want to do our duty towards our nation. In order to make our people love our country we who are in a position to do so must first make it lovely through nation-building sacrifices, not through demands for ever-increasing privileges and amenities of the expense of our rural poor, hard-pressed, disfigured, yet still the most productive sectors of our society.

In this connection, Mr Chairman, I wish briefly to refer, in passing, to the needless problem created by our doctors in the public service by charging fees in Government Hospitals, Health Centres and Clinics. As I have often state, my Administration is firmly committed to ensuring better working conditions for all in the public sector. We appreciate the sacrifices being made by our professionals such as engineers and medical personnel who have often had to work round the clock and make great sacrifices to keep such vital services as water, electricity and life-saving health services running. That was how the great inventors, explorers, reformers, nation- and even empire-builders earned their names.

Moreover, we should not run away from certain legal, moral and economic realities staring us in the face. As a Government we have never minced our words about the enormity of the economic problems facing us as a people. Indeed, we have continually informed the general public about our efforts to rehabilitate our institutions, which had been neglected until they have decayed beyond all recognition.

We have therefore viewed the problems facing our medical personnel in this light with much sympathy and have long asked in vain for proposals meant to ameliorate the situation. The plight and anger of our doctors should therefore not be visited on the general public or Government but on those who have ignored our request and repeated reminders for proposals. Ladies and gentlemen, a good case can easily be lost by intransigence, over-reaction and blatant illegalities. We must therefore implore our medical doctors to advise themselves and desist from committing any more illegalities or provoking public anger against themselves. We are aware of the hardships being encountered by our young doctors and the nursing staff in the areas of transportation and housing and have therefore been trying to provide relief in such areas despite the limits imposed on us by the meagre resources available to us. But I wish to re-emphasize that the case of medical doctors cannot be treated in isolation from those of other professionals in the public sector. That is why we have always tried to consider all claims on sectoral bases rather than treating them selectively and preferentially. It is for this reason that the claims of our medical doctors have been referred to your august Association for a more comprehensive assessment and review in the light of our present shattered economy. I therefore firmly believe that your Association should be given a fair chance to deliberate on these matters and make objective proposals and recommendations on them.

In this connection I want to express my gratitude to your Association for its prompt initial reaction to our request for the Association's intervention. I am happy to announce that Government has accepted your recommendation for the setting up of a Working Committee consisting of Ministers, representatives of the Ghana Medical Association, the Ministries of Health and Finance, the Public Services Salaries and Wages Commission and of the Association of Recognized Professional Bodies.

Detailed membership of the Committee will be announced as soon as consultations with the respective bodies have been completed. We also hope that the Ghana Medical Association will accept your recommendations to call off charging unauthorized consultation fees and thus create the right atmosphere for resolving the issues at stake. We appeal to the general public and all others directly or indirectly involved to exercise restraint and allow the matter to be resolved peacefully.

As far as the specific issue of the levying of hospital fees is concerned, my initial understanding was that this was meant to be a form of protest to draw public attention to the need to improve upon facilities available within the public health sector and also to change public policy which had long become unrealistic and impracticable. If so, then the point has been made and our doctors should therefore now refrain from unconstitutional, unprofessional and unethical activities which have so far tended only to create wrong impressions or impute bad motives to them.

I should like to repeat that my Administration is committed to improving upon our present health facilities, but not by illegal means. The levying of fees by doctors in the public service sector for themselves is unconstitutional and illegal and should therefore be stopped now. Doctors who want to charge fees ought to for private practice. Government hospitals are built and equipped at public expense so that they can provide medical services at minimum cost to the same public which has provided the infrastructure and continuing supplies. Moreover, all such charges can only be sanctioned by Parliament and not by individuals or groups. I therefore wish to remind all our doctros to realize the illegal, unprofessional and unethical nature of their conduct. Government has long recognized the need to improve upon the means of funding improvements in the spread and quality of medical services to be made available to the general public. We will therefore continue with our efforts in that direction, but illegality, which can easily provoke anarchy by other sectors also taking the law into their own hands, should stop.

Finally, Mr Chairman, I wish to congratulate your Association for the appropriate choice of theme for this year's Professional Week, namely, 'the Performance of the Various Arms of Government so far under the Third Republican Constitution'. The theme interests all our people and I therefore hope that critical, fair and objective analyses can be made of our performance as a nation in the past twenty months. I hope that such professional and objective analysis may help us to know our strong and weak points, our sins of omission and commission and thus enable us to avoid our failings, draw inspiration from our successes and go further to overcome the daunting problems still ahead of all of us.

To this end, I have great pleasure in declaring your Professional Week for this year open.

53

Graduation Parade, Ghana Military Academy, 31 July 1981

I am happy to be associated yet once more with Ghana Military Academy graduation parades, thanks to Intake Twenty-two of the Academy which has afforded me the pleasure of being the reviewing officer at this morning's function.

The smart turn-out, steadiness on parade, the brisk drill forms and excellent marching which we have just witnessed and appreciated, eloquently demonstrate the thoroughness of the training given to these cadets. I congratulate the Commandant and his staff and also the trainees on their hard work and endeavours and also thank them sincerely for a job well done.

To you, graduating cadets, I wish to avail myself of this singular opportunity to remind you and your colleagues in the various units of the Ghana Armed Forces that you may lead or command others who may be older than you and that therefore this demands such high leadership qualities as patience, tolerance and sensitivity while being firm. There is no alternative to leadership by example, just as a disciplinarian is one who disciplines himself first before he attempts to discipline others.

You should therefore be the first to show good examples of what you command others to do and always also remember that loyalty is one of the first and most important principles of military life and discipline.

You must be loyal to the nation, to Government, to your fellow officers and men and indeed to all fellow citizens. This is one of the ways in which you can elicit loyalty from those you may have the duty to command or lead, in line with the words of the Motto of this Academy, namely, 'Service, Devotion and Sacrifice'.

You should demonstrate absolute devotion to duty and be prepared to sacrifice in all your undertakings and service to the nation. In addition to the laudable motto of this Academy, I wish to remind you to read carefully and constantly the contents of your Commission Parchments as well as the Armed Forces Oath. The Commission Parchment requests you to discharge your duties carefully and diligently and to use your best endeavours to keep men placed under you in good order and discipline. You will succeed if you yourselves are of good behaviour, well disciplined, obedient to your superiors, loyal to both your superiors and subordinates and absolutely dedicated to your work.

I have every confidence that, with the training you have recently acquired in Intake Twenty-two, you are now equipped to assume your new jobs and roles in meeting the challenges of your calling and of our times. These challenges require maturity of mind, courage, a high sense of professionalism and all the other virtues associated with your martial bearing as the patriotic soldiers that you are expected to be.

In a developing nation such as Ghana, the Armed Forces are expected not only to play their traditional role of repelling external aggressors and helping, if necessary, to maintain internal peace, but much more than that. Modernization and development are very high priority demands of all Third World nations whose Armed Forces should be capable of making contributions in other areas than purely military. The organization and equipment of our Armed Forces should therefore be geared, as much as possible, towards the realization of our economic recovery, national reconstruction and growth.

I am happy to note that, as far as assistance to the civil community is concerned, the Ghana Armed Forces have made an appreciable impact on the national scene since my assumption of office as Head of Government, Head of State and your Commander-in-Chief. In this regard, the current exercise being undertaken jointly by the Army and the Police to restore law and order in the three districts we have very reluctantly had to declare disaster areas—the Army, Navy and Police exercise designed to restore discipline and security at our ports; the exercise 'Glad Tidings' being conducted against smuggling; and the Air Force air services assistance to the Ghana Airways—are but a few of the many ways in which the Armed Forces are making invaluable and much appreciated contributions towards reconciling our people and rebuilding our country.

The nation appreciates and thanks you for these services and hard work being rendered, often under the very difficult conditions that I have personally observed during my tour of the Nanumba and other areas of our country. Having rendered such self-abnegatory services in the Middle East since our attainment of independence under worse conditions, I have no doubt that they will perform even better at home in these areas.

Your Excellencies, the Chief of Defence Staff, the Inspector-General of Police, service commanders, distinguished guests, ladies and gentlemen, I now request you all to join me in congratulating the graduating cadets. May they build more and more on the sound foundations the Ghana Military Academy has just laid for them. Thank you.

54

Reception for incoming group of Peace Corps Volunteers, 5 August 1981

Ghana was the first country to host a batch of Peace Corps Volunteers when the Peace Corps came into existence at the instance of President John F. Kennedy.

The President paid tribute to the excellent record of the Peace Corps' contribution to Ghana's development, particularly in the sector of education. Peace Corps volunteers have worked even in the most remote rural areas where no utility facilities exist.

It is with great pleasure that I welcome this new group of Peace Corps Volunteers who have just arrived in Ghana for a two-year period of service. I hope that our new friends have, since their arrival, begun acclimatizing themselves to our country and our people. I am personally aware of and greatly appreciate the valuable contribution volunteers of the Peace Corps have made in Ghana since the inception of the scheme in 1961.

This contribution has been particularly remarkable in our educational efforts, in the members' understanding of our countryside and of our values, as well as in the good relations they have helped to foster between the peoples of the USA and Ghana. The Peace Corps therefore deserve special mention and praise, hence the exceptional gesture I have made by attending this reception, much against protocol and the numerous calls on my time, now more than ever before.

Your Excellency, I am quite sure that the late Osagyefo, Dr Kwame Nkrumah and Alhaji Imoru Egala who were directly instrumental in bringing the Peace Corps to Ghana to assist in the rapidly expanding education programme of the First Republic, would also have accepted your kind invitation were they alive today.

Twenty years old this month, it is with this group that we have the privilege and joy of observing this important anniversary of the birth of the Peace Corps.

Thus, the first fifty-two volunteers who responded to the late President John F. Kennedy's appeal to leave their comfortable lives of the Affluent American Society and go out to help the world's poor, landed in Ghana exactly twenty years ago this month. The members of this group, like all the others who have preceded them, will reinforce the special and, indeed unique relations that have always existed between Ghana and the USA since the fifteenth century. It may be recalled that Christopher Columbus stopped over here in Ghana for some time in 1492 on the momentous voyage which eventually ended in the discovery of the then New World of the West Indies or the USA.

It was therefore, perhaps, not an accident or surprising that the first batch of Peace Corps Volunteers ever sent out of the USA were the fifty-two who arrived in Ghana in August 1961. The realization of the idea and the whole future of the Peace Corps, as conceived by the late President Kennedy of blessed memory, depended on the success or failure of that pioneering or experimental group sent out to Ghana. Highly successful, that experiment was later extended to many other developing countries, thus forever giving relations between Ghana and the Peace Corps concept a unique character. It was from here that the experiment spread out, so much so that Peace Corps Volunteers can now be found not only in every part of the world but even in the United States where the parallel organization of VISTA has been established to render services to various communities.

We do not only justifiably share with the Peace Corps its feeling of fulfilment, but also deeply appreciate the contribution its volunteers have made, over the years, to our education which has, in turn, immensely aided our development in the social, cultural, economic and other fields.

I wish to avail myself of this opportunity to remind this fresh group of volunteers that the goals of the Peace Corps have been and will remain relevant to the world, namely, helping to promote, through service, world peace, international friendship and mutual understanding. During your stay in Ghana you will be sharing your knowledge, skills and experiences with us. But you will also be acting as ambassadors of your country in Ghana particularly among our rural communities.

In various institutions and communities you shall be helping to promote greater and better understanding between our two countries and peoples. You will therefore do well to learn as much as possible of our way of life, particularly in the rural areas where you will live very close to nature among our rural folk.

I hope that when you eventually leave us and return home, you will be our true friends and reverse your roles as Ghana's Ambassadors to the people of the USA. We shall look to you to promote increasingly better understanding between our two peoples, countries and continents. Indeed, I wish to go further and request you to be committed advocates and defenders of the cause of Ghana, of Africa and of the entire developing world. In this regard, I hope that past Peace Corps Volunteers still correspond with their Ghanaian friends.

DG-R

Since the Peace Corps believes in supplementing rather than supplanting the efforts of local peoples, I hope that wherever each one of you will be living and working, you will be able quickly to adjust to the harsh realities of our country, particularly at this stage in our socio-economic evolution and that you will also find enough local initiative, efforts and encouragement to assist you in your tasks to mutual advantage.

You shall be working in environments and under conditions that are completely different from those in which you were born, bred and have worked until now. I am convinced that you are not daunted by our peculiar circumstances but rather that you have already subsumed and accepted them in the new challenges you have freely opted to face as an integral part of your efforts to assist in our development process. You will also be widening your horizons, enriching your knowledge and experience. In all this, I wish you well and every success.

Ghanaians are a friendly and hospitable people. Our equanimity, smiles and good humour, even in adversity, puzzle foreigners, particularly some Americans. However, given our world as it is today, there does not appear to be any real alternative to our humaneness which is definitely better than cold commercial relations. If you ever face any difficulties, our friendship and assistance will be forthcoming.

While extending a hearty welcome to you once more, I wish you an exciting, fulfilling and happy stay and also a successful tour of voluntary service in Ghana.

55

The President Welcomes Members of Parliament, 20 August 1981

It is my singular duty and pleasure as Head of the Executive Arm of Government to organize this small function in your honour to mark the busy and successful end of the Second Session of Parliament under civilian rule.

Personally, I very much appreciate the role of Parliament in our civilian regime and therefore congratulate all of you on this second successful completion of your session which you readily prolonged in the light of urgent matters of State. I thank the Speaker and all Honourable Members very sincerely for heeding my request to extend your session and dispose of the urgent matters of our national interest and import which had earlier been placed before you.

There is no doubt that during the Parliamentary year which has just ended, major decisions affecting the lives of our people were taken. I was happy to observe that during debates on matters of crucial national importance, honourable members often rose to the challenges of our time and discussed issues in the best traditions of honesty, impartiality and sincerity. Thus, your contributions in passing the Investment Code and the Cocoa Council Bills into law deserve particular mention. These are two of the areas on which the very survival of our country depends. I wish therefore to strongly urge you, while in recess, to help educate the general public on the need for their total support of these Acts.

Honourable Members, one of the fundamental bedrocks of democracy is opposing views on which people may often 'agree or disagree'. Out of healthy rivalry and disagreements between political opponents emerges the truth and refined policy decisions. However, when this rivalry degenerates into intractable conflicts and needless confrontations, then the very foundation of democracy can be threatened.

It was to forestall such a development that before I travelled to Nairobi I requested the Vice-President and other national leaders to take action and bring what was becoming an unhealthy confrontation between the Executive and the Legislature to a speedy end. I therefore wish to take this opportunity to reiterate that the main objective of that meeting was to restore our mutual respect which I consider to be one of the major prerequisites for the successful practice of democracy. While thanking you all for your co-operation in the matter, I hope that the third parliamentary year of the Third Republic will be completely free of such incidents.

Honourable Deputy Speakers and Members of Parliament, as you go into recess I would like to draw your kind attention to some aspect of your parliamentary duties which seem to call for deep reflection, constant and careful analysis. As you are all very well aware, the first role and duty of Parliaments everywhere is the enactment of laws within a territorially demarcated national community but which laws also take account of the laws of other national communities the world over. The Executive administers the law within the limits of those other laws and the Judiciary interprets the municipal or domestic laws.

During the past two years I have persistently called for co-operation between these three arms of State and have been happy with positive responses from all sectors, now and then. However, this co-operation should not make us lose sight of our cardinal roles, nor should it be exploited to harm our national interests. As I have mentioned earlier, your main duty is the enactment of laws and not the administration of the nation which is the responsibility of the Executive. You may therefore wish to exercise caution so that we do not run two parallel executive arms of Government or foreign policies for one nation.

Of late, there have been incidents where Parliament has sought to direct the Executive on administrative matters. This has included directives to Ministers, Heads of Corporations and various institutions. The right of Parliament to show interest in matters affecting the nation is admittedly provided for under the constitution. Nonetheless, it is necessary to guard against the tendency of administering the nation from Parliament House. Premature utterances in Parliament also tends to wreck delicate international negotiations and you may therefore wish to ponder over this vital point.

With our past experiences of carelessness and irresponsibility in Government circles, I fully understand the desire of Parliament to pass every Government action through the crucible of critical examination. The People's National Party Administration is fully committed to the policy of open Government and participatory democracy and is therefore always prepared to submit itself to public examination. It is for these reasons that members of the Executive have often freely made themselves available to Parliamentary Committees at short notice in order to deal with issues at Parliamentary Committees on which they do not receive adequate prior notice. We hope this practice will be improved upon all the time. Parliament may also wish to recognize its own limitations and impose on itself a measure of self-censure on sensitive national issues, as the Executive has so far tried to do. The wilful abuse of confidentiality also harms our national interests and we should therefore all guard against this. I am confident that with tolerance and respect for each other's roles we shall achieve our objective of economic recovery and ensure progress and prosperity for our country and our people.

Finally, I appeal to you to take advantage of the period of your recess to revisit your constituencies, re-establish contact with your constituents and to renew their confidence in you. It will be your responsibility to explain to them the pieces of legislation that you have enacted during the Session so that they can the better appreciate our collective efforts to restructure our society, rebuild our economy and improve upon their lives. I wish each and everyone of you some rest and success in your individual endeavours.

I thank the Chairman and Members of the Council of State for working very hard indeed in reviewing and commenting on almost all the legislation passed during the year. Similarly, I must thank the Parliamentary staff, the Press and all who have rendered various services for their hard work and patience in often working far late into the night. Thank you all.

56

Seminar for PNP Lawyers

The President meets the PNP group of lawyers, 29 August 1981.

It is with trepidation that a layman dares to address such an august gathering of learned conferers as you. This may also be seen by some as temerity and yet by others as imposture. Howbeit, the theme for this Seminar being, 'the Party, the Government and the Lawyer' appears to suggest that knowledge of the intricacies and interpretation of the obscurities of the law will not be required. This has emboldened me to accept the invitation to address you in the role of, at least, the proverbial old adage of the trusted friend of the 'Reasonable Man'. Moreover, given the fact that I also happen to have studied Political Science, History, Constitutions and now head the Government, the People's National Party and the State, it should not be too daunting for me to address my learned comrades.

Mr Chairman, legal practice and the way Government operates have one feature in common, namely, the principle of reciprocity, as diplomats term it. To the layman and in ordinary language, this means the principle of give-and-take which underlines the topics discussed at this Seminar.

Thus, the first address delivered by Dr Ivan Addae-Mensah, our Party's General Secretary, dealt with 'The Executive Presidency and Party Pressure Group'. One may argue that I was, perhaps, better qualified to speak on this topic had I been free in terms of time to do so. However, I had no doubt that the General Secretary would do justice to the topic, not only as a political scientist, but even more importantly, as a 'scientific politician', that is, a chemist capable of subjecting not only natural but also social, economic and political matters to cold analysis. In any case a General Secretary is the faithful mouthpiece of the Party and the Leader, be he President or not. I therefore hope that you have been satisfied with my performance through him on that topic.

Learned comrades, seemingly opposing views on pragmatism, ideology and otherisms can, in the final analysis, also be reconciled through give-and-take or reciprocity which has enabled the great People's National Party to accommodate many shades of opinions, while remaining united, since its inception. In other words, artificially merged or grafted antagonistic and mutually exclusive ideas such as the merger of capitalists and workers has never and can never be an intractable problem for leftists, centrists, pragmatists and rightists among us, since we easily give and take within the general fold of our mass Party.

The Honourable Minister of the Interior, Professor Ekow Daniels, dealt with 'The Process of Law-making and the role of the Party under a system of the separation of powers'. Here again, reciprocity has been both implicit and explicit in the topic. In the process of law-making, it has mostly been the Executive, since September 1979, which has initiated policies and submitted bills to Parliament for debate and enactment. Thus, policy is formulated by laymen and women based on the wishes of the sovereign electorate, but the actual language of Bills embodying such policies is generally selected by lawyers, that is, legal draftsmen. These are again examined and criticized by Parliamentary laymen who also represent the wishes of the people. These are then finally shaped into law by legal draftsmen.

However, if the principle of reciprocity is to prevail, if our constitution is to survive and stand the test of time, then Bills reflecting the policies of the country's elected Government and Members of Parliament should not be so mangled that they emerge from the Parliamentary machine in an unrecognizable and impracticable form. Give-and-take is different from capitulation, the winner take all, intolerance or humbug when pushed too far.

Mr Chairman, the principle of the separation of powers even as the Baron de Montesquieu developed it in the abstract in the eighteenth century, presupposed the principle of give-and-take. It has never meant that each organ of State can be an island or a law unto itself. The esteem which the public accords the Judiciary and the Legislature depends very much upon the degree of mature reciprocity demonstrated between them and Executive. As the mathematician and philosopher, Bertrand Russell pointed out and as we have witnessed in Ghana since 1966, 'government can easily exist without law but law cannot exist without government'.

In a true democracy, as we have been trying to practise it since September, 1979, all the organs of State must work together towards the public and general good and not for narrow private, personal and selfish interests masquerading as the public interest.

What the separation of powers seeks to ensure is the realization of the legal principle that no one should be judge in his own cause, hence Bagehot's view that 'the unity and almost complete fusion of the Executive and Legislative parts characterized the British system more than Montesquieu realized or could grasp at the time of the 'Patriot King'. In France the King was expected to grant liberties in return for taxes voted for him to run his court or administration, or to refrain from issuing Letters de Cachet by himself alone instead of with the help of the parlements or courts of that time. These were the preoccupations and obsessions of Montesquieu in his *De L'Esprit des Lois* used by the Enlightenment philosophers to attack and destroy absolutist monarchy in the style of Louis XIV.

'The history of fundamental human rights and Executive expediency', Comrade Kwaku Boateng's topic, has admittedly not been particularly happy in Ghana. Neither has the history of land administration and national development. In the past, both of them have been marred by regimes which failed to observe or respect the rights of the vast majority of the people or promote the realization of their aspirations. In fact, reciprocity was reduced to the level where the people continually gave and the State continually asked for more, whether it meant sacrificing liberty or land.

The People's National Party was founded on the principle that the welfare of the people shall be the supreme law, that observance of the law, especially the fundamental law, that is the Constitution of the Third Republic, should be the eternal safeguard of liberty. Indeed, defiance of the law often tends to be a slow, but the surest, road to tyranny. That is why I have repeatedly stated that I will respect, uphold and defend the Constitution. The scrupulous observance of fundamental human rights and the equitable administration of the lands of Ghana which constitute our collective birthright, are among the guiding principles of my Administration.

Turning to Comrade Kofi Duku's topic of the 'Law and National Development', I wish to observe that the speech of the great Osagyefo at the opening of the Ghana School of Law on 4 January 1962, is as valid now in 1981 as it was nearly twenty years ago. I quote from that speech to refresh our memories:

> The lawyers needed in a developing State are, in the first place, those trained to assist the ordinary man and woman in his everyday legal problems and, particularly, in the new problems likely to arise through industrialization. For example, lawyers are required by the trade union movement to assist in making effective agreements with employers and seeing to it that the individual trade unionist obtains what is legally due to him if he is injured at work or if illegally dismissed. In the same way, lawyers are required throughout the country so that in small towns and villages, inexpensive but good advice can be had by the ordinary man and woman so that they are nót put at a disadvantage in dealing with wealthy trading or commercial firms.
>
> This is a very different conception to that of the lawyer of colonial days who lived in big towns and spent most of his time in court or chambers dealing with a very restricted class of clients. In consequence of the nature of his work, he was very liable to become subconsciously

262

an exponent of the views of colonial economic interests.

Secondly, and perhaps most important of all, we need lawyers in the service of the State to deal with treaties and commercial agreements and with questions of private and public international law. A modern State requires also in its public services an increasing number of persons with a legal education, not only as advisers and legal technicians, but also in the day-to-day administration of the country.

Given the present shattered state of our economy and abortive industrialization efforts since 1966 and our New Investment Code, the above views are in fact even more relevant now than in 1962.

Lawyers are needed in every sphere of public life, socio-economic relations and in every aspect of national development. Members of the learned profession must therefore never allow themsleves to be divorced from the aspirations of the masses who form the backbone of the People's National Party. You must never lose sight of the fact that there shall not be enough jails, nor enough policemen, nor enough courts to enforce the law if it is not supported by the people. Laws in aid of national development should neither be too retrograde nor too far ahead of public opinion.

In concluding my observations on the topic discussed at your Seminar, not as a learned lawyer, but as a commonsensible and reasonable man, I appeal to all of you and the entire population of Ghana to also appraise our present economy as reasonable men with common and practical sense. We all know what we desire but the hard truth is that economic miracles do not happen. All activities, policies and programmes begin and end with hard work and co-operation, particularly within the Party and between the Party, Government, Legislature and the Judiciary at all levels.

Comrades, this Seminar has been a unique occasion in the history of the PNP. The Interim Working Committee of the Council of Lawyers of the Party is therefore warmly commended and congratulated for organizing it. So innovative and unique have your efforts and this Seminar been that I shall not be surprised if, as usual, others start to ape you very soon. For this reason, I hope that you will also stop with this Conference.

I have noticed that all the topics selected for this Seminar have sought to re-examine the past and are also descriptive of present situations. This is a very good start for what we all always learn from hindsight and for our living daily experiences. However, your organization should also embrace study groups on law reform and be in all its endeavours forward-looking as an aid to the People's National Party, the Government and the people of Ghana. You have a great role to play in national development, a role in which complacency should be avoided.

After two years of operating the constitution of the Third Republic it may also now be opportune for you to re-examine it and ask yourselves as to how far it aids or hinders our socio-economic development. For instance, does it err on the side of rigidity or flexibility? Did its farmers leave us sufficient room to mould it according to the ever-changing needs of a developing society?

In your future studies and deliberations I hope that you will monitor the working of the Constitution and the Investment Code and thus assist the Government of the People's National Party to ensure that foreign investment does not lead to mere economic exploitation but serve as an aid to our economic recovery, national reconstruction and growth based on mutual trust, hard work and benefits.

The public image of the Lawyer in Ghana has hitherto left much to be desired. Here again, you have the chance to take the lead in improving upon this image so that the Danish proverb that 'Lawyers and painters can change black to white' is not applied in negative scenical and mechanical ways. In short, Mr Chairman and comrades, conferences, seminars and studies of this nature should aim at achieving these noble, bold, laudable and forward-looking objectives.

Hoping that you shall rise to these challenges, I wish you well and every success in your future endeavours. Thank you.

57

Silver Jubilee of the Ghana Boys' Brigade

The President was at home with the Boys' Brigade.

Members of the Boys' Brigade, twenty-five years in the life of any association such as yours, devoted to selfless service to society and moral upliftment, is a significant milestone about which we can all be justifiably proud. I therefore warmly congratulate you on this momentous occasion. In particular, I wish to pay a warm tribute to the crusading men whose untiring efforts have laid the firm foundation and nurtured your organization to this happy twenty-fifth birthday.

This occasion and the lessons it embodies should be of great importance not only to you as members but to the entire nation. From very humble beginnings, the Ghana Boys' Brigade has, through the hard work, commitment and perseverance of its members, grown into the present formidable movement, playing a very important role in the social progress of our people and country.

The need for a new moral awareness among our people has now become so crucial and urgent that your aim of working towards the advancement of Christ's Kingdom among boys and the promotion of sound habits of obedience, reverence, discipline, self-respect and all that tends towards true Christian manliness must be of immense interest to us all. The propagation of this message of discipline, devoted and selfless service benefits particularly the youth who, as leaders of tomorrow, need to acquire firm foundations in uprightness, strength of character and will-power.

In the present circumstances of low morality, especially among men and women in leadership roles, it has become more than ever necessary to bring up the youth who are the country's greatest asset now and our hope for the future. To this end, it is gratifying that the Ghana Boys' Brigade provides one of the best places for precisely this form of training.

Mr President of the Ghana Boys' Brigade, this movement is also significant in many other ways. It serves powerfully and permanently to forge a sense of unity and purpose among the youth by bringing them from different homes and backgrounds together on occasions such as this anniversary. It creates priceless opportunities for expanding and strengthening bonds of fellowship, brotherhood, friendship, solidarity and unity. By submitting the self to the larger interests of the group, young people also learn to submerge individual and personal interests in the larger societal interests of the nation. This example is worthy of emulation by our total population.

In congratulating the rank and file of the Ghana Boys' Brigade for their very exemplary code of conduct, I wish to re-emphasize that the role of the youth in national development should, in the present state of affairs, be more and more positive, constructive and productive.

The PNP Administration has unequivocally demonstrated its confidence in the ability of the youth to contribute to national development. We will continue to blend your youthful vigour and exuberance with the experience and studied wisdom of the older generation. Indeed, since the world of tomorrow belongs to the youth of today, it is in the national interest to involve them actively now in public affairs. However, for the youth effectively to influence the present and future course of events, they should also move from the realm of over-idealism to the level of practical everyday life problems of our time. The proper use of our feet, hands, head, ears and eyes builds up the body and sharpens perception. It is while we are young and malleable that we are best able to do this.

Youthful exuberance, excess energy and radicalism should also be harnessed for more productive activities than has hitherto been the case. It is absolutely necessary for the youth who have, perhaps justifiably become disillusioned with present-day society to accept practical and empirically viable alternatives. A society saved and reformed is better than a society destroyed without any known and tested system to replace it. We have all seen how very easily and quickly destruction is accomplished and how very difficult and costly it is to rebuild, whether it is the character and personality or the national economy and prestige.

All too often institutions and Government policies are subjected to hasty criticism by some youngsters who have no concrete alternatives to offer yet. Is it enough, for instance, merely to describe the present educational system as 'imperialistic' and to call for a 'radical new educational policy' without the remotest indication as to what the new policy should be? Is it enough to denounce the 'exploitation of our natural resources by foreign companies' without explaining just how such resources could be put to beneficial use without funds and the necessary technology which we now lack? Is it enough to condemn others as 'old and decadent' without bothering to find out how the older generation managed to out-live the rough old days of locust visitations, wars, famine and high infant mortality?

Members of the Ghana Boys' Brigade, these random questions are meant to suggest to you and all youngsters that the youth can best serve their own interest and that of the whole nation through practical involvement in the task of reconstructing our economy and country rather than being passive critics while demanding from society the very things they condemn in others. Many commonplace things which the youth can take for granted today were beyond the reach of the present older generation when they were young. All too often we fail to appreciate this real significance and gains of our independence.

Since assuming office, my Administration has taken the youth to be its most vital ally in the resuscitation of our economy and the reconstruction of the country. We have met many student and youth leaders for discussions. Many of them have often condemned wicked old men and women without realizing that these included their own parents also. Moreover, whenever we asked for practical suggestions for the solution of our national problems, we have been bombarded with a barrage of textbook theories many of which are not relevant to our needs and had, in fact, been tried, found wanting and abandoned long ago in their countries of origin. One young friend even once confessed that if I relied on him for any solution he could only complicate my problems for me.

This was, undoubtedly, very frank and honest but was it also very helpful and productive? I think that it was, in so far as the young friend refrained from complicating our already intractable existing problems. I must re-emphasize that I personally, and the Government of the PNP, believe in the youth as a positive force whose importance in the development of our country cannot be overestimated. The need to bring them into the mainstream of our national developmental efforts has therefore become greater now than ever before.

Some of my appointments have already started to take account of this fact. My very attendance at the present function also demonstrates the importance my Administration attaches to the youth of Ghana. I therefore urge all the youth of Ghana to close their ranks and offer Government and the nation the benefit of their resourcefulness, exuberance and youthful energies.

Mr President and Patrons of the Ghana Boys' Brigade, as these celebrations marking the Silver Jubilee of the Boys' Brigade unfold, I hope that members will highlight and emphasize the real significance of the occasion whose importance rises far above the merrymaking of an ordinary birthday anniversary. The central point of the celebration should be the re-assessment of the role of the youth in society and their rededication to the service of their country as future adults and potential leaders who have to take over the baton soon in the relay race of managing our affairs.

Through the appropriate agencies Government will continue to support the efforts of voluntary social organizations such as yours. I hope that individuals and organizations in the private sector will also step up their moral and material support for such voluntary organizations to help them play their proper roles in society more effectively.

May I, once again, on my own behalf as the National Patron and on behalf of the Government and our entire public warmly congratulate all the members of the Ghana Boys' Brigade for twenty-five years of selfless service to the community. On this note, distinguished ladies and gentlemen, I have the pleasure formally to launch these Silver Jubilee celebrations heralding and setting the tone for the Silver Jubilee celebrations of our independence and sovereign nationhood.